Nofsinger, *The Psychology of Investing*

Ogden/Jen/O'Connor, *Advanced Corporate Finance: Financing Policies and Strategies*

Rejda, *Social Insurance and Economic Security, Sixth Edition*

Rivera-Batiz/Rivera-Batiz, *International Finance and Open Economy Macroeconomics, Second Edition*

Scholes/Wolfson, *Taxes and Business Strategy: A Global Planning Approach, Second Edition*

Seiler, *Performing Financial Studies: A Methodological Cookbook*

Shapiro/Balbirer, *Modern Corporate Finance: A Multidisciplinary Approach to Value Creation*

Sharpe/Alexander/Bailey, *Investments, Sixth Edition*

Sinkey, *Commercial Bank Financial Management, Sixth Edition*

Taggart, *Quantitative Analysis for Investment Management*

Trivoli, *Personal Portfolio Management: Fundamentals & Strategies*

Van Horne, *Financial Management and Policy, Twelfth Edition*

Van Horne, *Financial Market Rates and Flows, Sixth Edition*

Van Horne/Wachowicz, *Fundamentals of Financial Management, Eleventh Edition*

Vaughn, *Financial Planning for the Entrepreneur*

Weston, *Cases in Dynamic Finance: Mergers and Restructuring*

Weston/Mitchell/Mulherin, *Takeovers, Restructuring, and Corporate Governance, Fourth Edition*

Winger/Frasca, *Investments, Third Edition*

Winger/Frasca, *Personal Finance: An Integrated Planning Approach, Sixth Edition*

For more information on Finance titles from Prentice Hall, visit us at
www.prenhall.com/finance

Entrepreneurial Financial Management

An Applied Approach

Jeffrey R. Cornwall

Belmont University

David O. Vang

University of St. Thomas

Jean M. Hartman

University of St. Thomas

PEARSON

Prentice
Hall

Upper Saddle River, NJ 07458

Library of Congress Cataloging-in-Publication Data

Cornwall, Jeffrey R.
    Entrepreneurial financial management: an applied approach / Jeffrey Cornwall, David
Vang, Jean Hartman.
    p. cm.
    Includes bibliographical references and index.
    ISBN 0-13-009411-0
    1. Business enterprises—Finance. 2. Entrepreneurship. I. Vang, David.
 II. Hartman, Jean. III. Title.

HG4026.C637 2003
658. 15—dc21   2002044988

Executive Editor: Mickey Cox
Editor-in-Chief: P.J. Boardman
Managing Editor (Editorial): Gladys Soto
Assistant Editor: Erika Rusnak
Editorial Assistant: Francesca Calogero
Media Project Manager: Victoria Anderson
Executive Marketing Manager: Debbie Clare
Marketing Assistant: Amanda Fisher
Managing Editor (Production): John Roberts
Production Editor: Kelly Warsak

Production Assistant: Joe DeProspero
Permissions Supervisor: Suzanne Grappi
Associate Director, Manufacturing: Vincent Scelta
Production Manager: Arnold Vila
Manufacturing Buyer: Michelle Klein
Cover Design: Bruce Kenselaar
Composition/Full-Service Project Management:
Progressive Publishing Alternatives/Bonnie Gladfelter
Printer/Binder: The Maple Press Company
Cover Printer: Phoenix Color Corp.

Credits and acknowledgments borrowed from other sources and reproduced, with
permission, in this textbook appear on appropriate page within text.

Pearson Education LTD.
Pearson Education Singapore, Pte. Ltd
Pearson Education, Canada, Ltd
Pearson Education–Japan

Pearson Education Australia PTY, Limited
Pearson Education North Asia Ltd
Pearson Educación de Mexico, S.A. de C.V.
Pearson Education Malaysia, Pte. Ltd

PEARSON
Prentice
Hall

10 9 8 7 6 5 4 3 2 1
ISBN 0-13-009411-0

CONTENTS

PREFACE

Courses in entrepreneurial finance are expanding rapidly across the country. The traditional approach to presenting entrepreneurial finance has often tended to place too much attention on venture capital and initial public offerings. Less than 1 percent of new ventures should even consider these financing vehicles. Entrepreneurial finance is not just about raising money and creating financial statements. Entrepreneurial finance should be an integral part of the basic management of any new venture.

Entrepreneurial Financial Management: An Applied Approach is written from an integrated, comprehensive perspective. The fundamental goal of this book is to present an applied, realistic view of entrepreneurial finance for today's entrepreneurs. This book provides an integrated set of concepts and applications, drawing from entrepreneurship, finance, and accounting, that will prepare aspiring entrepreneurs for the world they will most likely face as they start their new businesses. Although venture capital and public offerings are covered in this book, they have been put in their proper perspective. *Entrepreneurial Financial Management* is based on practical experience but is also informed by theory.

The book is designed for applied and experientially based teaching strategies in entrepreneurial financial management. Each chapter has been written with the goal of facilitating application of its contents to real-life businesses.

KEY FEATURES

- The structure of the book is designed to follow the life cycle of a new business venture. Topics are presented in the order that an entrepreneur would likely face them as they begin the process of business start-up and move into growing the business.
- Chapter 8 provides detailed information and techniques for *bootstrapping* new businesses. Most entrepreneurs learn that they must find creative methods for getting more "bang for their buck," as they rarely have access to unlimited funds.
- A comprehensive view of funding sources with discussion of how an entrepreneur works with each is presented in Chapters 10–12. Interviews with many of the funding sources are presented in "In Their Own Words . . ." boxes throughout these chapters.
- Numerous examples are presented throughout the text.

- A comprehensive computer spreadsheet financial template is available from the Companion Website. This tool allows many of the concepts to be applied to actual businesses. The tool can be a supplement to the process of developing a full business plan. Professors and students can access these resources from www.prenhall.com/cornwall.
- A self-assessment is included to assist student entrepreneurs in integrating their own personal aspirations into their financial and business plans.
- Opportunities for Application are included at the end of most chapters.

Acknowledgments

The authors would like to thank the following reviewers who provided constructive feedback that helped shape the manuscript as it developed: Susan Coleman, University of Hartford; Dixie Doughty, University of Nebraska–Lincoln; Robert W. Pricer, University of Wisconsin–Madison; Michael G. Mino, Clemson University; Charles B. (Chip) Ruscher, University of Arizona; and Richard S. Swasey, Jr., Northeastern University. Thanks as well to Katie Thayer for her work in conducting the interviews for the "In Their Own Words . . ." boxes throughout Chapters 10–12. Thanks to Alec Johnson and his students for their comments on early drafts of this text. Finally, we cannot possibly thank Betsy Lofgren enough. She not only did an incredible job in editing and layout throughout the writing of this book but also provided support, friendship, encouragement, and a wonderful sense of humor.

CHAPTER
1

Introduction

IMPORTANCE OF KNOWING THE NUMBERS

Imagine moving to a foreign country where the people speak a different language from your own. While you may be able to get by for a short time without learning the language of this country, you will be severely hampered. Asking for and receiving simple information will be a tedious and frustrating task. For example, assume you want to go to a movie. How do you get to the movie theater? How do you order a medium box of popcorn? What are the actors in the movie saying? More complex tasks are even a bigger challenge. Imagine trying to rent an apartment. What does the landlord expect from you as a tenant? The contract you are required to sign is completely unintelligible to you. Even an interpreter will only help so much. Your interpreter can translate, but the process is slow. And it would be impossible to rely on your interpreter all of the time.

Accounting is called the "language of business." Much of what is communicated about a business is done in this financial language. And yet to many entrepreneurs this is a language as foreign to them as the language was to the traveler in the previous story. Accountants who work with entrepreneurs often report that most entrepreneurs know very little about accounting or finance. And those entrepreneurs who do most likely have gained this knowledge from working in or from studying large publicly traded companies. The application of accounting and financial principles to entrepreneurial ventures creates unique challenges. And the success of new ventures is often dependent on entrepreneurs having the skills and knowledge necessary to manage this aspect of their businesses.

Financial statements tell us about the general financial condition of a business. How profitable is the business? Can it pay its bills on a timely basis? Can it pay its loans? What is the value of the business? All of these and many more questions can be answered through the financial statements of a company. This is critical information for outsiders, such as bankers and creditors, and for insiders, such as owners and managers.

Financial reports can also give critical insight into the operating effectiveness of a business. They are often critical to making the right decisions. Which of our products make money? Should we add a new type of service? When should we add more employees? Can we afford to expand our business right now? These are also questions that are answered through the language of accounting and finance. It is a myth that entrepreneurs can answer such questions simply based on intuition or gut feel.

This language is also the one used to communicate with those entities and people who provide funding for businesses. Bankers, venture capitalists, and investment angels all speak this language and expect the entrepreneurs with whom they work to be fluent in the language as well. None of these sources of funding will be satisfied with reports generated by a computer. All will want to have conversations with the entrepreneur in this language about where the business has been and where it is going.

Some entrepreneurs believe that they can get by with a good accountant who can speak this language for them—an interpreter, if you will. However, because this language of business is so fundamentally important to understanding any business venture, it is critical that entrepreneurs learn to speak it fluently themselves.

MEASURING SUCCESS

The language of business can help answer the fundamental question: How successful is my business? But to answer this question requires that entrepreneurs truly understand what success means to them. This is not as simple as it may first appear.

Certainly success means the ability to earn a living from a business. To most entrepreneurs, success is also measured by the ability to earn a profit from the business. Profits are important to sustain the business, to create additional income to the owners, to pay off debt, and to create value in the business (see Chapter 13 for a more thorough discussion of business valuation). To many entrepreneurs, success is also measured by the ability to create balance between work and family, work and leisure, or work and community activities such as volunteerism. Other entrepreneurs measure success through the jobs they are able to create. Every entrepreneur has their own unique definition of success.

The meaning of success is often derived from the entrepreneur's personal values and personal goals. For example, Bob Thompson, founder of a highway paving business, never felt very successful in his business in spite of incredible growth in sales and profits over many years. It wasn't until he sold his paving business and gave huge bonuses (many over $1 million) to many of his employees that he finally felt he had achieved real success. To him success came from the ability to share the wealth from his business with those who had helped him achieve that wealth. Another entrepreneur never felt she had fully realized success until she had the ability to use her own business success to help other women trying to start their own ventures.

It is important to note that not all entrepreneurs share such an altruistic measure of success. To some, success is measured solely by the profits they can put directly into their own pockets. Many of the dot-com businesses of the 1990s were criticized for this approach. Their only goal was to create enough hype to take their business public and realize a quick financial windfall. Many never created profits, and some never even created revenues, yet they were able to create wealth for themselves through a quick turn of their businesses.

Chapter 2 will present a process of self-assessment that can be used to help entrepreneurs understand what success really means to each of them. With this understanding, entrepreneurs are better able to know how to measure success for their unique businesses.

WHAT IS ENTREPRENEURIAL FINANCIAL MANAGEMENT?

Entrepreneurial finance is typically defined simply as raising funds for a business. How can an entrepreneur raise funds to support a business venture as it grows? How does the entrepreneur attract venture capital? What is the process of taking a business public? All of these can be critical questions that entrepreneurs may need to address for their businesses. However, when the topic is broadened to entrepreneurial financial management, many other critical issues emerge.

Entrepreneurial financial management is defined in terms of six general activities and functions in the business. First, entrepreneurial financial management includes setting clear financial goals for the business that are consistent with the aspirations of the entrepreneur who owns the venture. What are the income and wealth goals that the entrepreneur is pursuing through the business? How will the business need to perform to help the entrepreneur realize these financial goals? As will be discussed, the focus should not be on simply growing revenues as high and as quickly as possible. Instead, the focus should be on the profit goals that help the entrepreneur reach personal aspirations from the business venture. The process of setting financial goals and engineering these goals into the planning of the business will be examined in Chapter 2.

Second, using financial statements and reports to better manage a growing business and to make more informed decisions is a key element of entrepreneurial financial management. This is the process of becoming fluent in the language of business and being able to specifically apply this language to the unique circumstances found in each business venture. Chapter 3 will introduce the basic concepts of financial reporting, and Chapter 7 examines the process of monitoring financial performance.

Third, entrepreneurial financial management includes forecasting. The entrepreneur and the business team use forecasts as a guide to help assess the progress of the business and to determine how well it is meeting expected results. Forecasts are also used to communicate the potential of a business venture to outside funding sources such as banks and venture capitalists. Forecasting future financial results has been described as more art than science. However, there are tools and techniques that can drastically improve the accuracy of forecasts. Revenue forecasts (Chapter 4) should be developed hand-in-hand with the financial goals of the owners (what revenues will be required to reach the profit goals established for the business?). Also, revenue goals should be consistent with data obtained through the marketing plan. Expense forecasts are discussed in Chapter 5. Chapter 6 presents a spreadsheet model for forecasting financial statements that integrates the principles of effective revenue and expense forecasting.

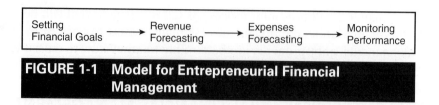

FIGURE 1-1 Model for Entrepreneurial Financial Management

Fourth, entrepreneurial financial management includes effective managing of what can be *the* most precious resource: cash. Cash flow is often described as the *lifeblood* of a business. Cash flow management includes both long-term planning for cash needs as well as day-to-day cash flow management. Chapter 9 examines various techniques and critical issues associated with cash flow management.

Fifth, entrepreneurial financial management does include raising funds for entrepreneurial ventures. However, before racing to obtain external funds, the entrepreneur must examine the impact of debt and equity on reaching goals. If managed properly, growing businesses can often "generate" funds internally through creative application of critical business functions such as marketing, staffing, operations, and so forth. Chapter 8 examines how a collection of techniques known as *bootstrapping* can help keep expenses lower and reduce the need to raise outside funding. Many businesses do need external support to grow. Chapters 10–12 provide a complete overview of the various sources of external funding, including both debt and equity sources of funds.

Finally, entrepreneurial financial management includes the process of how entrepreneurs exit the business that they founded. All entrepreneurs eventually leave their businesses—either through planned exits (e.g., selling the business, going public, or transitioning to the next generation in a family business) or through exits not subject to careful planning, such as the death of the owner or bankruptcy. Chapter 14 summarizes exit planning and the exit process, which, as will be seen, should actually start in the very beginning of a business venture. Chapter 14 also examines business valuation.

Figure 1–1 presents the model of entrepreneurial financial management used throughout this book. As shown, the process begins with a clear understanding of the financial goals of the entrepreneur, which is used to forecast and monitor performance. This model is based on the discovery-driven planning model developed by McGrath and MacMillan (1995), and includes the assumption that profit goals should be clearly established and then engineered into the plans for a new venture.

WHAT MAKES ENTREPRENEURIAL FINANCE SIMILAR TO TRADITIONAL FINANCE?

There are both similarities and differences between entrepreneurial finance and traditional corporate finance. Traditional corporate finance consists of three inter-related segments: the study of financial markets, the study of investments, and the study of financial management, which is sometimes called *business finance*. This book concentrates primarily on the area of business finance for entrepreneurial firms, but managers in such firms need to have an understanding of the other two areas in order to succeed. All of these areas are interrelated and the general principles of finance apply, but early-stage firms and investors have different challenges compared to well-established corporations.

Entrepreneurs need to have an understanding of financial markets, their institutions, and their structures, because either directly or indirectly they will have to access funds from them. Conceptually, financial markets can be divided into two general segments: capital markets and money markets. Capital markets are those that offer financing with a term of one year or more. Equity financing and longer-term business loans fall in this category. Such financing is very attractive for businesses that need to buy long-term (capital) assets. Capital financing also is attractive for firms that may need more "patient" financing that will last as a firm develops through a stage or stages where cash flows might not be large enough to immediately pay back the principal. Conversely, money markets involve instruments where the term is less than one year. The purpose of the loan in this case is to help a firm survive through a period of short-term negative cash flow, such as meeting this week's payroll. The assumption is that collections will soon cause cash flows to be positive again and the loan will be paid back.

The perspective of investors also needs to be considered by entrepreneurs. In order to gain access to funding, one needs to know the principles, expectations, and conditions that investors will have. In general,

1. Investors prefer less risk to more risk.
2. Diversified investors are primarily concerned with what is called *nondiversifiable, systemic,* or *market risk.*
3. Single-asset or nondiversified investors are concerned with the total risk of the investment, but such investors are relatively rare in the investment world.
4. Investors prefer more return to less.
5. Investors prefer the return to occur sooner rather than later.
6. Investors prefer more liquidity (the ability to turn an investment into cash) to less liquidity.
7. Investors face many different opportunities to invest their money, so raising funds is competitive (i.e., a request for funds must reasonably appear to offer less risk, more return, a faster return, or more liquidity than other requests).
8. No investors are immune to these principles, expectations, and conditions.

WHAT MAKES ENTREPRENEURIAL FINANCE DIFFERENT FROM TRADITIONAL FINANCE?

What potentially makes an early-stage firm different when compared to established, publicly traded corporations is its lack of history with which to assess risk, the inability to compare it with other firms because the industry may be so new, its lack of potential for making a profit in the immediate future, and its lack of liquidity. An entrepreneur has to convince investors that despite all these things, investing in the firm is in their best interest. As one can imagine, this is quite a tough sell.

Lack of Historical Data to Measure Risk

In a traditional finance textbook there is always an in-depth section on risk and return. A number of Nobel Prizes in Economics have been awarded for research in this area. The measures used to monitor risk, such as the standard deviations of stock returns and the stock's beta, are extremely helpful in observing and understanding investor behavior, with one caveat—historical data such as past stock prices are needed to calculate these risk measures. A recently started firm does not have tradable stock, or if it does, it does not have a long enough history of stock prices to allow one to perform statistical calculations. In addition, if a firm is creating a new product or service, then it cannot "borrow" data from the past history of firms that have gone down the same path. The framework of risk still exists, and investors view risk from this framework, but the means to accurately assess and measure it are not directly available.

Traditional Financial Concepts of Risk and Return

Total risk is sometimes called *stand-alone risk*. This is conceptually the amount of risk that an investor faces when holding ownership in only one asset. The investor's fortune rises and falls based on what happens to that one company. If a supplier balks, customers defect, workers strike, or a meteor falls from the sky and hits the building, the investor's entire net worth could be lost. An accepted proxy for total risk is the standard deviation of returns to the investment. For a stock the return, R, would be $(P_1 - P_0)/P_0$. P_1 is the price at the end of a time period and P_0 is the price at the start of a time period, so the return is the percentage increase or decrease in price during this period.

Squaring the difference between the return from one period and the period that follows, then dividing the sum of squared differences by the number of periods, results in a statistic called a *variance*.

$$\text{Variance} = \frac{\text{Sum}(R_i - R_{avg})^2}{N}$$

R_i = Return in a particular period
R_{avg} = Average or mean return calculated over all available periods
N = Number of periods of data available

Taking the square root of the variance results in a statistic called the *standard deviation*.

$$\text{Standard deviation} = \text{Square root of the variance}$$

The standard deviation is a measure of potential volatility from the average return on a stock. The greater the standard deviation value, the more variable the returns on the stock. In what statisticians would call a *normal distribution* or *bell curve,* returns that vary by 1 standard deviation or less from the average return on a stock have a 66% probability of occurring. Returns that fall 2 deviations or less from average have a 95% probability of occurring, and returns that fall 3 standard deviations or less from the average have a 99% probability of occurring. The implication is that if investors want to be 99% sure of what is going to happen to the investment in the coming year, they would calculate a range that starts at 3 standard deviations below the historical average return and ends 3 standard deviations above. If the standard deviation itself were a relatively large number, then this range of possible outcomes would be huge. Likewise, if the standard deviation were a very small number, then the range of possible outcomes known with 99% certainty would be somewhat narrow. Therefore, stocks with large standard deviations are riskier than stocks with small standard deviations, because the range of possible outcomes becomes so great that it is very difficult to forecast what is likely to happen to the stock in any given time period.

The vast majority of investors are not single-asset investors, however. Most investors have diversified portfolios. Either they own a number of different stocks or they own investments like mutual funds, which are already diversified. What happens is that from the investor's perspective, a substantial amount of the total risk "disappears." If the investor owns stock in 100 different companies, then the concerns about unique incidents such as a labor strike or a meteor smashing one particular company are less significant. As a matter of fact, a lot of these company-specific situations may actually cancel each other out. For every company with bad labor relations, there may be another one with good relations. For every firm that gets hit by a meteor, the odds are equally likely that some other firm will discover gold under the lawn at corporate headquarters. The portion of total risk that "disappears" when portfolios are created is called *diversifiable risk*. The main point is that because the vast majority of investors are diversified investors, the financial markets value stocks based upon the nondiversifiable risk. In other words, the relationship between risk and return is such that the markets price securities to compensate investors only for the nondiversifiable risk that exists in assets, not for the total risk. If investors are not willing or smart enough to painlessly protect themselves by diversification, then financial markets will not show them any mercy. Instead, because the vast majority of market participants are diversified investors, they price securities on the assumption that everyone else is diversified as well. If an investor is not diversified, then that is a personal choice and the consequences have to be accepted.

Total risk = Diversifiable risk + Nondiversifiable risk

A widely accepted measure used to proxy the nondiversifiable risk is called *beta*. Betas are usually estimated by regression analysis. Returns on a stock market are calculated for several periods in a row, and likewise, returns on a specific stock are calculated for those same time periods. Regression would help the analyst discover what is the average change in a company's return given an average size change in the stock market's return.

$$R_i = A + \text{Beta}(R_{\text{market}})$$

R_i = Return on company in period i
A = Constant from regression
R_{mi} = Return on the stock market in period i. Usually a market proxy such as the NYSE index or SP 500 Index is used to calculate this return.
Beta = Change in return on stock/ change in return on stock market

For instance, if the beta for a company is 2, then when the stock market's return increases, the return on the company is expected to increase by twice that amount. On the downside, if the stock market falls, then the stock would fall twice as fast. The beta of 2 indicates that the stock is twice as volatile as the stock market. High-risk companies have betas greater than 1, low-risk companies have betas of less than 1, and average-risk companies have a beta of 1. The comparison of an asset's return is made to the most diversified investment that one can have—a portfolio that mirrors the entire stock market. Hence, beta is a measure of nondiversifiable risk because it is a relative measure compared to the most diversified portfolio available. Conceptually, when averaged over a long enough time period, it should reflect just the nondiversifiable (market-related) risk and none of the diversifiable (company-specific) risk.

An asset's *required rate of return* is the minimum return necessary to compensate an investor for risk. The relationship between nondiversifiable risk and an asset's required rate of return is denoted by a concept called the *Security Market Line*.

$$\text{Required rate of return} = R_f + \text{beta}(R_m - R_f)$$

R_f = *risk-free rate* such as found with U.S. government T-bills
R_m = average return on market portfolio proxy

Verbally, this says that an investor should demand to earn at least the risk-free rate (which can be proxied by the rate on U.S. government T-bills). If one wants the investor to accept more risk, then the return should also include a *risk premium* or additional compensation above the risk-free rate. The size of this risk premium is thought to be equal to the beta times the *market risk premium* or the difference between the return on the stock market and the risk-free rate:

$$\text{Market risk premium} = R_m - R_f$$

For instance, if a stock has a beta of 2 (meaning it is twice as volatile as the stock market), then the investor should demand a risk premium that is twice the size of the market risk premium. Likewise, if a stock's beta is .5 (meaning it is only half as volatile as the stock market), then the investor should demand a risk premium that is half the size of the market risk premium.

The beauty of the concepts of traditional finance is that they provide a framework for investors to understand that there are two kinds of risk, and the market will most likely consider only the nondiversifiable risk in estimating an asset's required rate of return. The drawback is that while these concepts provide insight, they are not always easily measured and quantified.

Lack of Historical Data and Liquidity Complicate the Practice of Finance in Early-Stage Firms

The financial concepts of risk and return as presented here are extremely valuable in understanding the perspective of investors who supply the funds necessary to start and grow early-stage firms. For established firms with publicly traded stock, these concepts not only provide insight but can also be applied to historical data to measure such things as an asset's return, variance, standard deviation, beta, and required rate of return.

For early-stage firms that do not have a past history of stock prices and other data, these measurements cannot take place and must be inferred and estimated instead. Further complicating the calculations is the fact that even if prices, returns, and so on could somehow be substituted or borrowed from other, similar firms, the relevance would still be highly questionable. First, there is the difficulty of finding truly comparable firms, which happen to be publicly traded. Second, the mere fact that an early-stage firm is not tradable means there will be a huge difference in value and accuracy of the calculations because of the liquidity difference. Conceivably, there can be a difference of as much as 50% between a firm that has tradable stock and one that does not.

Therefore, trying to use traditional, mathematically based finance techniques when there is a lack of historically measurable data as well as a lack of liquidity is like a carpenter building a house by measuring timber with a micrometer, marking a line with chalk, and then cutting with an ax. The general principles of building a house are the same whether or not one has access to a laser-guided saw or an ax, but if access to the high-tech saw is a physical impossibility, then this must be taken into account. For entrepreneurial finance, the situation is the same. If historical data are not available, the option of using mathematically sophisticated techniques is not available; instead, general principles and benchmarks must be used.

An entrepreneur competes for funding from investors who have a wide universe of investment options. And while these principles are derived from traditional finance theory, for the entrepreneur the challenge is the application of these principles without the advantage of direct access to the data and tools that a traditional finance person would have.

ETHICS AND ENTREPRENEURIAL FINANCE

A common challenge faced by all entrepreneurs is identifying and putting into practice the basic ethical standards that will guide their businesses. Ethical issues and challenges arise in all aspects of entrepreneurial financial management. A

BOX 1-1

The CEO of a fast growing software company was three weeks away from facing a payroll he knew he wouldn't be able to meet. Then a check for $94,000 showed up on his desk. That amount . . . was more than enough to cover a full payroll period, relieving him of an oppressive burden and ensuring that his six-year-old company would stay intact. Until the next payroll came due, anyway. . . . But the order had come from a customer looking for a customized version of the company's software. It was a product, the CEO well knew, that his company couldn't possibly deliver. . . . So what was he to do? . . . His chief financial officer, concerned about cash flow, wanted to cash the check. The vice-president of sales, whose compensation was tied to revenues, expressed a similar sentiment. But the vice-president of client services thought it was a bad idea to alienate a big customer. But note what was absent: nobody talked about whether misleading the customer was the ethical thing, the right thing to do. (Seglin, 1998).

---

common framework that helps navigate ethical issues is based on a stakeholder analysis. Stakeholders are interested parties beyond the owners of a business who have a stake in the decisions made in that business and in the outcomes of those decisions.

The first step in a stakeholder analysis is to identify the relevant stakeholders. There is no standard list, as this can vary from business to business. The list can also vary based on the values of each entrepreneur. For example, one entrepreneur in the southeastern United States had a strong commitment to his employees. Common stakeholders for entrepreneurs can include family, partners, investors, employees, customers, suppliers, creditors, and the local community. The list can often become more complex and include interest groups, trade associations, and unions. Each entrepreneur needs to clearly identify the stakeholders based on the demands and relationships created by the business and personal values.

The second step is to determine the basic ethical principles and values that guide the entrepreneur's interaction with each of these stakeholders. These may be shaped by generally held beliefs of right and wrong, religious convictions, or a general moral code. It is important to develop specific applications of these principles and values as they apply to each stakeholder. In the preceding example, whenever the entrepreneur made a major decision, such as expanding the business, he wanted to make sure that any employees that were hired would have their employment with his company protected. He believed that his commitment to employees was long-term, and he had a no-layoff policy.

The third step is to apply these principles specifically to the process of the financial resource management of the business. In our example, the entrepreneur always insisted on careful review of financial forecasts to ensure that any new employees hired for expansion could be supported financially by his business even under a worst-case scenario. Table 1-1 displays an example of how these three steps might look for a hypothetical business. Note the level of specificity that is achieved by the third column. This specificity ensures that the principles will more likely be put into action by the entrepreneur and by his employees. Many entrepreneurs find it helpful to write these principles down in order to communicate them to all employees and even the stakeholders themselves.

TABLE 1-1   Example of Stakeholder Analysis

Stakeholder	Ethical Principle or Value	Application for Financial Resource Management
Family	Create balance between work demands and family time.	Establish a more moderate financial growth goal to allow for time with family.
Investors (e.g., angel investors, venture capitalists)	Deal with all investors openly and honestly.	Develop a financial reporting system that provides full and accurate historical information as well as realistic forecasts.
Employees	Share financial success with those that helped create it.	Modify financial goals and expense forecasts to allow for programs such as profit sharing, stock option plans, phantom stock, ESOP, etc. while still meeting goals of entrepreneur.
Customers	Fair pricing.	Establish revenue forecasts that are realistic given this pricing principle.
Suppliers	Prompt payment for money owed.	Establish cash forecasts that are based on an assumption of prompt payment of all invoices submitted by suppliers/vendors.
Banker	Honest disclosure of information.	Ensure timely and accurate financial reporting and reasonable financial forecasting.
Community	Company should be source of reliable employment for the community.	Manage cash flow to allow for stable employment even during times of temporary slowdowns.

Over the long term, the challenge to the entrepreneur is to create a culture that is based on the ethical principles used while building his business. As the business grows, the entrepreneur must rely on this culture to guide the actions of employees. No entrepreneur can be all places at all times. But it is important to remember that the culture of a business is created with the very first actions and decisions of the entrepreneur. To expect an ethical culture and ethical actions by employees, the entrepreneur must embody these same ethics in every action taken.

SUMMARY

This chapter has presented the basic foundation and model of entrepreneurial financial resource management that will guide the rest of this book. Part I, which begins with the next chapter, will discuss the process of building a financial forecast. Part II examines various aspects of managing the financial resources of an entrepreneurial venture. Finally, Part III presents issues related to planning the transition of the entrepreneur out of the business. Also included in this book are a self-assessment instrument to help begin this critical part of financial planning for the venture and a financial template that will help create financial forecasts.

DISCUSSION QUESTIONS

1. Why is accounting considered the language of business? Why is it important for the entrepreneur to learn this language?
2. How will you measure your success in your business/entrepreneurial career?
3. What are the six activities that make up entrepreneurial financial management, and why are they important?
4. How is entrepreneurial finance both similar to, and different from, traditional finance?

OPPORTUNITY FOR APPLICATION

1. Interview an entrepreneur to learn how he or she measures success in their career. Is it only in financial terms, or are there other yardsticks used to measure success?

REFERENCES

Brigham, E. F., and Daves, P. R. *Intermediate Financial Management,* 7th ed. Cincinnati, OH: South-Western College Publishing.

McGrath, R., and MacMillan, I. (1995, July–August). Discovery-driven planning. *Harvard Business Review,* pp. 4–12.

Naughton, M., and Cornwall, J. The good entrepreneur and the role of virtue. 11th International Symposium on Ethics, Business and Society, July 2001, Barcelona, Spain.

Seglin, J. (1998, January). Always a payroll to meet. *Inc. Magazine,* p. 31.

CHAPTER

2

Setting Financial Goals

In the excitement of starting and growing a business, many entrepreneurs fail to systematically evaluate their own personal goals in relationship to their business ventures. What income do they need? What are their long-term income goals? When do they want to retire? What lifestyle will they want in retirement? How much money will they need to set aside for their children's education? These are just some of the personal financial goals that need to be integrated into the business plan. There are many nonfinancial goals involving family, hobbies, friends, and community groups that are important as well. This chapter offers a framework that helps the entrepreneur to integrate a personal assessment with the business planning of the entrepreneurial venture.

WEALTH VERSES INCOME

Before presenting the process of setting financial goals, it is critical to understand that there are two types of goals that the entrepreneur must consider: income and wealth. By understanding how a business creates income and wealth, the entrepreneur is better able to "engineer" personal financial goals into the business plan. Simply put, entrepreneurs consider income to be the cash that is available from the business to pay their salaries, whereas wealth is thought of as the value of the business itself. Certainly, entrepreneurs may also build wealth through savings from the salary they draw, but for most entrepreneurs their single most valuable asset by far is their business.

Income is fairly simple to understand, as it is the means to meet the day-to-day, month-to-month, and year-to-year monetary needs of the entrepreneur and his or her family. The entrepreneur should not only plan for short-term income needs but also long-term needs. It is a myth that bankers are impressed by business plans that show the entrepreneur taking no income from the business for a long period of time. In fact, to many bankers and other investors, this is a red flag. They have seen too many entrepreneurs who give up on a business that does not create enough cash to adequately pay the entrepreneur. Certainly, they do not want to find excessive salary being paid early on, as they may be funding part or all of this

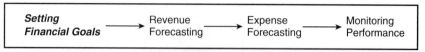

FIGURE 2-1 Model for Entrepreneurial Financial Management

salary through their loans or investments. On the other hand, a business plan that includes a modest and reasonable salary for the entrepreneur is not only accept-able but also desirable for most financial backers.

Stanley and Danko (1996) published a best-selling book, *The Millionaire Next Door,* that gives insights into the differences between wealth and income. They point out that many confuse wealth with the trappings of wealth. Living in a big house or driving an expensive car may give the impression that someone is wealthy. However, many people rely heavily on debt to fund such purchases and have little actual wealth.

Wealth is actually the difference between what someone owns less the debts that are owed. Therefore, if the big house and expensive car are purchased mostly with debt, there is little true wealth. Stanley and Danko (1996) refer to this situa-tion with an old Texas saying: "big hat, no cattle." While the house and car give the illusion of wealth (the big hat) there is no real wealth (the cattle). In their book, they report the results of their research on millionaires, how they live, and how they created their own wealth. Two-thirds of the millionaires they studied are self-employed, and three out of four of these consider themselves entrepreneurs (the other one-fourth are self-employed professionals, such as physicians or lawyers). Most of the entrepreneurs they studied, such as contractors, auctioneers, farmers, mobile home park owners, pest controllers, coin and stamp dealers, and office building cleaning services, owned "dull" businesses rather than high-tech, high-growth ventures. Most live on a fairly modest median taxable income of $131,000, given their average wealth of $1,600,000. They live in typical upper-middle-class neighborhoods with an average home value of $320,000, although they average about 6.5 times the wealth of their neighbors. Most reported that they buy inex-pensive suits and drive American cars that are at least a couple of years old.

Because most of the wealth of an entrepreneur comes from the value of the business, it is important to understand how businesses are valued. Formal business valuation uses a variety of financial models (this will be covered in Chapter 13). Such formal valuation is critical when buying or selling a business. However, many entre-preneurs find it helpful to use what is known as a "quick and dirty" method of valua-tion to monitor progress in building value in their businesses as they grow. Most forms of valuation, whether formal or quick and dirty, share a common assumption. The real value of a business is its potential to generate profits or, more specifically, cash in the future. A very simple form of quick and dirty valuation works as follows:

1. Start with the most recent year-end profits of the business. Add to this any unusually high bonuses or other extra compensation beyond a normal salary paid to the owners.
2. Evaluate the growth potential of the business based on recent growth in profits over the past three years.
3. Evaluate any important industry or market trends that might either improve or decrease profits in the next three years.
4. Assign a profit multiple, which is a number that is used to multiply the profits of a business to estimate the value of future profits. The profit multiple typically ranges from 3 to 8 times profits, based on the estimate of future profits. A profit multiple of 3 to 4 generally indicates that profits are expected to remain steady or may decline, 4 to 5 that profits will remain steady or increase modestly, and 6 and higher that profits are expected to increase significantly.
5. Multiply the profits by the profit multiple to determine the value of the business.
6. Finally, subtract bank debt such as lines of credit or mortgages to determine the estimated value of the business *to the entrepreneur*.

For example, assume a business had profits of $250,000 last year, and the entrepreneur took a bonus of $50,000 over the normal salary that same year. While the business had strong profit growth over the past several years, there are strong indications that this growth may be difficult to sustain due to changing market conditions. The business had about $100,000 in long-term bank debt. Given the positive impact of historical growth in profits, tempered by the less than positive outlook in the industry, the entrepreneur decided to use a middle-range multiple of 5 times profits. The calculation would look like this:

Profits	$ 250,000
Plus: one-time bonus	50,000
Adjusted profits	$ 300,000
Times: earnings multiple	× 5
Value of business	$1,500,000
Less: business debt	100,000
Quick and dirty estimate of value of business to owner	$1,400,000

Remember that this is not considered a formal valuation. Rather, it is simply a means for the entrepreneur to create an estimate. Formal valuations can often lead to very different estimates due to factors not addressed in this quick and dirty approach. For example, one entrepreneur had estimated the value of his prototyping business to be about $3 million. However, when he began negotiations to sell his business, he was shocked that the initial offer was more than twice that figure. Apparently, he had created a strong market niche and very loyal customers for which the buyer was willing to pay a premium. On the other hand, another entrepreneur who owned a counseling center was greatly disappointed by the offer she received. She had estimated the value of her business to be about $800,000. However, prospective buyers were concerned that most of the profit was tied to her own services in the center. The only way that future profits would continue would be if she continued to work as hard as she always had. Because the potential buyers all thought that she was using the sale to work into retirement, they all made offers that were less than half of what she had estimated. Valuation will be discussed more fully in Chapter 13.

Planning for specific goals for wealth can be difficult, particularly when first starting a business. However, for many entrepreneurs it is the wealth that they create from their businesses that will be used for long-term needs such as retirement. Therefore, it is important for the entrepreneur to at least make an estimate of a retirement date (i.e., early or at a more traditional age) and how much wealth will be needed for the desired lifestyle during retirement. The self-assessment process can help the entrepreneur begin to think about these types of issues more concretely and to then build them into the criteria used to evaluate potential business ventures. However, before moving to the specifics of the self-assessment, it is important to recognize that there are nonfinancial goals that should also be considered.

INTEGRATING NONFINANCIAL GOALS

. . . (The entrepreneur) was a gifted computer specialist. He came for assistance in getting his cash flow and financing under control. He had identified a market niche for a computer application he had been developing with his previous employer. The employer was not interested in the idea, so the entrepreneur gained permission to take the idea and start his own company to develop and market the product. He had methodically refined the concept and done a remarkable job in making the program operational and ready for market. He reported that he was on the verge of breaking through into the market, but was "dealing with some financial distress." If he could raise a little more money, he would be able to make the business profitable. When asked how bad his financial condition was, he matter-of-factly stated that he had funded his start-up primarily through his life savings (i.e., cashed his retirement accounts) and through a second mortgage on his home. He had gotten "a little behind" on his loan repayment and lost his house. This frustrated his wife, who took their children and left him. And, oh yes, he was about to have his car repossessed. But he only needed to raise another $50,000 and he could deliver his product to several customers. He did raise the funds and did become financially successful. However, at what cost? He . . . left behind a trail of damage to his family, friends, creditors, and many others. (Naughton and Cornwall, 2001).

Cathy Cotton works like a maniac. From 9 A.M. until midnight, Cotton toils away at Meta-Search Inc., her two-year-old . . . technical recruiting company. At midnight an alarm in Cotton's . . . office goes off—her way of reminding herself to quit working. But more often than not, she ignores the clock and keeps going. She typically heads home between 2 A.M. and 4 A.M. (Gruner, 1997).

Many entrepreneurs create ventures, such as those in the preceding examples, that consume all of their time and focus. It is understood that many jobs go through periods where long hours are required. This is very common when starting a new business, as well. However, the woman in the example has a business that is now two years old and shows no sign of changing her behaviors. There is growing recognition of the importance of creating a more balanced life, even during an entrepreneurial start-up. Without addressing the issue of balance, the entrepreneur risks damaging physical and mental health, as well as relationships with family and friends.

In addition to the financial goals we have discussed, entrepreneurs should establish specific nonfinancial goals. How much time does the entrepreneur want to spend with family? What other interests or hobbies does the entrepreneur want to be able to continue to pursue? Should formal education be continued? Are there other aspirations to pursue at some point in life? One entrepreneur made a goal that whenever he was in town he would always be home for dinner with his family. Sometimes this meant that he would have to go back to work to finish an important project, but he made sure to integrate this commitment into his work.

These nonfinancial goals can be even more important than the financial goals for some entrepreneurs. Another entrepreneur was faced with the possibility of an initial public offering for his business. Experts told him that he could expect a large personal return from the offering. However, he realized that if he did take his business public, this would mean a great deal of travel that would keep him away from his family. Instead, he chose to find a buyer for his business so he could spend even more time with his children before they grew up. Although the sale resulted in a good financial return, it was a fraction of what he could have received from a public offering. To him, however, the trade-off was well worth it.

These goals can be integrated into business planning. Business growth is one of the major drains on the entrepreneur's time. When planning the business, the entrepreneur may choose to plan for growth that allows for more balance in life, rather than planning for the maximum growth the market will allow.

IMPORTANCE OF SELF-ASSESSMENT

The process of self-assessment plays an important role throughout the life of an entrepreneurial venture. Aspirations for income and wealth can change over time, so it is important to revisit the process of self-assessment periodically. The entrepreneur may have a change in a family situation, such as getting married or having children. Such changes often require an adjustment to both short-term and long-term financial goals. These changes can also create new nonfinancial goals that become increasingly important, such as having time to spend with children as they grow up. Changes in aspirations also can occur as a result of changes in the business. Often, ventures can either exceed or fall well short of initial expectations, and entrepreneurs may need to adjust their expectations accordingly. For example, if the goals are unrealistic given the current prospects for the business, the entrepreneur may need to either bring financial goals in line with this reality or even choose to sell the venture and pursue a more promising one.

Businesses go through distinct phases of development (Churchill, 1983). During each stage, both the entrepreneurial venture and the entrepreneur go through transitions and changes. The first stage is pre-venture, during which the business plan is developed and all of the work necessary to open the business occurs. The second stage is start-up. This is when the venture is launched and begins basic operations. This stage can last until the business has well over $1 million in revenue. The third stage is growth. This is when revenues and, it is hoped, profits begin to grow much more quickly. The fourth stage is maturity, which can include the exit of the entrepreneur from the business. Although the exit of the entrepreneur can actually occur at any stage in development of a business, maturity is the most common stage at which it occurs.

Self-assessment can play a prominent role in the planning of a new venture, which occurs during the pre-venture stage. In evaluating opportunities and conducting feasibility analyses, the primary criterion is the financial viability of the business idea under consideration. Some mistakenly assume that breaking even equates to financial feasibility. In reality, to be financially viable the new venture must not only meet breakeven but also meet the financial needs and expectations of the entrepreneur and other investors. Many entrepreneurs fail to factor in their own financial goals during this critical step in evaluating opportunities. "Making a lot of money" or "providing for my family" are not specific enough goals to integrate into the new-venture planning process. Entrepreneurs should take the time to assess the specific expectations they have for income and wealth from their business venture and integrate that into the feasibility analysis and business planning. It is hard to imagine that someone applying for a management position in a publicly traded company would go into negotiations for the job without a salary and benefit goal in mind. And yet, many entrepreneurs do just that when planning their own ventures.

The start-up of any business can be a time of much excitement and confusion. Many entrepreneurs suddenly identify additional opportunities that were not part of their original plans. There also is a tendency to take on any orders that come through the door to help cash flow. While this may be necessary, it is important to have a well-developed plan formed by the entrepreneur's thoughtful self-assessment to keep the business focused and headed in the desired direction. Entrepreneurs who stray off-course from their plans to reduce their anxiety over cash flow can sometimes lock themselves into a business model that will not let them achieve the personal goals and objectives they hoped to achieve through their businesses. Therefore, any change in direction for a new start-up business should be carefully evaluated.

The growth phase of a business can be one of the most perilous periods for an entrepreneurial venture. The business can begin to experience many stresses and strains on systems and staff. Flamholtz (1990), in his book *Growing Pains,* calls this the transition from an entrepreneurship to a professionally managed business. During this transition, the entrepreneur's role begins to change within the business. No longer can the hands-on, day-to-day management style used during the start-up be followed. Management and operating systems need to be put in place and upgraded to manage growth effectively. The management team begins to grow and take on ever-increasing responsibilities. One entrepreneur who successfully navigated this transition stated that his "business took on a life of its own." This is a common feeling. Growth is pursued simply because the business can grow. The reason the entrepreneur started the business—the personal goals and aspirations—can become blurred and even secondary in importance to the growing body of decision makers. It becomes crucial for the entrepreneur to reinstill personal goals and vision for the business into the business. This may not be as easy as it might appear. However, it is still the entrepreneur's business. Flamholtz (1990) discusses how the entrepreneur's role transitions to one of leadership based on a strong vision of where the business is headed. This vision should be fundamentally based on the entrepreneur's own goals and aspirations, which may require revisiting the self-assessment process to make sure that any changes in the entrepreneur's goals and aspirations are accurately reflected.

At some point in time, every entrepreneur exits a business. This can happen in a variety of ways, including selling the business, transitioning to the next generation in a family business, bankruptcy, or even through the death of the entrepreneur. The process of preparing for this departure is called *exit planning*. Most experts recommend beginning the exit planning process at the very beginning of a business venture. They recommend that the entrepreneur be clear on what is wanted from the business, how long to be involved in the business, and what should happen to the business once the entrepreneur leaves. Clearly, the exit process, if well executed, relies on careful and thoughtful self-assessment. It is important to note that most ventures do not evolve exactly as planned and that exits do not always happen as the entrepreneur originally intended. However, that does not diminish the importance of such planning. Chapter 14 will examine the exit process in more detail.

THE SELF-ASSESSMENT PROCESS

There are many ways in which an entrepreneur can evaluate goals and aspirations. In this book, we draw upon a self-assessment model developed by Cornwall and Carter (1999) for the John M. Morrison Center for Entrepreneurship at the University of St. Thomas. The self-assessment can be found in the Appendix at the end of this chapter.

The first section of the self-assessment helps the entrepreneur begin the process of identifying and prioritizing those things that are most important. In this section, the entrepreneur is asked to specifically identify financial goals, which include both income goals and wealth goals. These goals should be very specific and measurable (e.g., being "really rich" is not a measurable goal). These personal financial goals become the basis for setting the financial goals of the entrepreneur's business. For example, an entrepreneur starting a business right out of college may set an income goal of reaching the average salary of college classmates that went into traditional industry jobs by the third year of the business venture, recognizing that in the first two years there will likely be less personal income due to the demands of start-up. By the fifth year, the goal is to make 50 percent more than former classmates. The wealth goals include having enough wealth to retire at 50 so that other interests in life could be pursued and having enough invested to pay for the children's college expenses no matter where they want to go to school.

But the self-assessment moves well beyond financial goals. Nonfinancial goals are also included in the questionnaire. One entrepreneur realized after completing his self-assessment that his preoccupation with rapid growth and success had caused him to forget how important his family was to him. He stated that he had not been able to spend any time with his children for the past year. After this realization, he decided to build more family time into his business planning in the future. He had reached a point of financial stability but needed to spend more time addressing his family's stability. As simple as these questions may first appear, they can provoke powerful discernment if approached with honesty and careful thought. There are several questions in this section that help entrepreneurs define success on their own terms. Success in business, family, and friendship is a part of a single "equation." And each entrepreneur evaluates success in a different way. The end of this section challenges the entrepreneur to clearly identify the core values being brought to the business. These are the values that will shape the business ethics of the entrepreneur (see Chapter 1).

The second section of the questionnaire raises more specific questions regarding personal readiness and personal preferences that can shape how an entrepreneur approaches the new business. These personal preferences and characteristics also should be integrated into the business planning process. For example, entrepreneurs have varying tolerances for risk. All businesses include some degree of financial risk, but entrepreneurs need to consider other, nonfinancial risks, such as reputation, career advancement, and additional stress on a family. Some can tolerate much more risk than others. The level of risk tolerance can be used to determine if a particular venture is the right one for a given entrepreneur to pursue. Risk tolerance should also be considered in planning how large a venture will become and how rapid a growth plan should be pursued.

Self-assessments often include items that address additional areas, such as idea-generation exercises, thorough evaluations of skills, knowledge and competencies, personality assessments, and vocational assessments. Although these are important processes to go through in pre-venture planning, they move beyond the scope of setting financial (and nonfinancial) goals for the business. Setting financial goals is the foundation of entrepreneurial financial management.

THE BUSINESS PLAN

Once the entrepreneur has a clear understanding of the financial goals and the business goals needed to achieve personal goals, these goals should be used to generate the business plan. The business plan is a comprehensive document that

FIGURE 2-2 Business Plan Outline

I. Executive Summary (one-page summary of the entire plan)

II. The Business Concept

    A. Vision of company   C. Core values

    B. Mission statement

III. Industry Analysis

    A. Size   C. Trends

    B. Status (growing, mature, declining)   D. Barriers to entry

IV. Marketing Plan

    A. Target market   B. Competitive analysis

       • Description   C. Pricing

       • Results of market research   D. Promotional plan

       • Entry strategy   E. Distribution

V. Operating Plan

    A. Map out the flow of all aspects of   B. Team

        the business   C. Advisors

       • Raw materials and supplies   D. Space requirements and costs

       • Making the product or providing   E. Basic staffing plan as you grow

         the service

       • Sales process—customer contact

         from beginning to end

       • Bookkeeping and billing

VI. Growth Plan

    A. Growth goals: long- and short-term

    B. Growth strategies

    C. Growth requirements

VII. Financial Plan

    A. Complete list of key assumptions for most-likely case scenario

    B. Complete list of key assumptions for worst-case scenario

    C. Income statements for both scenarios

       • Monthly for at least three years

    D. Balance sheets for both scenarios

       • Monthly for three years

    E. Statements of cash flows (direct method) for both scenarios

        (see Chapter 9 for discussion of this statement)

       • Monthly for three years

VIII. Appendices

describes the intended course that the entrepreneur wants the business to take. Figure 2-2 displays a sample outline for a comprehensive business plan. Such an outline is just an example, as each business plan should be tailored to its specific use. For example, business plans used to generate equity financing (Chapters 11–12) should include more detail throughout. Generally, any business plan should include the same comprehensive and fully integrated set of financial forecasts as will be generated by following the process presented in Chapters 3–6.

SUMMARY

This chapter presented a model for financial goal setting and examined the difference between income and wealth. The importance of thoughtful and thorough personal self-assessment to assist in setting goals for the business was outlined for each stage of the business life cycle. Finally, a model for self-assessment was presented. The next chapter provides an understanding of the basic financial statements used in all business ventures.

DISCUSSION QUESTIONS

1. Discuss the differences between wealth and income. Why is this distinction important for an entrepreneur to understand?
2. What nonfinancial goals are important to you? How would you integrate these goals into your career planning?

OPPORTUNITY FOR APPLICATION

1. Complete the self-assessment in the Appendix. What did you learn about yourself from completing this questionnaire? How will you integrate what you learned into your business planning?

REFERENCES

Churchill, N. (1983). Entrepreneurs and their enterprises: A stage model. In *Frontiers of Entrepreneurship Research,* J. A. Hornaday, et al. (eds). Babson Park, MA: Babson College, pp. 1–22.

Cornwall, J., and Carter, N. (1999). *University of St. Thomas Entrepreneurial Self-Assessment: Start-up.* St. Paul, MN: John M. Morrison Center for Entrepreneurship, University of St. Thomas.

Flamholtz, E. (1990). *Growing Pains*. San Francisco: Jossey-Bass.

Gruner, S. (1997, October). Get a life! *Inc. Magazine.*

Naughton, M., and Cornwall, J. The good entrepreneur and the role of virtue. Presented to the 11th International Symposium on Ethics, Business and Society, July 2001, Barcelona, Spain.

Stanley, T., and Danko, W. (1996). *The Millionaire Next Door*. Atlanta, GA: Longstreet Press.

---------------------------**A P P E N D I X   1**---------------------------

University of St. Thomas
Entrepreneurial Self-Assessment[1]

Section I. Personal Aspirations and Priorities

What gets you excited, gives you energy, and motivates you to excel?

What do you like to do with your time?

What drains energy from you?
    In the work you do:

    In personal relationships:

How do you measure success in your personal life?
    Family:

    Friends and relationships:

    Personal interests/hobbies:

    Contributions to community/society:

What do you consider success in your business/career?
    Short-term:

    Long-term:

What are your specific goals for your personal life?
    Family:

    Friends and relationships:

    Personal interests/hobbies:

    Contributions to community/society:

What are your goals for your business/career?
    Income/lifestyle:

    Wealth:

---

[1]This self-assessment is adapted from the Cornwall, J., and Carter, N., "Entrepreneurial Self-Assessment: Start-up" from the John M. Morrison Center for Entrepreneurship, University of St. Thomas, St. Paul, MN with permission.

Free time:

Recognition/fame:

Impact on community:

Other:

What do you want to be doing:
In one year:

In five years:

In ten years:

At retirement?

Start your Personal Entrepreneurial Plan with a summary of what you described above, making sure to identify priorities and time frames.

Core Values

List the core personal values that you intend to bring to your business (e.g., treating people fairly, giving something back to the community). Where do each of these core values come from (religious faith, family, etc.)? Why are each of these important to you?

Integrate your core values into your Personal Entrepreneurial Plan.

Section II. Personal Entrepreneurial Readiness

What are the major reasons you want to start a business?

How many hours are you willing and able to put into your new venture?

How would you describe your tolerance for uncertainty and risk?

Do you easily trust other people working with you on a common activity? Why or why not?

How much financial risk are you willing to take with your new venture (personal assets, personal debt, etc.)?

Assume you decide not to start your business. A short time later, you see that someone has started the same business and is doing well. How would you feel? Why?

What are the nonfinancial risks for you in starting a new business?

How do you react to failure? Give examples.

How do you react in times of personal stress? How do you deal with stress in your life?

How much income do you need for your current lifestyle?

How long could you survive without a paycheck?

How much money do you have available to start your business?

Which of your personal assets would you be willing to borrow against, or sell, to start your business?

Whose support (nonfinancial) is important for you to have before starting your business (family, spouse, etc.)?

CHAPTER

3

Understanding Financial Statements

Chapter 1 described accounting as the language of business. This chapter provides an overview of basic accounting. The entrepreneur should understand the impact of a business decision on both the income statement and the balance sheet prior to making the decision. This chapter is intended as a review for those who have already been exposed to accounting in previous courses. With this review, the reader will be better prepared for the remaining chapters in this book, but it may be skipped if the reader feels comfortable enough with the relationship between the income statement, the balance sheet, and the cash flow statement to use the integrated financial statement model presented in Chapter 6.

There are two main types of accounting: financial and managerial. Financial accounting deals mostly with reporting what has happened historically. Users of financial accounting include investors, creditors, potential employees, customers, and government agencies such as the Internal Revenue Service and the Securities and Exchange Commission. Financial accounting reports are prepared using generally accepted accounting principles (GAAP). This allows users to make comparisons between companies, knowing that they are accounted for on the same basis.

Managerial accounting refers to accounting information prepared internally to help managers make decisions for the business. Examples include gross profit analysis by product, unit cost analysis, and department budget compared to actual expense analysis, just to name a few. The basis of managerial and financial information is the same. It all comes from recording transactions in the accounting system.

THE ACCOUNTING EQUATION

The basis of all accounting is the following equation:

$$Assets = Liabilities + Owners' Equity$$

Every financial business transaction can be put in this format to assess the impact on the business. Assets are resources owned by an entity: cash, accounts receivable (amounts owed by customers), prepaid expenses, inventory, land, equipment, patents, copyrights, and so on. Liabilities are amounts owed to others: accounts payable (amounts owed to suppliers), wages payable, taxes payable, notes payable, bank loans, and so on. Owners' equity represents the ownership rights of the investor(s); it is the owners' claims to assets after all liabilities have been satisfied. In other words, if the company assets were used to satisfy the liabilities, the remaining balance of the assets would belong to the owners. Other terms for owners' equity include *stockholders' equity, net assets,* or *book value* of the company.

Owners' equity consists of two primary components: the investment in the business by the owners and the retained earnings of the business. Retained earnings represent the earnings of the business (prior years' earnings plus the current year's income) that have been retained for use in the business rather than disbursed to stockholders as dividends or to owners as withdrawals.

AN EXAMPLE

The accounting process results in recording the transactions for the company for a period of time as they affect the accounting equation. Periodically—be it monthly, quarterly, or yearly—a company will sum these transactions and issue the financial statements. Working through an example is the easiest way to understand the accounting equation and the interrelationship of the financial statements. For our example, "The Company" is the name of a new merchandising business that buys inventory and then sells it to customers. Table 3-1 displays a more detailed version of the basic accounting equation.

Dennis Becker, an entrepreneur, sells shares of stock to investors in The Company for $100,000. This means The Company now has $100,000 in cash and the owners have shares of stock. This transaction would increase the asset cash while at the same time increasing common stock, a part of owners' equity (see Table 3-2).

$$\text{Assets} = \text{Liabilities} + \text{Owners' Equity}$$
$$(\$100,000) = \$0 + \$100,000$$

TABLE 3-1

	Assets					=	Liabilities			+	Owners' Equity		
	Cash +	Accounts Receivable +	Inventory +	Equipment –	Accum. Deprec.	=	Notes Payable +	Accounts Payable +	Wages Payable	+	Common Stock +	Retained Earnings +	Revenues – Expenses
Balance						=							

TABLE 3-2

	Assets					=	Liabilities			+	Owners' Equity		
	Cash +	Accounts Receivable +	Inventory +	Equipment –	Accum. Deprec.	=	Notes Payable +	Accounts Payable +	Wages Payable	+	Common Stock +	Retained Earnings +	Revenues – Expenses
	100,000					=					100,000		
Balance	100,000					=					100,000		

TABLE 3-3

	Assets					=	Liabilities			+	Owners' Equity		
	Cash +	Accounts Receivable +	Inventory +	Equipment –	Accum. Deprec.	=	Notes Payable +	Accounts Payable +	Wages Payable	+	Common Stock +	Retained Earnings +	Revenues – Expenses
	100,000					=					100,000		
	(36,000)			36,000		=							
Balance	64,000			36,000		=					100,000		

The Company then buys a piece of equipment for $36,000 in cash. This transaction reduces the asset cash but increases the asset equipment. After this transaction, assets still equal $100,000, but there are two categories of assets, cash and equipment (see Table 3-3).

$$\text{Assets} = \text{Liabilities} + \text{Owners' Equity}$$
$$(\$64,000 + \$36,000) = \$0 + \$100,000$$

Now The Company decides to borrow money from the local bank. The loan is for $15,000 and the entrepreneur signs a note agreeing to pay the bank back the principal and annual interest of 8% at a future date. The impact of this transaction is to increase the asset cash and to increase the liability notes payable (see Table 3-4).

$$\text{Assets} = \text{Liabilities} + \text{Owners' Equity}$$
$$(\$79,000 + \$36,000) = \$15,000 + \$100,000$$

The Company purchases inventory to be resold to customers. It buys $40,000 of inventory on account. "On account" means it has not yet paid for the inventory but will do so later. The impact of this transaction is to increase the asset inventory and increase the liability accounts payable (see Table 3-5).

$$\text{Assets} = \text{Liabilities} + \text{Owners' Equity}$$
$$(\$79,000 + \$40,000 + \$36,000) = (\$15,000 + \$40,000) + \$100,000$$

The Company is now ready to open for business. During the first month, it sells $10,000 of the inventory it previously purchased, for $35,000 on account. In this case "on account" means that the sale was on credit; that is, the customer will be paying at a later date. However, accrual accounting under GAAP says the sale should be recorded in the same period that the customer receives the goods or services. Therefore, the sale is recorded with an increase to accounts receivable instead of cash. Because the customer has the inventory, a second entry is required to reduce inventory for its cost, $10,000 and to show the expense or "cost of goods sold" of $10,000 (see Table 3-6).

$$\text{Assets} = \text{Liabilities} + \text{Owners' Equity}$$
$$(\$79,000 + \$35,000 + \$30,000 + \$36,000) = (\$15,000 + \$40,000) + (\$100,000 + \$35,000 - \$10,000)$$

Assets increased by a net $25,000 while equity increased by a net $25,000. Revenues increase equity because they increase income. Expenses decrease equity because they decrease income. The minus sign in front of the expenses means that as expenses increase, equity decreases.

The next transaction involves the payment of $10,000 for rent for the month. Rent is one of the costs of running a business, which are called *expenses*. Because

TABLE 3-4

	Assets					=		Liabilities		+	Owners' Equity		
	Cash	+ Accounts Receivable	+ Inventory	+ Equipment	– Accum. Deprec.	=	Notes Payable	+ Accounts Payable	+ Wages Payable	+ Common Stock	+ Retained Earnings	+ Revenues	– Expenses
	100,000					=				100,000			
	(36,000)			36,000		=							
	15,000					=	15,000						
Balance	79,000			36,000		=	15,000			100,000			

TABLE 3-5

	Assets					=		Liabilities		+	Owners' Equity		
	Cash	+ Accounts Receivable	+ Inventory	+ Equipment	– Accum. Deprec.	=	Notes Payable	+ Accounts Payable	+ Wages Payable	+ Common Stock	+ Retained Earnings	+ Revenues	– Expenses
	100,000					=				100,000			
	(36,000)			36,000		=							
	15,000					=	15,000						
		40,000				=		40,000					
Balance	79,000	40,000		36,000		=	15,000	40,000		100,000			

TABLE 3-6

	Assets				=	Liabilities			+	Owners' Equity			
Cash	Accounts Receivable	Inventory	Equipment	Accum. Deprec.	=	Notes Payable	Accounts Payable	Wages Payable	+	Common Stock	Retained Earnings	Revenues	Expenses
100,000					=					100,000			
(36,000)			36,000		=								
15,000					=	15,000							
		40,000			=		40,000						
	35,000	(10,000)			=							35,000	(10,000)
Balance 79,000	35,000	30,000	36,000		=	15,000	40,000			100,000		35,000	(10,000)

TABLE 3-7

	Assets				=	Liabilities			+	Owners' Equity			
Cash	Accounts Receivable	Inventory	Equipment	Accum. Deprec.	=	Notes Payable	Accounts Payable	Wages Payable	+	Common Stock	Retained Earnings	Revenues	Expenses
100,000					=					100,000			
(36,000)			36,000		=								
15,000					=	15,000							
		40,000			=		40,000						
	35,000	(10,000)			=							35,000	(10,000)
(10,000)					=								(10,000)
Balance 69,000	35,000	30,000	36,000		=	15,000	40,000			100,000		35,000	(20,000)

the rent is for the current month, it is recorded as an expense in the current month. Paying rent reduces the asset cash and reduces equity because expenses have increased (see Table 3-7).

$$\text{Assets} = \text{Liabilities} + \text{Owners' Equity}$$
$$(\$69{,}000 + \$35{,}000 + \$30{,}000 + \$36{,}000) = (\$15{,}000 + \$40{,}000) + (\$100{,}000 + \$35{,}000 - \$20{,}000)$$

The Company receives a utility (heat and lights) bill for $2,000, which it will pay the following month. Under accrual accounting, the expense is recognized when it is incurred even though it will not be paid until the following month. The impact on the equation is to increase the liability accounts payable and to increase expenses, which reduces equity (see Table 3-8).

$$\text{Assets} = \text{Liabilities} + \text{Owners' Equity}$$
$$(\$69{,}000 + \$35{,}000 + \$30{,}000 + \$36{,}000) = (\$15{,}000 + \$42{,}000) + (\$100{,}000 + \$35{,}000 - \$22{,}000)$$

The Company receives a check in the mail for $10,000 as partial payment of the account receivable owed by their customer. The asset cash increases by $10,000 while the asset accounts receivable decreases by $10,000 (see Table 3-9).

$$\text{Assets} = \text{Liabilities} + \text{Owners' Equity}$$
$$(\$79{,}000 + \$25{,}000 + \$30{,}000 + \$36{,}000) = (\$15{,}000 + \$42{,}000) + (\$100{,}000 + \$35{,}000 - \$22{,}000)$$

The Company makes a $20,000 partial payment to the supplier of the inventory. The asset cash goes down by $20,000, and the liability accounts payable also decreases by $20,000 (see Table 3-10).

$$\text{Assets} = \text{Liabilities} + \text{Owners' Equity}$$
$$(\$59{,}000 + \$25{,}000 + \$30{,}000 + \$36{,}000) = (\$15{,}000 + \$22{,}000) + (\$100{,}000 + \$35{,}000 - \$22{,}000)$$

At the end of the month, The Company owes its employee $5,000 in wages, which it will pay at the beginning of the next month. The employee has been working in the current month and is therefore owed the wages for the services performed. The Company must record the cost of those services as an expense and will record a liability called wages payable to show that it owes the employee for those services (see Table 3-11).

$$\text{Assets} = \text{Liabilities} + \text{Owners' Equity}$$
$$(\$59{,}000 + \$25{,}000 + \$30{,}000 + \$36{,}000) = (\$15{,}000 + \$22{,}000 + \$5{,}000) + (\$100{,}000 + \$35{,}000 - \$27{,}000)$$

TABLE 3-8

		Assets			=		Liabilities		+		Owners' Equity		
Cash	Accounts Receivable	Inventory	Equipment	Accum. Deprec.	=	Notes Payable	Accounts Payable	Wages Payable	+	Common Stock	Retained Earnings	Revenues	Expenses
100,000					=					100,000			
(36,000)			36,000		=								
15,000					=	15,000							
	35,000				=		40,000						
		40,000			=							35,000	
(10,000)		(10,000)			=								(10,000)
				(10,000)	=		2,000						(10,000)
					=								(2,000)
Balance 69,000	35,000	30,000	36,000	(10,000)	=	15,000	42,000			100,000		35,000	(22,000)

TABLE 3-9

		Assets			=		Liabilities		+		Owners' Equity		
Cash	Accounts Receivable	Inventory	Equipment	Accum. Deprec.	=	Notes Payable	Accounts Payable	Wages Payable	+	Common Stock	Retained Earnings	Revenues	Expenses
100,000					=					100,000			
(36,000)			36,000		=								
15,000					=	15,000							
	35,000				=		40,000						
		40,000			=							35,000	
(10,000)		(10,000)			=								(10,000)
				(10,000)	=		2,000						(10,000)
					=								(2,000)
10,000	(10,000)				=								
Balance 79,000	25,000	30,000	36,000	(10,000)	=	15,000	42,000			100,000		35,000	(22,000)

■ 33 ■

TABLE 3-10

	Assets					=	Liabilities			+	Owners' Equity			
	Cash	Accounts Receivable	Inventory	Equipment	Accum. Deprec.	=	Notes Payable	Accounts Payable	Wages Payable	+	Common Stock	Retained Earnings	Revenues	− Expenses
	100,000					=					100,000			
	(36,000)			36,000		=								
	15,000					=	15,000							
			40,000			=		40,000						
		35,000				=							35,000	
			(10,000)			=								(10,000)
	(10,000)					=								(10,000)
						=		2,000						(2,000)
	10,000	(10,000)				=								
	(20,000)					=		(20,000)						
Balance	59,000	25,000	30,000	36,000		=	15,000	22,000			100,000		35,000	(22,000)

TABLE 3-11

	Assets						Liabilities			Owners' Equity		
Cash	+ Accounts Receivable	+ Inventory	+ Equipment	– Accum. Deprec.	=	Notes Payable	+ Accounts Payable	+ Wages Payable	+ Common Stock	+ Retained Earnings	+ Revenues	– Expenses
100,000					=				100,000			
(36,000)			36,000		=							
15,000					=	15,000						
		40,000			=		40,000					
	35,000				=						35,000	
		(10,000)			=							(10,000)
(10,000)					=							(10,000)
					=		2,000					(2,000)
10,000	(10,000)				=							
					=			5,000				(5,000)
(20,000)					=		(20,000)					
Balance 59,000	25,000	30,000	36,000		=	15,000	22,000	5,000	100,000		35,000	(27,000)

The Company now needs to record depreciation on the equipment. Depreciation expense represents the allocation of the initial cost of a piece of equipment to expense over its useful life. Through recognition of depreciation expense the income statement reflects the cost of using equipment in the business. The process of recording depreciation expense is not meant to reflect the equipment at market value. Most companies use the straight-line method to record depreciation in their financial statements. Under straight-line depreciation, the cost of the equipment less its trade-in value (if any) is divided by the number of months the company expects to use it. The Company plans on using this piece of equipment for 36 months and does not expect it to have any trade-in value at the end of the 36 months. Therefore, it will record $1,000 of depreciation every month ($36,000/36 months = $1,000). Depreciation is recorded by setting up a contra-asset account (an account that reduces assets) called accumulated depreciation. This account will accumulate all depreciation until the piece of equipment is sold or discarded. The other account impacted will be depreciation expense. Depreciation expense reduces income, reflecting the fact that the company had to use this equipment to run its operations (see Table 3-12).

$$\text{Assets} \quad = \quad \text{Liabilities} \quad + \quad \text{Owners' Equity}$$
$$(\$59{,}000 + \$25{,}000 + \$30{,}000 = (\$15{,}000 + \$22{,}000 + (\$100{,}000 + \$35{,}000$$
$$+ \$36{,}000 - \$1{,}000) \qquad + \$5{,}000) \qquad - \$28{,}000)$$

Finally, the entrepreneur needs to record the interest paid on the note payable. The interest for one month is determined using the interest formula:

$$\text{Interest} = \text{Principal} \times \text{Rate} \times \text{Time}$$

In this case, the interest for one month would be $15,000 × .08 × 1/12, or $100. Cash would decrease by $100 and interest expense would increase by $100. The increase in expense results in a decrease to owners' equity (see Table 3-13).

$$\text{Assets} \quad = \quad \text{Liabilities} \quad + \quad \text{Owners' Equity}$$
$$(\$58{,}900 + \$25{,}000 + \$30{,}000 = (\$15{,}000 + \$22{,}000 + (\$100{,}000 + \$35{,}000$$
$$+ \$36{,}000 - \$1{,}000) \qquad + \$5{,}000) \qquad - \$28{,}100)$$

A typical company records many more transactions in any given month. The intent of the example is to show how transactions impact the accounting equation. Some transactions impact only the balance sheet, while others impact the income statement and the balance sheet. The entrepreneur needs to understand the impact his or her decisions have on the financial statements. For an in-depth review of accounting transactions, the reader should review any introductory accounting textbook.

TABLE 3-12

	Assets					=	Liabilities			+	Owners' Equity			
	Cash	+ Accounts Receivable	+ Inventory	+ Equipment	– Accum. Deprec.	=	Notes Payable	+ Accounts Payable	+ Wages Payable	+	Common Stock	+ Retained Earnings	+ Revenues	– Expenses
	100,000					=					100,000			
	(36,000)			36,000		=								
	15,000					=	15,000							
			40,000			=		40,000						
		35,000				=							35,000	
			(10,000)			=								(10,000)
	(10,000)					=								(10,000)
						=		2,000						(2,000)
						=			5,000					(5,000)
	10,000	(10,000)				=								
	(20,000)					=		(20,000)						
					(1,000)	=								(1,000)
Balance	59,000	25,000	30,000	36,000	(1,000)	=	15,000	22,000	5,000		100,000	35,000		(28,000)

TABLE 3-13

	Assets						Liabilities				Owners' Equity			
	Cash	+ Accounts Receivable	+ Inventory	+ Equipment	− Accum. Deprec.	=	Notes Payable	+ Accounts Payable	+ Wages Payable	+ Common Stock	+ Retained Earnings	+ Revenues	− Expenses
	100,000					=				100,000			
	(36,000)			36,000		=							
	15,000					=	15,000						
		35,000	40,000			=		40,000				35,000	
	(10,000)		(10,000)			=							(10,000)
	(10,000)					=		2,000					(2,000)
	10,000	(10,000)				=							
	(20,000)					=		(20,000)					
						=			5,000				(5,000)
	(100)				(1,000)	=							(1,000)
						=							(100)
Balance	58,900	25,000	30,000	36,000	(1,000)	=	15,000	22,000	5,000	100,000		35,000	(28,100)

BASIC FINANCIAL STATEMENTS

The next step in the accounting cycle would be to prepare the financial statements. A company has four basic financial statements. The *balance sheet* reports what a company owns and owes at a given point in time. It also is known as a statement of financial position. The *income statement* tells how a company has performed, that is, its income or loss for a period of time. The *statement of changes in owners' equity* summarizes any investments by owners and earnings of the company, less any distributions made to owners, for a period of time. The *statement of cash flows* reports how the entity produced and used cash for a period of time.

Income Statement

The first statement to be prepared is the income statement, which is a scorecard for a *period* of time. It answers basic questions about the performance of the business: Did the company make money? What were the financial results of its operations for the most recent time period? It is prepared following GAAP as discussed at the beginning of this chapter.

There are only two categories on the income statement: revenues and expenses. Revenues are created when the entity sells a product or provides services and receives cash or creates a receivable in return. There are many terms for revenues, including *sales, net sales, net revenues,* and *fees.*

Expenses are outflows, the using up of assets or incurring a liability for services or goods received. They may be recognized with the revenues that relate to the expense (e.g., "cost of goods sold"). Expenses may also be recognized in the period they are incurred (e.g., rent, administrative salaries). Finally, expenses may be recognized to reflect an allocation of cost to the period (e.g., depreciation). The income statement for The Company example is displayed in Exhibit 3-1

Gross profit is the difference between sales and the cost of goods sold. It is usually expressed as a percentage of sales and serves as an important measure of whether a company is generating enough profit margin to cover operating expenses and provide income. However, it is not a measure used by companies that provide services. Operating Expenses may be classified into selling, general and administrative, research and development, and other. Internally, a company may classify them as direct or indirect, variable or fixed. In the income statement in Exhibit 3-1, each expense was listed individually instead of being grouped into categories. EBIT, or **E**arnings **B**efore **I**nterest and **T**axes, equals gross profit less operating expenses. It is usually considered a key measurement of management's ability to utilize a firm's assets to generate income.

Interest expense (and/or interest income) is usually shown as a separate line item. Most users want to know this amount because it is a contractual obligation. EBIT less interest equals EBT, or **E**arnings **B**efore **T**axes. This book will not address the topic of income tax expense. How taxes are calculated and recorded is dependent on how the company has been organized (i.e., sole proprietorship, partnership, limited liability corporation, subchapter S, or C Corporation). An entrepreneur should

EXHIBIT 3-1		

The Company
Income Statement
Month ended April 30, 2002

Sales	$35,000	100.0%
Cost of Goods Sold	10,000	28.6
Gross Profit	25,000	71.4
Operating Expenses		
Rent expense	10,000	28.6
Utilities expense	2,000	5.7
Wages expense	5,000	14.3
Depreciation expense	1,000	2.8
Total Operating Expenses	18,000	51.4
Earnings Before Interest and Taxes (EBIT)	7,000	20.0
Interest expense	100	.3
Earnings Before Taxes	$ 6,900	19.7%

consult a legal and tax advisor as to the optimum method of organization for his or her personal circumstances. Another measurement of income is **Earnings Before Interest, Taxes, Depreciation and Amortization**, or EBITDA. The Company's EBITDA is $8,000 ($7,000 of EBIT plus $1,000 of depreciation). EBITDA is often used by entrepreneurs and bankers as a quick measure of cash flow.

The percentages provide a type of vertical analysis of the income statement. The Company was able to generate 71.4 cents of gross profit for every dollar of sales. Out of the 71.4 cents, 51.4 cents was used to cover operating expenses, leaving 20 cents of every dollar of sales in EBIT. Companies can then compare their EBIT to last year's, the budget, or the industry average to determine if they are operating efficiently or as planned. See Chapter 7 for an in-depth discussion of financial statement analysis.

Balance Sheet

The second basic financial statement is the balance sheet, which is displayed in Exhibit 3-2. This statement records the assets, liabilities, and equity of the company at a point in time. It is usually prepared monthly but at a minimum is done annually.

A balance sheet classifies assets and liabilities as either current or long-term. Current assets are cash or assets that can be turned into cash or used up within one year of the balance sheet date. Current liabilities are liabilities that must be paid within one year of the balance sheet date. *Working capital* refers to the difference between current assets and current liabilities. Management issues concerning current assets and liabilities relate to seasonal cycles, which dictate a need for

---

EXHIBIT 3-2

The Company
Balance Sheet
April 30, 2002

ASSETS	
Current Assets	
Cash	$ 58,900
Accounts Receivable	25,000
Inventory	30,000
Total Current Assets	113,900
Fixed Assets	
Equipment	36,000
Less: Accumulated Depreciation	(1,000)
Net Fixed Assets	35,000
TOTAL ASSETS	$148,900
LIABILITIES	
Current Liabilities	
Notes Payable	$ 15,000
Accounts Payable	22,000
Wages Payable	5,000
Total Current Liabilities	42,000
STOCKHOLDERS' EQUITY	
Common Stock	100,000
Retained Earnings	6,900
Total Stockholders' Equity	106,900
TOTAL LIABILITIES & STOCKHOLDERS' EQUITY	$148,900

planning cash inflows and outflows, investing excess cash and borrowing cash when needed. Liquidity is having enough cash on hand to meet cash flow needs.

ASSETS

Cash is the liquid monetary asset a company has on hand or in checking/savings accounts. Cash equivalents are short-term investments that mature within 90 days or less. If the company has excess cash, the entrepreneur may choose to invest it in debt (bonds) or equity (stocks) securities. These investments are often called *marketable securities,* and they result in interest and/or dividend income.

Accounts receivable represents sales to customers on credit. Under accrual accounting, a sale is recognized when the product or service is delivered to the customer. The timing of the receipt of cash impacts the cash flow statement, but not the income statement. GAAP requires accounts receivable to be recorded at net realizable value, which is the amount expected to be collected. Therefore, an estimate of what is uncollectible needs to be made at the same time the sale is made. This results in creating a contra-asset account called allowance for bad debts. The company records an expense for the amount it estimates will not be collected in the future. The net effect is that the income statement reflects both the sales and the bad-debt expense related to the sales that will not be collected, in the same period. When a receivable is written off in the future because it has been determined to be uncollectible, the asset and the allowance are both reduced and net income is not affected.

Inventory is merchandise held by a company to be sold to its customers, and it is typically the most significant asset for merchandising or manufacturing firms. Inventories for a manufacturing company consist of raw materials, work in process (WIP), and finished goods. Inventories are recorded as an asset until sold. Upon a sale, the inventory account is reduced and the expense account called cost of goods sold (or cost of sales) is increased. A company has a choice of methods to record cost of goods sold and ending inventory under GAAP, the three most common being FIFO (first-in, first-out), LIFO (last-in, first-out), and average cost. FIFO describes how costs flow from inventory to cost of goods sold, *not* how the physical product moves. This method assumes that the oldest costs in inventory are moved to cost of goods sold first; the result is that ending inventory consists of the most recent costs. LIFO assumes that the newest costs in inventory are the first ones moved to cost of goods sold, resulting in the oldest costs remaining on the balance sheet. In times of inflation, as the cost of new inventory purchases is increasing, LIFO increases cost of goods sold, thereby reducing taxable income. Companies choose the LIFO method because by reducing income, they reduce their income tax expense and increase cash flow. Average cost means that the average cost of all the purchases is used to determine the cost of goods sold. The entrepreneur should work with a tax accountant to determine which method is the most appropriate.

Noncurrent assets are assets that have a useful life longer than one year. For most entrepreneurs, these assets consist of land, buildings, equipment, furniture, and fixtures. These are tangible or physical assets that are used by the company in the production or sale of inventory or in providing goods and services. They are recorded on the balance sheet at their acquisition cost, which includes the invoice price, freight, sales tax, assembly, and installation. Another term for these costs is *capital expenditures*. A capital expenditure means that an asset is recorded on the balance sheet if it has a life longer than one year. However, the dollar value is also considered. A relatively small expenditure is usually expensed in order to minimize cumbersome record keeping. Most companies have a capitalization policy of capitalizing all expenditures over a certain dollar amount if they have a life longer than one year. The entrepreneur should work with an accountant to develop this policy.

Depreciation is a systematic method of allocating the original cost of a long-term asset to expense over the asset's expected life. Land is never depreciated because it has an infinite life. Depreciation *does not necessarily* indicate a decline in market value. The two methods commonly used to depreciate an asset are straight-line and an accelerated method called MACRS (modified accelerated cost recovery system). Most companies use the straight-line method for their financial statements because of its simplicity and its resulting constant level of depreciation expense. However, the IRS allows companies to use accelerated methods (MACRS) for tax purposes, which permits them to expense a greater amount of depreciation in the early years, thus saving on income taxes and cash flow, and a lesser amount in later years. A company may use one method for its financial statements and a different method on its tax return.

Straight-line depreciation is calculated as follows:

$$\frac{\text{Historical Cost} - \text{Salvage Value}}{\text{Years of Use}} = \text{Annual Depreciation Expense}$$

From our previous example with The Company, this resulted in an annual depreciation charge of $12,000, or $1,000 per month.

$$\frac{\$36,000 - \$0}{3 \text{ years}} = \$12,000 \text{ annually, or } \$1,000 \text{ per month}$$

A company may finance a capital expenditure by leasing a building or piece of equipment. There are two types of leases, operating and capital. An operating lease has no attributes of ownership and is not reflected on the lessee's balance sheet. The lease payment is shown as an operating expense. Under a capital lease, the lessee assumes the benefits and risks of ownership. Buildings and equipment purchased under a capital lease are reflected on the balance sheet as an asset with an offsetting liability. An accountant or leasing company can help determine whether a lease is a capital or operating lease. Leasing is a financing tool. A company may choose to lease a piece of equipment rather than buy it for three reasons: it reduces the risk of obsolescence, it gives the company more flexibility, and it helps with cash flow.

Intangible assets represent the company's right to something. Examples are patents, copyrights, and trademarks. Goodwill is also an intangible asset. Goodwill is only recorded when one company purchases another company for more than its fair market value (i.e., the value of its assets less its liabilities). Intangible assets are amortized (written off to expense) except for goodwill, which is only reduced if it is impaired.

LIABILITIES

Liabilities are the claims of creditors to the assets of a company that usually arise due to an expense or the purchase of an asset. Current liabilities are those that are due within one year of the balance sheet date. An entrepreneur may have several types of current liabilities, for example, a working capital loan, which is short-term credit obtained to finance the buildup of accounts receivable or inventory in a seasonal business. Once the inventory is sold and accounts receivable are collected, the loan is repaid. A revolving line of credit is a predetermined, maximum amount of credit that is flexible in the timing and amount of borrowing.

Current liabilities also include obligations where the exact amount owed will not be known until a later date. An example is warranty expense. Under GAAP, a company needs to accrue an estimate of what the warranty may cost in the future if it warranties its products or services. The warranty expense and the related liability are recorded when the sale is recognized, just as we discussed with bad-debt expense. When warranty work is done, the liability and the asset impacted to service the warranty are reduced; there is no impact on net income.

Current maturities of long-term debt represent the principal payment due on the debt within the next year. Current maturities usually occur because funds borrowed on a long-term basis are often repaid in monthly installments. On all debt, interest must be accrued and recognized in the period it is incurred, whether or not it is paid. The interest rate charged will be based on the lender's rating of the risk associated with the loan and the current prime rate, which is the interest rate established by lenders for their "most creditworthy" borrowers.

Accounts payable are amounts owed to suppliers for goods and services. Chapter 10 will discuss trade debt as a financing tool. Accounts payable are based on an invoice that has been received. Accruals are obligations a business has incurred but for which no formal invoice has been received, such as wages, payroll taxes, sales taxes, and property taxes.

Unearned revenues, also called *deferred revenues,* occur when customers pay for products or services in advance. These are recorded as liabilities because the company has the cash up front but has done nothing to earn the payment. Instead, the company owes the customer the product or service in the future. Examples are magazine subscription payments received by a publisher or season ticket payments received by a sports team. Collecting cash up front is a method of improving cash flow by using the cash collected to fund costs incurred prior to a sale.

Long-term liabilities are those obligations that are not due within the current year. They may include funds borrowed from banks or the issuance of bonds. See Chapter 10 for a discussion of debt-financing strategies.

OWNERS' EQUITY

Owner's equity represents the claim of the entity's owners to the assets on the balance sheet. For a corporation, it is called *stockholders' equity.* If the corporation is dissolved, stockholders' liability is limited to the amount they have invested in the stock. Equity consists of two main categories, contributed capital and retained earnings. Contributed capital is the original investment in the company by the owners. In a corporation, the investment by the owners is usually called *common stock*. In a partnership or sole proprietorship, this investment is called *capital*.

Retained earnings (R/E), as discussed earlier, represent the net income of the company since its inception that has not been disbursed back to the owners in the form of dividends or withdrawals. Retained earnings *do not represent a cash account*.

Beginning R/E + Net Income − Dividends (or Withdrawals) = Ending R/E

The statement of changes in owners' (stockholders') equity (not included here) reconciles the change in the common stock account and retained earnings account from the beginning of the year to the end of the year.

Statement of Cash Flows

The last of the basic financial statements is the statement of cash flows, which tracks the sources and uses of cash in the company. Chapter 9 will discuss the issue of cash flow management and the statement of cash flows in detail.

LIMITATIONS OF BUSINESS FINANCIAL STATEMENTS

Financial statements have limitations. For one thing, not all assets of a company are included (e.g., employees or brand names). The research and development costs leading to a patent or trademark are also not reflected as an asset but are expensed as they are incurred. Most assets are reflected at historical cost, that is, their purchase price instead of current market value (except in the case of marketable securities). Historical cost is an objective measurement but it is less useful.

There are many estimates reflected in the financial statements that impact both the income statement and the balance sheet. These estimates include the lives used for depreciation, the collectibility of accounts receivable, the salability of inventory, and the amount of warranty liability outstanding. These estimates are only as good as the methods used to calculate them and the assumptions used by management in the calculations. The numbers reflected in financial statements are also affected by the choice of accounting methods—FIFO, LIFO, or average cost—which can again impact both the income statement and the balance sheet.

SUMMARY

Accounting is the language of business, and therefore a working knowledge of this language is key to understanding entrepreneurial finance. This chapter discussed the basic workings of the accounting equation and how this equation impacts the basic financial statements and their interrelationships. The next two chapters will examine the process of forecasting revenues and expenses. The final chapter in this section will present an integrated spreadsheet model that can be used to create financial forecasts for new ventures. The remainder of this book will build on the basic understanding of accounting presented in this chapter.

DISCUSSION QUESTIONS

1. Discuss the importance of entrepreneurs understanding their financial statements.
2. How does net income affect the balance sheet?
3. What does an income statement communicate about a business?

4. What does a balance sheet communicate about a business?

5. How would you define Assets? Liabilities? Owners' equity?

6. What is the definition of revenue? An expense?

OPPORTUNITIES FOR APPLICATION

1. Practice Makes Perfect, Inc. was started on July 1 of the current year. Practice Makes Perfect provides piano lessons for students of all abilities. You are the founder, president, office manager, and so on. You have not yet hired an accountant but your bank is asking for an income statement and balance sheet for the first month of operation.

    a. Using the following information, put each transaction in the equation format given. (Table 3–14)

    Transactions:

    1. You started your company with $100,000 that you raised by selling stock in Practice Makes Perfect, Inc. to your family and friends.

    2. Knowing that you would need additional funds, you presented your business plan to the bank and were able to get a $50,000 loan at 10 percent.

    3. You purchased three pianos for $16,000 each, paying cash. You believe these pianos will last five years before you replace them. At the end of the five years, you think you can sell each piano for $1,000.

    4. You spent $2,000 on supplies, which you charged on account.

    5. The newspaper bills you $500 for the advertisement you ran. You plan on paying the bill next month.

    6. Rent for the space you have leased is $1,000 a month, which you paid.

    7. The first month, you bill students $2,000 for lessons.

    8. You pay your two part-time piano teachers $500 each at the end of the month.

    9. One of your students paid the $200 invoice you sent earlier in the month.

    10. You write the check for the interest owed for the month.

    11. You adjust the supplies account for $300 of sheet music that you gave to students.

    12. You record one month of depreciation on the pianos.

    b. Prepare a simple income statement and balance sheet to present to the bank.

2. Make a list of the assets and liabilities you would want to keep track of in a company you owned. What types of revenues would you have? What types of expenses would you want to track?

3. Look on the Internet for the financial statements of a publicly held company. (If you own stock in a company, look for the financial statements in the last annual report you received.) Or ask your employer if you can look at a set of financial statements.

    a. Create the accounting equation for the balance sheet. Does it balance?

    b. What is the company's EBIT?

    c. Identify an asset or a liability you are not familiar with and look it up in an accounting or finance resource.

TABLE 3-14

Assets		=	Liabilities		+	Owners' Equity		
Cash + Receivable + Supplies + Pianos − Deprec.	Accounts ... Accum.	=	Notes Payable +	Accounts Payable +		Common Stock +	Retained Earnings +	Revenues − Expenses

CHAPTER

4

Revenue Forecasting

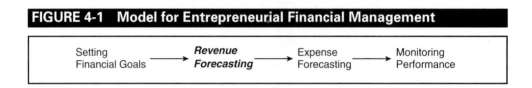

FIGURE 4-1   Model for Entrepreneurial Financial Management

Setting Financial Goals → **Revenue Forecasting** → Expense Forecasting → Monitoring Performance

This chapter examines the second major component in the model for entrepreneurial financial management used in this book: revenue forecasting. To achieve the financial goals discussed in Chapter 2, specifically the profit goals, a venture must achieve a certain level of revenues. Sound financial management requires that the entrepreneur develop a model of revenue forecasting that helps the venture to realize these revenue levels.

COMMON FORECASTING MISTAKES

Before examining how more reliable and accurate revenue forecasts are developed, it is important to identify the three common mistakes found in unreliable and inaccurate revenue forecasts. All three can be found in business plans ranging from the simplest small business start-up plan to the most elaborately developed business plans seeking millions of dollars in funding from venture capitalists.

1.   *The linear forecast mistake.* The most basic mistake in revenue forecasting is to assume a simple linear growth in revenues. This is a common mistake of entrepreneurs who have a strong technical knowledge base that has led them to start their businesses and of entrepreneurs who start their businesses because of a passion they have for their ideas. For example, assume an entrepreneur is developing a plan to open a software company to develop and produce a software application that his current employer is not interested in developing. He has spent countless hours perfecting the software and its applications. When it comes time to pursue the funding he needs to bring the software into full production and to the marketplace, he sits down to develop his forecasted income statement. First he estimates the expenses, which he knows in detail from his previous job at another software company. Then he estimates revenues. He assumes that he will sell 5 units in the first month, 10 in the second month, 15 in the third, and so on. He has no support for his revenue

growth model. He simply assumes that sales will grow by 5 units a month because it seems reasonable to him and then he develops an income statement based on that assumption. There are many risks to using such an oversimplified assumption. Sales may grow much slower than he assumed, and he may run out of funds before he reaches breakeven. On the other hand, sales may grow much faster than he assumed, and he may run out of product, thus risking angry customers. An even larger, yet hidden, risk is that the entrepreneur has not developed any knowledge of what will generate sales. He assumes that if he builds a good product the customers will find it and buy it. Very few new ventures have ever had the luxury of a product that "sells itself." Most successful businesses result from a thorough knowledge of the customers and what they want from the product.

2.   *The hockey stick forecast mistake.* A mistake that is very similar to the linear forecast, but even riskier, is the hockey stick revenue forecast. In this case, the entrepreneur assumes that sales will begin slowly and then will suddenly increase dramatically for no documented reason other than blind faith in the new business. Bankers and others who work with new businesses are very wary of such forecasts, as they are based on nothing more than the optimism of the entrepreneur.

3.   *The 20/80 versus 80/20 mistake.* Even entrepreneurs who take the time to develop more sophisticated revenue forecasts than the two methods discussed thus far may make the third type of mistake. The 20/80 versus 80/20 mistake in forecasting refers to the allocation of time between forecasting the two main sections of the income statement, revenues and expenses. When establishing income statement forecasts, it is common to observe that as little as 20 percent of time spent on developing the forecast is dedicated to developing the revenue portion of the forecasts, while as much 80 percent is spent on detailing the expenses. Accurately developed expense forecasts are vitally important. However, the information used to develop expense forecasts is relatively straightforward to identify and research. (Chapter 5 will examine expense forecasting in more detail.) It is information that may be very familiar if the entrepreneur has worked in the industry before starting the venture.

Revenue forecasts are not as easy to build. Unfortunately, rather than spend the time necessary to develop more accurate revenue forecasts, the entrepreneur will often make a few simple assumptions and establish revenue forecasts that seem to "make sense." For example, assume that an entrepreneur has established an income statement forecast that shows steady growth in revenues but allows for the seasonal variability that occurs each year. While enough information was gathered to support the seasonal aspect of the forecast, there is no specific justification for either the level of sales or the growth in sales that underlie the revenue model. Some research was completed on revenues but not enough to have confidence in the numbers.

Clearly, the point is not that entrepreneurs should spend *less* time on the expense forecast—in fact, they should not. On the contrary, entrepreneurs should be spending much more time on the revenue forecast using the methods presented in the following sections of this chapter. Avoiding mistakes in income statement forecasting may require that as much as *four times* as much time be spent on revenue forecasts as on developing accurate expense forecasts. The increased time spent on revenue forecasts is dedicated to developing a marketing plan, as outlined in the next section, which includes more accurate and detailed market data. These data are then used to create a more sophisticated and robust revenue forecast.

THE LINK BETWEEN THE MARKETING PLAN AND REVENUE FORECASTS

Those who regularly evaluate business plans, such as investors and bankers, follow a similar and consistent pattern. Their first step is to evaluate the executive summary to determine if the plan is one they want to read about in more depth. This decision may be based on a variety of factors, including the nature of the business, the management team, the industry, and revenue and profit potential. If the executive summary catches their attention, the focus then shifts to the marketing plan. After careful review of the marketing plan, they immediately move to examine the revenue forecasts in the pro forma financials. What they look for is a consistent story between the marketing plan and the forecasted revenues. Their experience has shown them that a strong link between these two parts of a business plan reduces the types of risk just outlined. Revenue forecasts based on a sound marketing plan reduce the risk of the business venture that results from failing to meet projected revenues. The link between the marketing plan and the revenue forecast, as illustrated in Figure 4-2, creates what is known as the *backbone of the business plan*.

There are three main aspects of the marketing plan within a business plan that are of concern in evaluating the strength of the link with the revenue forecast.

1. *Identifying industry and market trends.* Market and industry trends can help lend support to the financial projections in a business plan. If the industry and/or local markets that a business operates in are forecasted to have significant future growth, this can help justify growth projections for a specific business within that industry or market. Conversely, if an industry or market is forecast to experience a downturn, it will be difficult to argue that a new venture could operate contrary to those trends. Data on industry and market trends are available from a variety of public domain sources. Also, the entrepreneur can gather data on a specific market by networking with potential customers and suppliers and with others familiar with the local market environment. Business plan readers, such as bankers and investors, will often seek independent research to confirm the industry and market trends cited within the marketing plan.

2. *Market research.* A marketing plan should clearly demonstrate that the entrepreneur understands the needs, wants, and buying behaviors of potential customers.

FIGURE 4-2 Backbone of an Effective Business Plan

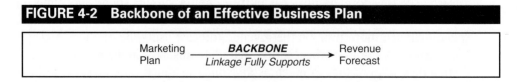

Many entrepreneurs assume that their customers will think the way they do. However, this is often not the case. For example, an optometrist who was planning to set up a series of privately owned retail eyeglass outlets was committed to providing the absolute highest quality. He was convinced that quality was all that mattered. However, the customers in his market were equally concerned with price and were looking for retail outlets that offered "value" (i.e., good quality for a reasonable price). The optometrist failed to understand how his potential customers thought and behaved, and consequently his business closed before he could even open his second store. Effective market research is critical to understanding the thought process and behavior of potential customers.

Entrepreneurs rarely have the funds to support a sophisticated market study, such as those conducted by large corporations. However, useful and reasonably accurate market research is possible on even the smallest budget. Entrepreneurs can gain important insight into how their potential customers think by getting out and talking to them. The conversation should be approached with an open mind and without any leading questions. By networking with just a few potential customers, entrepreneurs can begin to discern consistent patterns that should help create a venture that will succeed in attracting the necessary customers to reach their business financial goals.

3.   *Competitive analysis.* Accurate revenue forecasting requires a thorough understanding of the competitive environment. This knowledge helps develop a clearer picture of the potential market share, which is the proportion of a given market that buys a given company's products or services. Market research helps the entrepreneur gain a better understanding of customer preferences; competitive analysis compares that understanding with the product/service offerings of each business within a given market. A competitive analysis is generally constructed as follows:

- Generate an inventory of all competitors that do business in the market. Make sure to include current competitors, potential competitors (i.e., companies that are planning to enter the market), and any businesses that offer a close substitute product or service that can easily be chosen by the customer as an alternative (e.g., a bus service can serve as a substitute for a taxi cab company).

- Estimate the market share for each competitor. This can be calculated by estimating the sales for each competitor, adding the sales of all competitors to estimate the size of the market, and then dividing each competitor's sales by the total market sales to get the percentage of market share for each company. If sales cannot be estimated, a surrogate (such as number of customers) can be substituted for sales.

- The data gathered through market research should be used to identify features that the customers like and do not like about the competitors' products and services. If possible, the entrepreneur should visit competitors to understand how a customer experiences interacting with these companies and to determine how each performs in terms of the

	Cleanliness of Facilities	Hours of Operation	Selection	Price
Joe, Inc.	Good	8:00–6:00	Moderate	Moderate
Jane, Co.	Excellent	8:00–8:00	Large	High
Sally & Jim's Shop	Fair	9:00–4:00	Limited	Low
Your Own Business (your planned approach to each)	Excellent	7:00–9:00	The largest	Moderate

FIGURE 4-3   Sample Competitive Grid

important products and services. Finally, the entrepreneur should talk to customers to determine how they rate the competitors on the important traits and features.

- Create a competitive analysis grid. To do this, list all competitors along the left side of the grid and key customer needs and preferences along the top of the grid. Rate or describe each competitor for each customer need and desired feature within the grid. It is important to be honest in the evaluation. Avoid the temptation to belittle or underrate the competition. Figure 4-3 displays an example competitive grid.

- Identify the competitive strategies to be pursued given this analysis. Through this analysis, the entrepreneur should be able to create an estimate of potential market share, which can then be used to estimate revenues. Also, it is important to estimate how long it may take to build up to that market share based on a perception of customer loyalty and on how well the competition is meeting the needs and wants of the customers.

CREATING SCENARIOS

Once the revenue forecasts are validated through the marketing plan, the entrepreneur will usually create multiple scenarios. Most bankers and investors want to see a presentation of best-case, worst-case, and most-likely-case scenarios. To accomplish this, the assumptions that were used to develop the marketing plan and any additional ones used in creating the revenue plan should be listed. The entrepreneur should then rate the probability of each assumption. Only those that are highly probable or even certain should be used to create the worst-case scenario. All other assumptions should be ignored, and the revenue assumptions should be adjusted to reflect this change. Under the best-case scenario, all assumptions should be included. This scenario assumes that almost every assumption will go in favor of the entrepreneur. Finally, in the most-likely-case scenario, the entrepreneur strikes a balance between the first two scenarios. For example, an entrepreneur named Bill Robertson has made an assumption that he can add two new customers each month during the first two years. This growth assumes that he gets an equal share of new customers entering the market. This is what he considers his most likely scenario. Under his best-case scenario, he decides that he might be able to add three new customers each month. This would be an aggressive growth model, and it would require that he could take away existing customers from his competitor, rather than just growing by adding new customers entering the market. Bill's worst-case scenario is that he will only be able to attract a small fraction of new customers, which he assumes would create a growth rate of one new customer every other month. He is reasonably certain that his product is different enough from the competitors' to gain at least this much new business. Three different scenarios of revenue growth that reflect each of these cases are then created, resulting in three sets of financial statement projections.

THE LINK BETWEEN THE REVENUE FORECAST AND THE CASH FLOW FORECAST

When forecasting revenues, it is important to identify the cash flow associated with those revenues. Although revenues are important, it is the actual receipt of cash or cash flow from those revenues that is critical to the entrepreneur. If credit is not extended to customers, then the sales projections will equal the cash receipts projections. However, if credit is extended (i.e., accounts receivable are recorded when the sale is made, but cash is collected at a later point in time), then the cash collections will lag the recognition of sales on the income statement. This is called *accrual accounting*. Sales and expenses are recorded when the business delivers the product or service or benefits from the expenses incurred, but the cash does not exchange hands until a later point in time. Chapter 9 will discuss cash flow in more detail. There are three key steps in transforming revenue forecasts to cash flow forecasts.

First, the entrepreneur needs to determine whether to extend credit to customers. Part of the competitive analysis discussed earlier should include gaining an understanding of the standards for payment within the industry. In some industries, such as most manufacturing businesses, for example, extension of credit to customers is expected. The entrepreneur has no real choice but to extend credit to customers. In other businesses, credit may be optional. An example of this would be health care providers, such as medical clinics. Some extend credit to clients while others expect payment at the time of service. In this case, credit can be used as a competitive feature offered to customers, but it is important in the competitive analysis to determine if credit is actually something the customers want. Other businesses operate on a cash basis with payment received at the time of the sale. Most retail operations operate in this manner. In today's electronic age, credit card sales are like cash. However, there is a cost to accepting credit cards that can range from 2 to 7 percent of the sale.

Second, if credit is extended, the entrepreneur should estimate the percentage of the sales that will be on credit and the percentage that will be cash. Many businesses that extend credit have a portion of sales that are immediate cash collections due to the preferences or past bad credit history of the customer.

Third, the entrepreneur will need to determine how long it will take to collect credit sales. Average times for collection of accounts receivable are available for most industries either through industry associations or publications such as those of Robert Morris Associates. An assumption will also need to be made about what percentage of accounts receivables will never be collected. Industry averages for this percentage also are available. The financial statement template included in Chapter 6 incorporates those assumptions when calculating the cash flow projections.

A cash flow forecast is a key component of a business plan. The entrepreneur will want to demonstrate to a potential lender or investor an understanding of the future cash needs of the company.

THE IMPACT OF BUSINESS TYPE ON REVENUES

Forecasted revenues should be adjusted to reflect the differences that will occur for companies in different types of business. This section will examine how revenue forecasting will differ between manufacturing firms and service firms, and how commission-based selling and seasonal sales affect forecasting models. The examples used in this section are all for small businesses that are already in operation. For start-ups, this data can be estimated with industry data that are often readily available through industry trade associations or economic development agencies. Other entrepreneurs can use their experience gained by working in the industry to create these estimates.

Manufacturing Firms

Revenues in manufacturing firms are limited by their production capacity, which is the maximum number of units that can be produced with a given number of machines, employees, and raw materials available. An assembly line can run for only 24 hours per day and can make only so many units per hour; moreover, the line can only run as long as there is enough raw material to feed it and employees to run the machines. In addition, downtime must be factored into any estimate to allow for needed service and maintenance of the assembly equipment. Therefore, if an owner is unwilling to buy the equipment for a second line and is even resistant to opening up a second or third shift on the same line, then there are natural limits to the number of units and, therefore, revenue that can physically be produced. It would not make sense to have unit sales projections that are a simple extrapolation of a past trend which results in a number greater than the amount the firm can physically produce.

For example, an assembly line can produce 50 units per hour assuming normal downtime. Currently, there is only one shift of workers, and the owner does not want to use space in the warehouse to set up a second assembly line. What is the maximum number of sales possible per month if a second shift were to be added one month and a third shift the next, assuming each shift operates eight hours?

	Month 1	Month 2	Month 3
First shift	8 × 50	8 × 50	8 × 50
Second shift		8 × 50	8 × 50
Third shift			8 × 50
Max. # sales	400 units	800 units	1200 units

The number of units sold in the preceding example represents the maximum number of units that can be produced. There likely will be a time lag between when these units are produced and when they are actually sold. In addition, if sales are made to customers on trade credit, there can be a further time lag before the firm actually receives payment for the units sold. In the meantime, the firm will have to pay suppliers for raw materials and employees for their labor. Hence, a period of rising production and sales will probably correspond to a period of net cash out-flows until the revenues climb above the current cost of production.

Service Firms

For service firms such as law firms, accounting practices, or even lawn services, the firm's capacity to provide the service should be established to calculate accurate forecasts. Service firms bill in different ways, such as hourly and per job completed, and this also should be factored into any forecast.

Billing by the Hour

The specialized skill required by some service firms, such as law firms and auto repair shops, may be something that by its nature is not easily transferred. This trait limits the capacity for expansion of revenues. Therefore, there are some general characteristics that these types of businesses have in common:

1. Typically, specialized services can be billed by the hour or by the job based upon how many hours a typical job should take. Per job fees become very close substitutes for per hour fees in this framework.
2. There are approximately 2000 work hours in one year, which equates to approximately 160 work hours in one month.
3. No employee can physically be 100% involved in billable time. Depending on the industry and whether the employee is expected to perform sales or administrative duties, the utilization ratio (the percentage of time in billable work) could be as low as 40 percent or as high as 80 percent. Factors such as travel time or ongoing required training will lead to lower utilization ratios.

For example, the owner of a lifestyle consulting firm wants to hire one asso-ciate per month during the growth phase of the business. Associates can work at 70 percent utilization. The owner can work only at 20 percent utilization due to administrative work that must be completed. Each new associate has to be trained, so they average only 35 percent utilization for the first month. The service is billed at $100 per hour. Assume that there are 160 work hours per month.

Revenue per Employee = 160 Hours per Month × Utilization × $100 per Hour

	Month 1	Month 2	Month 3
Owner	160 × .20 × 100	160 × .20 × 100	160 × .20 × 100
Associate #1	160 × .35 × 100	160 × .70 × 100	160 × .70 × 100
Associate #2		160 × .35 × 100	160 × .70 × 100
Associate #3			160 × .35 × 100
Total Revenue	$8,800	$20,000	$31,200

Thus, we have a month-by-month sales revenue forecast based on the firm's ability to deliver the service. As was discussed in the previous section, sales revenue is not necessarily the same thing as cash flow. In this example, for instance, if customers are granted a 30-day deferral before payment is due, then each of the monthly revenue numbers would be collected in the next month (i.e., $8,800 would be collect in Month 2, not Month 1, etc.). On the expense side, the associates would have to be paid their monthly salary almost immediately, even though the revenue they generated would not be collected until the next month.

Billing by the Job

Similar to the hourly example, the owner of a business that bills by the job must still understand that because there are only so many hours in a day, there is a limit to the number of jobs that can be generated per employee.

For example, suppose an information technology (IT) firm has one owner who is planning to add associates to meet forecasted revenue growth. When an employee is trained and at full productivity, the typical IT software installation takes about 25 hours. For a new employee it takes twice as long. Each job is priced at $2,000, and the owner wants to hire one associate per month. The productivity measures are the same as in the previous example (employee utilization rate is 70 percent at full efficiency, with the owner at 20 percent).

Revenue per Employee = $2,000 per Job × Number of Jobs per Month
Number of Jobs per Month = 160 Hours per Month × Utilization/Number of Hours per Job

	Month 1	Month 2	Month 3
Owner	2000 × 160 × .2/25	2000 × 160 × .2/25	2000 × 160 × .2/25
Associate #1	2000 × 160 × .7/50	2000 × 160 × .7/25	2000 × 160 × .7/25
Associate #2		2000 × 160 × .7/50	2000 × 160 × .7/25
Associate #3			2000 × 160 × .7/50
Total Revenue	$7,040	$16,000	$24,960

The sales numbers are on a prorated basis, because an employee cannot perform a fraction of a job and still get paid. Similarly, some job installations are started in one month but completed in the next. Also, just as in the hourly billing example, the reader should keep in mind the cash flow effect. In other words, the revenue amounts are booked in their respective months but are actually received in the following month if 30-day payment deferral is extended to customers.

Recurring Revenue Firms

Some businesses provide a service that is used by the customer repeatedly. Wire-based and wireless services such as paging, digital telephone, cable, and Internet access are some examples.

A typical recurring revenue firm requires that a customer sign a contract for a particular term of service. Depending on the nature of the service or product, the customers may be able to physically disconnect from the service during the contract period. In other words, just because customers have signed a one-year contract, they may not stay with the company for the full year. It could also be the case that rigorous collection activities may not be economically justified to enforce the customer contract because (1) there is no asset to be repossessed or (2) the dollar amount of monthly revenue is less than the cost of enforcement. Therefore, an entrepreneur cannot automatically forecast and base plans on the assumption that each customer represents a full contract worth of revenue and cash flow.

Because customers can potentially disconnect no matter what a contract says, a measurement tool is needed to assist in monitoring customer behavior and to help forecast revenues. This measurement is called the *disconnect rate*. The disconnect rate is the inverse of the average customer's economic life.

$$\text{Disconnect Rate} = (1/\text{Avg. Customer Life in Months})$$

For instance, if the disconnect rate is 10 percent, it means that the average customer disconnects after 10 months worth of service. If the disconnect rate is 10 percent = (1/customer life in months), customer life must be (1/disconnect rate) = (1/.10), which is 10 months.

Put another way, if a company loses 10 percent of its previous month's customers each month, then after 10 months the company has essentially replaced all of its customers with new ones. Likewise, if the disconnect rate is 5 percent, then losing 5 percent of the previous month's customers means that the company replaces all of its customers over 20 months, which is the average customer life. If the disconnect rate is 5 percent, or .05 = (1/customer life in months), then customer life is (1/.05) = 20 months.

It might be more accurate to keep track of every single customer to project and monitor revenue, but if the business in question has a very high volume, then that might not be feasible. All that is needed to create an estimate of the disconnect rate is the gross number of customers this month, the gross number of customers on service last month, and the number of new customers added this month.

$$\text{Disconnect Rate} = [(\text{Number of Customers This Month} - \text{Number of New}$$
$$\text{Customers} - \text{Number of Customers Last Month})/$$
$$\text{Number of Customers Last Month}]$$

Because customers may be able to unilaterally disconnect (i.e., without notifying the company) from the service by not paying their invoice, the number of customers that a company *truly* has in a particular month would have to be estimated by dividing the actual revenue collected in that month by the monthly average price charged per customer. Because of the potential for customers to simply stop paying for a service, there can be a time lag before the company's customer information system can recognize that it has lost a customer. This could cause the firm to overestimate its actual number of customers at any one time and therefore overestimate its revenue projections.

For example, sales revenue last month for I-Can't-Quite-Hear-You Wireless, Inc. (ICQHY) was $10,000. The price ICQHY charges for service is $10 per month. Revenue for this month is $11,000. The sales division told the company that it added 150 new customers this month.

Estimated # customers last month = ($10,000/$10) = 1000
Estimated # customers this month = ($11,000/$10) = 1100
New customers = 150
Disconnect rate = [(1100 – 150 – 1000)/1000] = .05, or 5 percent

What ICQHY learned from this is

- 50 customers disconnected last month (1100 – 150 – 1000)
- 5 percent is the disconnect rate
- The average customer is disconnecting after 20 months
  (1/Disconnect Rate) = Avg. Customer Life
  (1/.05) = 20 Months

The understanding of the disconnect rate can now be applied to forecasting revenue. For example, ICQHY had 1000 paying customers last month at a monthly service fee of $10. The sales force believes that they can add 150 new customers each month based on the number of salespeople and its commission structure. ICQHY believes that the disconnect rate is 5 percent (or that the average customer life is 20 months).

Number of Customers		
Month 1	Month 2	Month 3
$(1000 + 150) \times (1 - .05)$	$(1093 + 150) \times .(1 - .05)$	$(1181 + 150) \times (1 - .05)$

Revenue per Month		
Month 1	Month 2	Month 3
$1093 \times \$10$	$1181 \times \$10$	$1264 \times \$10$
$10,930	$11,810	$12,640

Recurring revenue firms frequently have cash flow challenges due to fixed costs that must be paid up front to establish service for a new customer. Once a customer is established, the marginal cost of providing the service or product decreases. Therefore, a high disconnect rate (or short customer life) means that the firm is constantly paying that start-up cost. The company would be making a larger profit at the same level of revenue if customer turnover rate was reduced.

Commission-Based Selling Firms

A similarity between commission-based selling and service industries is that sales revenue is partially a function of the number of employees. The difference is that in commission-based selling firms, the employees are salespeople rather than consultants or service providers.

A typical arrangement is that a salesperson is required to sell a set number of units or dollars, called the *base,* which is considered by the company to be a minimum level of acceptable performance. If this base is exceeded, then the salesperson is eligible for a commission. In some firms, a salesperson works entirely on commission, but this depends on the industry norm and the potential supply of employable salespeople.

Given the typical situation, a sales forecast can be crudely established by multiplying the number of units for the base by the number of salespeople. The base should be determined as the number of units necessary to justify the fixed cost of a sales employee. It also can be set at the number of units that are considered acceptable for sales professionals in that industry. Hopefully, the industry standard is greater than what is necessary to cover the fixed costs. Additionally, the standard amount of commission that is paid per unit must be less than the profit margin on each unit. Otherwise, a company would be selling each unit at a net loss.

For example, the Harmon Company plans to hire one new salesperson per month during the first five months of the start-up year. The base level of sales is 100 units per month per salesperson. It takes three months for a salesperson to be fully effective (i.e., they sell 33 units in the first month, 66 in the second, and their full quota of 100 in the third). The price per unit is $50.

	Month 1	Month 2	Month 3	Month 4	Month 5
Salesperson 1	33 × 50	66 × 50	100 × 50	100 × 50	100 × 50
Salesperson 2		33 × 50	66 × 50	100 × 50	100 × 50
Salesperson 3			33 × 50	66 × 50	100 × 50
Salesperson 4				33 × 50	66 × 50
Salesperson 5					33 × 50
Revenue	$1,650	$4,950	$9,950	$14,950	$19,950

Of course, if a salesperson cannot meet the minimum base number of sales, then the actual sales would be less than the projection. Similarly, if a salesperson were productive enough to earn commissions, then the projections would be underestimated. Unless the method of sales can be changed or expanded, such as through the Internet, retail stores, and so on, the amount of sales primarily will be a function of the number of salespeople.

Cyclical or Seasonal Sales Firms

Some businesses, whether service, manufacturing, or commission-based, may have customers that are seasonally based. Some classic examples are snowmobile manufacturers, tax preparers, and ski resorts. The key element is not to count on a sustainable level of revenue (and certainly not growth) during months that a firm physically cannot have any customers.

For example, Sammy's Ski-Jumping School can only operate in the months of December, January, and February. The price for instruction is $100 per day, and only five students can be taught per day. Because of holidays and bad weather conditions, the school typically is open only 12 days in December, 18 days in January, and 17 days in February. What is the maximum amount of revenue per month?

	Nov.	Dec.	Jan.	Feb.	Mar.	April
	0	5 × 12 × 100	5 × 18 × 100	5 × 17 × 100	0	0
Sales	$0	$6,000	$9,000	$8,500	$0	$0

Seasonal firms have to be particularly careful about cash flow management, especially if they have expenses that must be paid throughout the year.

QUANTITATIVE FORECASTING TECHNIQUES

Established businesses often use sophisticated statistical forecasting techniques such as regression analysis, exponential smoothing, and moving averages. However, this is almost impossible for a start-up firm because the entrepreneur does not have the historical data needed for these techniques. Regression is an extremely useful tool with which to quantify the relationships between sales (the dependent variable) and factors (the independent variables) that a manager may have some control over. These relationships incorporate such elements as prices and level of advertising spending, as well as elements that a manager cannot control, such as the population of an area and the state of the economy. For an entrepreneur, this sounds like very valuable information—which it is. However, there is a catch. A regression cannot be performed unless the firm has been in business for a sufficient length of time to collect the amount of data necessary for statistical significance. For instance, one cannot mathematically approximate the effect of price changes on the quantity sold unless the business has been in operation long enough to have undergone at least one price change during its existence. However, the principles that have been discussed in this chapter of (1) linking the marketing plan to the revenue forecast by identifying industry and market trends, (2) market research, and (3) competitive analysis can be used to create estimates that can be used as substitutes for historical data. An example of how to use a quantitative approach to apply these principles to forecast sales revenue follows.

American One-Way, Inc. has been a paging company for several years. It has recently begun exploring a new handheld, wireless, two-way, personal communications device. This device would require an all-new system of transmitting and receiving towers and will have totally different capabilities from a traditional pager. Therefore, American One-Way, Inc. intends to create an all-new venture with a different brand and organization to reduce customer confusion and to raise capital. An estimate of costs suggests that the price of the service has to be at least $120 per year in order to cover costs and earn an adequate profit, but that over five years the price can be phased down to $100. Because no such device has ever been offered in the market, the forecasting process must start from scratch.

First, the marketing department consulted the U.S. Census Website to find the population of the counties in which American One-Way intends to build the necessary towers and offer the service. It also found that the population of these counties has been growing at 5 percent a year.

Second, because the product is a communications device, the marketing team looked at the history of paging and cell phone use and found that given enough time, communications devices eventually achieve a penetration rate of 32 percent. This means, for instance, that at the most mature phase of the product's life, 32 percent of the population will own the newest version of a cell phone. However, it takes roughly five years for this level of acceptance to occur. Given no other data, it was assumed that market penetration of this new product might follow a similar pattern.

Third, a competitive analysis suggested that for the first two years American One-Way's new venture will be the only one with this new device. However, after two years competitors will probably have their towers up and running, and American One-Way's market share will fall to 80 percent in the third year, 60 percent in the fourth, and 55 percent in the fifth.

For American One-Way, Inc. the forecasted revenue for a particular year would first require estimating the population of the counties and multiplying this by the estimated penetration rate to get the estimated total potential market for this product. Next, the total potential market is multiplied by market share to get the theoretical number of American One-Way's customers. The final step would be to take the number of customers and multiply this by price to get the estimated sales revenue. These steps are illustrated in Table 4-1.

This particular case demonstrates that a quantitative approach can be used despite the absence of direct historical data for the product. A potential strength of this approach is that one can actually see (and therefore evaluate) the assumptions that are necessary to achieve particular sales levels. For instance, the actual level of sales achieved by any company is a function of macro factors, such as the number of people in a geographic area and the rate of acceptance of a new product. It is also a function of factors specific to the company, such as the firm's market share and the price the company charges.

IMPORTANCE OF REVENUE FORECASTING

The consequences of missing revenue targets can be devastating for an entrepreneurial venture. Any number of decisions may be based on the revenue assumptions in the entrepreneur's business plan. Banks may have lent money based on

TABLE 4-1

Population 5,010,000 =	Year 1	Year 2	Year 3	Year 4	Year 5
	5,010,000 × 1.05	5,260,500 × 1.05	5,523,525 × 1.05	5,799,701 × 1.05	6,089,686 × 1.05
	5,260,500	5,523,525	5,799,701	6,089,686	6,394,171
Penetration rate	5%	10%	20%	27%	32%
Total potential market =	5,260,500 × 0.05	5,523,525 × 0.10	5,799,701 × 0.20	6,089,686 × 0.27	6,394,171 × 0.32
	263,025	552,353	1,159,940	1,644,215	2,046,135
One-Way market share percentage	100%	100%	80%	60%	55%
One-Way customers =	263,025 × 1	552,353 × 1	1,159,940 × 0.80	1,644,215 × 0.60	2,046,135 × 0.55
	263,025	552,353	927,952	986,529	1,125,374
Pricing	$120	$120	$115	$110	$100
One-Way revenue forecast =	263,025 × $120	552,353 × $120	927,952 × $115	986,529 × $110	1,125,374 × $100
	$31,563,000	$66,282,360	$106,714,480	$108,518,190	$112,537,400

revenue forecasts. If the targets are not met, the business may become a problem loan for the bank. One commercial real estate company faced such a crisis. Its loans were based on growth that matched its historical rate of 20 percent. However, due to a variety of unforeseen factors, including a hurricane and the departure of a major local employer, vacancies rose and revenues actually declined slightly, causing the company's key financial ratios to fall below the range that a bank can accept from its customers (see Chapter 10). Even though the company still had positive cash flow, the bank was forced to call in its loans. Fortunately, the company found alternative funding.

Inventory assumptions are made based on revenue forecasts. A small midwestern company that manufactured mittens and scarves had projected a significant increase in sales due to positive negotiations under way with a major retailer. The company had to commit to raw material purchases nine months in advance of the ultimate sale to customers at retail outlets. Based on the positive forecast, the company placed a large order for raw materials in January. It would take possession of the materials by April so that manufacturing could take place from April through August, when the orders were to be shipped. By late July, however, it became clear that the large order it had planned on was not going to occur after all due to a projected softening of the economy. Retailers were cutting back on new product orders. The company was left with a large amount of finished and partially finished inventory that was likely to go unsold. The company ultimately had to liquidate its assets in bankruptcy (see Chapter 14).

Revenue forecasts also are used to make commitments to increased staffing and additional space. A Web site consulting business had just rented a large new office and hired several high-priced staff, many with six months of severance guaranteed in their contracts (a standard practice at the time). Unfortunately, these commitments were made only two months before the dot-com stock crash. After the crash, many of the company's major customers went out of business as their stock values became worthless. Soon, the entrepreneurs in this firm were faced with major commitments to staff and space that they could not meet with their much reduced cash flow. Only through drastic measures and an infusion of money from a family member was this business able to stay open.

Investors, such as angel investors and venture capitalists (see Chapters 11 and 12), make their investments based on expectations created by forecasts. An entrepreneur who had developed a process for converting farm waste into energy faced a crisis due to the unmet expectations of his investors. Although the business was doing fairly well, it was nowhere near meeting the 100 percent per year growth forecast in his business plan. He had accepted a significant amount of venture capital, and the venture capital firm decided that the business could meet the projected growth, but not with its current management. As permitted by the investment agreement, the venture capital firm removed the entrepreneur from his management role and brought in outside executives to run the company.

Revenue forecasts are important because so many decisions rest on the assumption that these numbers are accurate. The examples given here clearly demonstrate the impact of missed revenue forecasts. Basic guidelines that should be followed when making revenue forecasts are:

1. Conduct enough market research to ensure the quality of the assumptions behind the revenue forecasts.
2. Validate assumptions with more than one source of data. Do not ignore conflicting data, for it is a sign that further research may be required.
3. Although you may hope to meet optimistic forecasts, planning should be based on more conservative assumptions. It is much easier to adjust to higher-than-expected revenues than to try to deal with the consequences of missed revenue targets.

SUMMARY

This chapter presented an overview of revenue forecasting for entrepreneurial ventures. It covered the critical linkage between the marketing plan and accurate revenue forecasts and the importance of taking into account features of the business, including type of business and sales patterns. Although not as accurate as when used in businesses with historical data, quantitative techniques can help a start-up venture to achieve more accurate revenue forecasts. Missed revenue forecasts can be devastating to an entrepreneurial venture. The next chapter will examine the second major category of forecasting: expenses.

DISCUSSION QUESTIONS

1. What are the linear forecast and hockey stick forecast mistakes, and why would they be common among inexperienced entrepreneurs?
2. Given how crucial sales revenue is to the survival of a business, why is there a natural tendency for an entrepreneur to make the 20/80 versus 80/20 mistake?
3. What are the three main parts of the marketing plan, and why is linking the marketing plan to the revenue forecast so important?
4. What is the value of creating scenarios?
5. What is the difference between revenue and cash flow, and why is the distinction so important?
6. When should an entrepreneur take into account the productive capacity of the facility when making a revenue forecast?
7. In what type of businesses do customers gained in the past have the most impact on revenue today and why?
8. How do the following factors relate to revenue forecasting: population, penetration rate, market share, and price?
9. Why are sophisticated statistical techniques difficult to perform in an entrepreneurial environment?

10. What would be the potential risk of not directly linking a marketing plan and a financial forecast?

OPPORTUNITIES FOR APPLICATION

1. Mortinson Manufacturing plans to open one assembly line per month for the next seven months. Each assembly line is capable of manufacturing 14,250 toys per day. When at full capacity seven months from now, what will be the maximum total revenue that Mortinson Manufacturing could achieve if the toys could be sold for 35 cents apiece?

2. The Andersonian Consulting Company currently has five employees. The best-case situation is for the employees to be at 70 percent utilization. At 160 hours per month and a billing rate of $55 per hour, what is the maximum revenue that can be achieved?

3. Assume that a lawn service company collected $127,000 last month; it charges a typical customer $100 per month for its service. This month, the revenue is $134,000 and the sales department claims to have added 300 new customers.
   a. How many customers did the company actually have and collect from last month?
   b. How many paying customers does the company have this month?
   c. How many customers probably disconnected from the company's service in the past month?
   d. What is the disconnect rate?

4. The Extron Company sells a home electronics convergence device for $1,050 each. It uses commission-based selling and the quota per salesperson is 40 units per month. If it has three employees who are new and only expected to hit 50 percent of quota, two employees who can hit 75 percent of quota, and five experienced people who can consistently reach 100 percent, then what should be this month's anticipated level of sales revenue?

5. The Wankel Publishing Company is planning to start a new magazine on girl's high school basketball and has the following information: Census data indicate that one of the states where it wishes to introduce the magazine has a population of 1 million females between the ages of 13 to 18. A national study found that 42 percent of high school females compete in sports, and the High School League Annual Report suggests that 20 percent of high school female athletes play basketball. Wankel Publishing has found through past experience in specialty magazines that it can have monopoly status in a market for at most three years (100 percent market share). Under a best-case scenario it plans to have 4 percent market penetration in year 1, 8 percent in year 2, and achieve 12 percent in year 3.
   a. What will be the peak number of subscribers in the best-case scenario in each of the next three years?
   b. What will be the number of subscribers in each of the next three years under a worst-case scenario? (Assume that the worst-case scenario has a penetration rate of 1 percent in year 1, 2 percent in year 2, and 3 percent in year 3.)
   c. If the most likely case scenario is one-half of the best-case scenario penetration rates, calculate the number of subscribers for years 1, 2, and 3.

6. Micki Manufacturing's market study suggests that 1,200,000 novelty dolls can be sold per year through carnivals and county fairs. If an assembly line at maximum capacity

can produce 15,000 dolls a month per shift, can the company meet its sales goal for the year if it runs only two shifts?

7. The recently started law firm of Dewey, Cheetum, and Howe has three partners. Because of "rain making" work to get business and administrative duties, the partners believe that the average utilization rate is only 40 percent at best. At a billing rate of $200 per hour on a 40-hour work week, what is the maximum revenue per week?

8. How many new sales are necessary to average 1,200 customers if the disconnect rate is 4.5 percent?

9. If you need to pay an average of $4,000 per month in order to attract automobile sales employees, then what must the per employee monthly quota be to achieve commission, given the following information?
   a. Cars sell for approximately $24,000.
   b. The manufacturer charges your dealership $21,000 per car on average.
   c. Your dealership needs about $2,275 per car in gross profit to cover fixed costs and generate an adequate return to the investors.
   d. What is left over after the gross profit can be used to pay the commission to the salesperson.

10. If your product sells for $200 per unit, the population of your area is 10 million people, and the penetration rate for the product is 50 percent, then what must be your firm's market share in order to achieve a sales goal of $1 million?

CHAPTER

5

Expense Forecasting

Once profitability goals have been established and the revenue forecasts determined, the final component of the income statement, expenses, should be forecast. This chapter presents several methods for expense forecasting. The key to understanding expenses is to understand the possible behavior of the costs. That is, how will a particular cost react or adjust as changes occur in the level of activity of the business? As long as there is an understanding of how costs behave, the entrepreneur will be better able to predict what will happen under various operating circumstances and within different types of businesses.

DEFINING COSTS

Expenses are the costs of being in business and providing a product or service to a customer. In a business that sells products, expenses are generally classified as cost of goods sold, selling, general and administrative, and other.

Cost of goods sold represents the cost of the product to the seller. In a manufacturing firm, this would include the cost of the raw materials, direct labor, and overhead costs to run the manufacturing plant, such as rent, utilities, production supervision, and so on. In a merchandising firm, the cost of goods sold would represent the cost of the product to the entrepreneur when it was purchased. A company selling services would not incur cost of goods sold.

Selling expenses represent costs related to selling the product or service. They may include advertising, sales salaries and benefits, commissions, travel and entertainment, retail store operations costs, marketing, and so on.

General and administrative expenses include the entrepreneur's salary, office personnel salaries and benefits, office supplies, insurance, accounting and legal fees, depreciation on office equipment, and any other costs incurred in running a business.

Other expenses would be costs incurred in addition to the costs just discussed. Typically, interest expense (or interest income) and any losses (or gains) incurred on the sale of equipment would be included in this category.

Capital expenditures also represent a cost for companies. Examples of capital expenditures include the purchase of a piece of equipment or a building. As discussed in Chapter 3, these types of purchases are not expensed immediately but are allocated to expense over their useful lives. Depreciation expense therefore reduces income on an accrual basis but does not impact monthly cash expenses. The entrepreneur must identify and budget for these capital costs because they can have a huge impact on cash flow in the month of purchase. How capital expenditures are funded will also impact cash flow and the income statement in terms of the interest costs.

The accurate forecasting of expenses is critical to the establishment of reliable budgets and as input for various business decisions that must be made during the start-up and growth of a business venture. Without accurate expense forecasting and a good understanding of how costs behave, an entrepreneur may be unable to manage the business financially as events unfold. Simply constructing a budget is never enough for an entrepreneurial venture, for there are too many unknowns and unforeseen events that make a budget an inaccurate barometer of the financial performance of an emerging business. The entrepreneur needs to understand the behavior of costs so that, as events change, midcourse adjustments can be made to any budget or forecast that has been created. An entrepreneur makes an assumption about the number of employees and amount of materials needed for a project under bid, for example. After winning the project and beginning the work, the entrepreneur realizes that due to outside events, another employee and more materials are needed. What will this mean for profits on this project? Will there be enough cash to finish the project? What can be done, if anything, to ensure that profit targets are met and cash is not depleted? An understanding of cost behavior can help to answer these questions while also assist in making sound decisions as a new business develops.

COST BEHAVIOR

Typically, costs can be defined as variable, fixed, or mixed in terms of how they react to changes in output.

Variable Costs

The first type of costs, called *variable*, change in direct proportion to the level of activity of the business. Activities that change variable costs can be very specific or can be as general as the number of units being produced. For example, sales commission expense is directly related to the level of sales. Direct materials costs change directly in relationship to units produced. An airline operating a flight will have the variable cost of meals tied to the number of passengers. The cost of fuel will be dependent on the length of the trip. With variable costs, the total cost changes with the change in activity while the cost per unit remains the same. Using the airline example, the longer the trip, the higher the total cost of the fuel. However, the cost per mile will stay the same. Table 5-1 displays some examples of expenses and the activity base that might be used to estimate those expenses.

A small manufacturer of snowshoes is an example of variable cost behavior. Assume that the cost of materials for each pair of snowshoes is $20. The total

TABLE 5-1	Examples of Activity Bases for Variable Costs	

Type of Expense	*Activity Base*
Sales commissions	Sales
Materials cost	Units produced
Health insurance expense	Number of employees covered
Wages expense	Number of hours worked
Payroll tax expense	Dollars of wages paid

variable cost at different levels of activity, in this case the production of snowshoes, would then be as follows:

Number of Units Produced (Pairs)	Materials Cost per Unit	Total Materials Cost
5,000	$20	$100,000
7,500	20	150,000
10,000	20	200,000

The cost of materials per pair of snowshoes does not change. However, the total cost changes with the change in level of production. At 5,000 pairs, the total materials cost is $100,000. When production doubles to 10,000 pairs, the total cost also doubles, to $200,000. When determining variable costs, care should be taken to make certain that the actual activity base that drives the cost has been identified. In this example, the total cost of materials does not vary with the number sold but rather with the number produced. Figure 5-1 displays a graph of the behavior of the variable cost of materials in this example.

Fixed Costs

The second basic type of costs, called *fixed,* remain constant in total dollar amount within a relevant range of activity. That is, these are costs that do not change with a

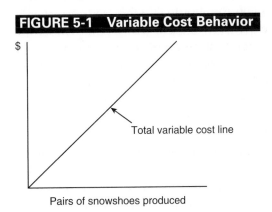

FIGURE 5-1   Variable Cost Behavior

$

Total variable cost line

Pairs of snowshoes produced

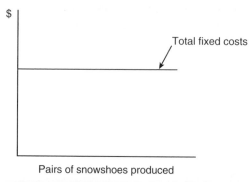

FIGURE 5-2 Fixed Cost Behavior

given activity such as sales or units produced. Figure 5-2 displays the behavior of fixed costs.

An example of a fixed cost is rent on a manufacturing plant. No matter what the production level, the amount of rent stays the same. Even though the total amount of fixed cost does not change, the cost per unit decreases as the activity level increases. In the case of rent, the more units produced, the lower the cost of the rent per unit, for the amount of rent does not change but is now spread over more units. At some point the company may outgrow its facilities and rent will increase as additional space is needed, but until that happens the cost of rent is fixed.

As stated in the definition, fixed costs remain the same within the *relevant range* of activity. As an example, consider the fixed cost of a production supervisor. Ten production workers can be hired before another supervisor will need to be hired. At the point when another supervisor is needed, we have moved out of the relevant range for that cost. The relevant range for a fixed cost is the range of activity over which the graph of the cost is flat. In this example, the relevant range is ten production workers for each supervisor; that is, the cost of supervision is fixed within this range.

Returning to the snowshoe example, assume the company rents manufacturing space at $5,000 per month. The cost of the space is $5,000 whether it manufactures 5,000 pairs of snowshoes or 10,000 pairs. Therefore, the cost per pair can vary from $1.00 ($5,000/5,000) to $.50 per pair ($5,000/10,000) while the total cost remains the same, $5,000 per month. However, if production jumped up to 15,000 pairs, the company might have to rent additional space. The 15,000 pairs are said to be "outside the relevant range"; that is, the fixed costs are fixed only up to a certain range of production.

One category of fixed costs is termed *committed fixed costs*. Two key traits of committed fixed costs are that they are long-term in nature and are difficult to cut back to zero without impacting profitability or long-term goals. Generally, committed fixed costs include investments in facilities, equipment, and the basic infrastructure. The resulting costs include depreciation of buildings and equipment, real estate taxes, and insurance. Because a committed fixed cost is by definition difficult to cut, an entrepreneur needs to be careful when adding such a long-term obligation for the business. Many examples exist where a company builds a new office building only to experience an economic decline, thereby causing the failure of the business due to its inability to pay for the new committed fixed cost.

A second category of fixed costs is *discretionary fixed costs*. The key trait of a discretionary fixed cost is that it is usually annual in nature and can be cut back for short periods of time without too much impact on the company.

Management strategy and the culture of the business often have a lot to do with whether a cost is committed or discretionary. For example, if plant workers are considered to be discretionary costs, they will be laid off more quickly than if they are considered committed costs. Why would employees be considered committed costs? The entrepreneur may have created a culture in the business in which employee layoffs are avoided at almost any cost. Commitment to employees is considered a cornerstone of the company culture. Treating plant worker costs as committed can also be economic in nature. The cost of hiring, training, and getting new workers to be fully productive can be greater than keeping employees through a business downturn.

Mixed Costs

Many costs do not behave simply as fixed or variable costs. Such costs are termed *mixed costs,* as they have both a fixed component and a variable component. Telephone expense is a good example of a mixed cost. There is a basic cost, a monthly charge, which must be paid just to have telephone service available. However, there is an additional variable portion of telephone expense that is based on the actual service used, that is, the long distance charges. Sales staff salaries may also be mixed. The company may pay each salesperson a base salary along with a commission that is based on number of units sold. When forecasting a mixed cost, the estimate should include the fixed portion and the variable component based on the appropriate activity base.

In summary, it is critical to identify the type of cost behavior—variable, fixed, or mixed—for each expense in a forecast. The activity base for the variable costs and the relevant range for the fixed costs should then be determined. Too often, start-up businesses will miss profitability estimates because the entrepreneurs made the simple assumption when making forecasts that all costs are variable with sales. Also, many entrepreneurs fail to realize that variable costs may vary with a variety of activities, not just sales. Cost behaviors should be documented and included in the assumptions for the forecast used in making financial projections (see Chapter 6). For costs directly related to sales, document the percentage relationship between that cost and sales. For indirect costs, document the total dollars of cost. Exhibit 5-1 shows how a merchandising company might set up an income statement. The cost of goods sold and the selling expenses are considered direct expenses, and of these only the cost of goods

EXHIBIT 5-1   Example—Merchandising Company

			Assumptions Used
Sales	$100,000	100.0%	
Cost of goods sold	65,000	65.0	65% of sales
Gross profit	35,000	35.0	35% of sales
Sales salaries	15,000	15.0	# of salespeople × monthly base
Sales commissions	1,500	1.5	1.5% of sales
Store rent	3,000	3.0	Monthly rent
Total selling expenses	19,500	19.5	
Office rent	2,500	2.5	Monthly rent
Office salaries	12,000	12.0	# people × monthly pay
Depreciation	500	.5	Cost of equipment/months of life
Total gen. & admin.	15,000	15.0	
EBIT	500	.5	

sold and sales commissions are variable. The general and administrative expense is considered indirect and in this case is fixed because the dollars will not vary with sales.

BREAKEVEN ANALYSIS

Breakeven analysis is a way to look at costs and revenues to assess the likelihood of profitability. Basically, it is the calculation of the minimum number of units of product or service that a firm must produce and sell in order to cover all of its variable and fixed expenses. Beyond this level of sales the firm starts to make a profit. It should be emphasized that the breakeven quantity is *not* an optimum; it is a minimum. If a firm's marketing projection suggests that it cannot sell at least the breakeven level of production, then the firm should abandon this endeavor before any money has been wasted. If a firm's marketing projection suggests that more than this minimum amount can be produced and sold, then further analysis should be conducted to determine whether the level of profit that is anticipated is acceptable. Breakeven analysis can sometimes be thought of as a "back-of-the-envelope" type of calculation to assess possible feasibility before a significant amount of time and energy has been invested in a business.

As an example, suppose a firm makes standard-sized signs for businesses. The entrepreneur can buy the sign material for $50 a piece and hire part-time workers to paint it for $20 per sign. Therefore, the variable cost per sign is $70. In addition, the firm has to rent a warehouse to do the work at a cost of $1,000 per month. Also, the monthly fee to the accounting firm to handle the sign company's books is $500 a month, so the fixed costs add up to $1,500 a month. The signs can be sold for $100 each. Profit on a before-tax basis would be

$$\text{Profit} = (P \times Q) - (V \times Q) - F$$

P = price per unit, $100
Q = quantity produced and sold
V = variable cost per unit, $70
F = fixed cost, $1,500

Therefore, we can solve for minimum number of units by setting the profit equal to zero and solving for Q:

$$Q = F/(P - V)$$
$$Q = 1500/(100 - 70), \text{ or } 50 \text{ units}$$

If the firm makes and sells less than 50 units, the level of profit would be negative. At 50 units, the level of profit is exactly zero; at more than 50 units, the profit becomes positive and increases with each additional unit produced and sold. In this example, the difference between price and variable cost ($100 – $70) is $30 per unit. Therefore, the firm has to make 50 units just to cover the fixed costs of $1,500, which the firm would be paying whether or not any units were produced. The term *contribution margin* is used to describe the difference between price and variable cost. It is the amount contributed to covering fixed costs.

EXPENSE FORECASTING—THE IMPACT OF BUSINESS TYPE ON EXPENSES

Manufacturing Firms

The expenses of a manufacturer would typically include the following: the raw material cost, the direct labor cost, overhead costs, and administration and selling or distribution costs. Different products require different proportions of expenditures. Some manufacturing schemes are so automated that direct labor is a very small part of total expenses; other manufacturers require a very labor-intensive technology where direct labor is the largest component. Manufacturing firms also provide some of the best examples of fixed versus variable costs. Direct labor and raw material costs are variable, meaning that they vary with the level of production. Administrative expenses such as accounting, secretarial help, and managers are usually fixed expenses, as is the cost of leasing equipment or a building. As discussed earlier in the chapter, fixed expenses such as these do not vary with the level of production, at least in the short term. To demonstrate the general expense characteristics of a manufacturing firm, the assembly line example from Chapter 4 for revenue forecasting will be used again here.

Assume an assembly line can produce 50 units per hour. The plan is to open up a second shift in the second month and a third shift in the following month. The product requires $25 per unit in materials to make. Each assembly line requires one employee, who is paid $20 per hour and works 20 days per month. The owner is also the manager/accountant and collects a salary of $4,000 per month. Benefits amount to $200 per employee per month. The Social Security tax contribution for the company is 7.65 percent. The final product sells for $100 per unit. What are the monthly expenses and resulting net cash flow?

	Month 1	Month 2	Month 3
Owner salary	$ 4,000	$ 4,000	$ 4,000
Employee #1	3,200	3,200	3,200
Employee #2		3,200	3,200
Employee #3			3,200
Benefits (200 empl.)	400	600	800
Social Sec. (7.65%)	551	796	1,040
Materials	200,000	400,000	600,000
Total expense	$208,151	$ 411,796	$ 615,440
Revenue	$800,000	$1,600,000	$2,400,000
Net cash flow	$591,849	$1,188,204	$1,784,560

In this example, labor expense was only a very small portion of the total expenses. Because cash flow is being measured, depreciation expense on equipment is not included, but if net income were being measured, depreciation expense would be included, resulting in income lower than cash flow.

In nonmanufacturing firms certain expense attributes may exist that someone from a manufacturing background may not anticipate. The next set of discussions will highlight some of these attributes.

Service Firms

Firms that provide a service, such as consulting companies, law firms, accounting firms, and lawn care, typically have employee salary/wages as one of their most significant (if not *the* most significant) expenses. And typically, this is an expense that behaves like a fixed cost. For instance, a fairly standard practice is to pay an employee a fixed salary plus a bonus on a periodic (yearly) basis. A wise way to handle the bonus aspect is to calculate it based on some measure of end-of-year profit. That way, the firm does not have to commit itself to paying bonuses when experiencing a loss.

In Chapter 4, the revenue characteristics of a service firm were discussed; we will now use that same example to describe the expense side. Assume a lifestyle consulting company has one associate and one owner. The plan is to hire one associate per month during the growth phase. The owner is collecting a base salary of $4,000 per month. Associates can be hired for $4,500 per month with a bonus at the end of the year *if* the firm makes a profit. For now, we will concern ourselves with only the month-to-month expenditures. Benefits are

$200 per month per employee and the employer must contribute 7.65 percent of an employee's salary for Social Security. In addition, associates are paid their base salary even though they are not at peak efficiency until they have worked for two months or more. Office rental is $2,000 per month and computer lease and phone costs are $100 per month per employee. What are the monthly expenses and resulting cash flow?

	Month 1	Month 2	Month 3
Owner salary	$ 4,000	$ 4,000	$ 4,000
Associate #1	4,500	4,500	4,500
Associate #2		4,500	4,500
Associate #3			4,500
Benefits (200 empl.)	400	600	800
Social Sec. (7.65%)	650	995	1,339
Office rent	2,000	2,000	2,000
Computer/telephone	200	300	400
Total expenses	$11,750	$16,895	$22,039
Revenue projection	$ 8,800	$20,000	$31,200
Net cash flow before taxes	($ 2,950)	$ 3,105	$ 9,161

Note that in this example expenses related to the number of employees are the most significant. Also notice that salaries have to be paid even when an employee is too new to be fully productive in producing revenue. Hence, the firm experienced a negative net cash flow in the first month before enough employees were generating sufficient revenue to "carry" the new employee cost.

Recurring Revenue Firms

Recurring revenue firms such as wireless communications, paging, and cable services frequently have relatively large expenses at the front end of service and then somewhat lower recurring expenses as the service is provided. For instance, a fixed wireless or cable company typically requires an employee to install an electronic device at a job site, which can sometimes be an expensive endeavor. In addition, a salesperson may also have to be compensated with a commission. Once the service is up and running, however, the monthly cost and effort to provide the service could be quite low.

We will estimate the expenses for I-Can't-Quite-Hear-You Wireless, Inc. from Chapter 4. The company requires $23 in labor costs in order to hook up a new device. The salesperson, who is hired as a subcontractor, also gets a commission equal to three months' revenue for each new customer. In order to maintain growth in revenues, 150 new customers must be added each month to make up for the 5 percent disconnect rate. Monthly revenue is $10 per customer and the firm starts out with 1,000 current customers. The monthly cost of providing the service is $1 per customer per month for airtime. Finally, salary for the owner is $4,000 per month with benefits of $200 and a Social Security tax contribution of 7.65 percent. Office rental is $2,000. What is the monthly expense flow and the resulting cash flow?

	Month 1	Month 2	Month 3
Hook up cost (150 × $23)	$ 3,450	$ 3,450	$ 3,450
Commission (3 mo. revenue for each new customer	4,500	4,500	4,500
Airtime cost (# old customers + 150 new) × (1 minus 5% disconnect) × ($1/month)	1,093	1,181	1,264
Owner salary	4,000	4,000	4,000
Benefits	200	200	200
Social Sec. (7.65%)	306	306	306
Total expenses	$13,549	$13,637	$13,720
Revenue	$10,930	$11,810	$12,640
Cash flow before taxes	($ 2,619)	($ 1,827)	($ 1,080)

Clearly, having a lot of new customers creates a large amount of one-time expenses. Therefore, when a firm is in a period of trying to grow its customer base, it winds up experiencing negative cash flow. New growth means new customers, and new customers mean large up-front expenditures. Therefore, this type of business model may result in losses when the company aggressively pursues sales growth, and ironically, the firm will be more likely to experience profits when sales growth is stopped or at least slowed. However, this does not mean that firing all the salespeople is the way to achieve long-term profits, because 5 percent of the customers disconnect each month. Eventually, all of the revenue will disappear unless customers are continually replaced with new customers.

Commission-Based Sales Firms

The commission-based selling model typically requires that salespeople take part or all of their compensation in the form of a sales commission. The expense of paying a commission can be forecasted simply by multiplying the number of units forecasted to be sold by the commission per unit. A key element is setting a commission structure that attracts people into the sales profession and at the same time is not so generous that the firm ends up operating at a loss just to pay the commission.

We will use the example from Chapter 4 to analyze the expense side of a commission-based company. The Harmon Company plans to hire one new salesperson per month during the first five months of the start-up year. The base level of sales expected from each salesperson is 100 units per month. It takes three months for a salesperson to be fully effective (i.e., sell 33 units in the first, 66 in the second, and 100 in the third). The price per unit is $500, and salespeople are paid a commission equal to $50 per unit. The wholesale cost per unit is $100. The owner is to be paid $4,000 per month, the benefit package costs $200 per employee, and the

TABLE 5-2

	Month 1	Month 2	Month 3	Month 4	Month 5
Salesperson 1	33 × $50	66 × $50	100 × $50	100 × $50	100 × $50
Salesperson 2		33 × $50	66 × $50	100 × $50	100 × $50
Salesperson 3			33 × $50	66 × $50	100 × $50
Salesperson 4				33 × $50	66 × $50
Salesperson 5					33 × $50
Commissions	$ 1,650	$ 4,950	$ 9,950	$ 14,950	$ 19,950
Owner salary	4,000	4,000	4,000	4,000	4,000
Social Sec. (7.65%)	432	685	1,067	1,450	1,832
Benefits (200/empl.)	400	600	800	1,000	1,200
Telephone/computer	200	300	400	500	600
Office rent	2,000	2,000	2,000	2,000	2,000
Wholesale cost	3,300	9,900	19,900	29,900	39,900
Total expenses	$11,982	$22,435	$38,117	$ 53,800	$ 69,482
Revenue	$16,500	$49,500	$99,500	$149,500	$199,500
Net cash flow	$ 4,518	$27,065	$61,383	$ 95,700	$130,018

employer's Social Security contribution will cost 7.65 percent of the gross payroll. Office rent is $2,000 per month. Telephone and computer leasing cost is $100 per month per employee. What are the monthly expenses and resulting cash flow?

Table 5-2 shows that the salespeople were officially made employees of the firm. As a result, benefits had to be paid for each new salesperson added and Social Security taxes had to be calculated and paid on the salesperson's commissions. Note the difference from the I-Can't-Quite-Hear-You Wireless example, in which a commission was paid to a salesperson for each new customer and the salesperson was considered a subcontractor. The salesperson for ICQHY Wireless was *not* an employee but a separate business that performed the sales function in exchange for a fee. Out of that fee, the salesperson was responsible for paying Social Security taxes, insurance, and so on. Hence, benefits and Social Security taxes were not paid for by ICQHY, which demonstrates a possible advantage of outsourcing some of the functions of the firm rather than always hiring employees to do everything "in house." Subcontracting out functions such as sales, accounting, human resources, payroll, and so on will not always be the most efficient way to handle a particular business function, but frequently it can be effective in reducing the amount of time, paperwork and legal responsibilities of an entrepreneur.

Cyclical or Seasonal Firms

It is important for businesses that have only a seasonal demand for their product or service not to count on a sustainable level of revenue (and certainly not growth) during months that they cannot maintain customers.

Sammy's Ski-Jumping School, for example, (from Chapter 4) can only operate in the months of December, January, and February. Because there is only one ski jump in the entire state, the number of students that can be taught is limited, (only five students can be taught per day at a fee of $100 per student) and because of holidays and lift times, the school is only open 12 days in December, 18 days in January, and 17 days in February. The ski resort that has the ski jump has agreed to make Sammy the official ski-jumping instructor. In return, however, the resort demands an annual fee of $4,800 to reserve the ski jump, payable on a monthly basis of $400. Sammy works as a construction worker during the spring, summer, and fall months. What are the monthly expenses and the resulting cash flow?

	Nov.	Dec.	Jan.	Feb.	Mar.	Apr.
Fee to resort	$400	$400	$400	$400	$400	$400
Total exp.	400	400	400	400	400	400
Revenue	0	6,000	9,000	8,500	0	0
Net cash flow	(400)	5,600	8,600	8,100	(400)	(400)

The key point to consider in this situation is that somehow the entrepreneur must be prepared to survive during the times of the year when revenue is not coming in. In this case, Sammy runs this business only during the peak winter months and has alternative employment to meet his living expenses for the other times of the year.

REDUCING EXPENSES THROUGH BOOTSTRAPPING

For many entrepreneurs, simply understanding cost behavior and using accurate forecasting techniques is not enough. Because of limited resources or a desire to keep control of their business, these entrepreneurs may need to find ways to "sharpen the pencil" and bring expenses down below their initial forecasts. At first this may seem an impossible task. However, there are a variety of techniques and tools that can help achieve the same outcomes while greatly reducing costs. This process is known as *bootstrapping*.

Initial marketing for a new venture can often be costly when using traditional techniques employed by larger corporations. For example, a typical market study conducted by larger organizations can cost tens of thousands of dollars, which exceeds the entire start-up funding of many entrepreneurs. There are a variety of tools that can be used, however, to bootstrap the necessary marketing, including market research and promotion. Employee costs are another large expenditure item for new businesses, yet there are several steps that can be taken to reduce the cost of human resources. Overhead expenses, which were described in this chapter as indirect costs, can choke entrepreneurial ventures with expenses that do not directly create revenues and profits. One entrepreneur went so far as to describe overhead expenses as the start-up entrepreneur's "worst enemy!" While this may be a bit of an overstatement, it is true that the management of overhead expenses is critical, and there are a variety of bootstrapping techniques that can help keep overhead expenses to a minimum. Chapter 8 will examine bootstrapping management techniques in more detail and provide examples of a variety of tools and techniques that can help reduce expenditures in all categories.

SUMMARY

Forecasting expenses requires an understanding of how costs behave, that is, as variable, fixed, or mixed costs. Expense behaviors also differ by type of business and type of sales cycle. Bootstrapping is a means of managing expenses by creatively reducing costs without reducing the impact of the activity. The next chapter will integrate the financial model built in the first five chapters into a spreadsheet format that can be used to forecast financial statements for new and growing ventures.

DISCUSSION QUESTIONS

1. What are the three different types of costs, and how do they differ?
2. What would be the relationship between sales revenue and profit when a firm operates with a very high degree of fixed expenses and very little variable costs?
3. How are profit and revenue related in a business where almost all the expenses are variable?
4. Why would an entrepreneur need to know the operation's breakeven point if the goal is to make a profit?
5. How are the expenses and the resulting cash flow likely to differ for a service company such as a law firm compared to a service company with recurring revenue that has an up-front hook-up expense and thereafter can provide the service almost for free?
6. What is the key challenge to a seasonal firm in terms of revenues versus expenses?
7. What is bootstrapping, and why is it important to a start-up firm?
8. Given a long enough time frame, can expenses always be fixed?
9. Having all sales employees working on a totally commission-based compensation plan has certain advantages for a firm. What might be some of the difficulties an entrepreneur could face in trying to implement such a plan?
10. What is the difference between expenses and cash flow?

OPPORTUNITIES FOR APPLICATION

1. If a product can be sold for $1,000 per unit, the variable cost per unit is $550, and fixed costs are $2,000,000, then how many units must be produced and sold before the firm can break even?
2. If an employee has a salary of $50,000 per year, benefits cost the company $7,200 per employee per year, and the employer's share of the Social Security tax is 7.65 percent then what is direct cost per year for this employee?
3. Suppose a salesperson in a recurring revenue firm is paid the equivalent of 2.5 months' sales revenue for each new customer added. Also, the charge for the service is

$120 per month, and providing the service costs the company $50 per month per customer. It costs $25 to initially hook each new customer up. What would be the effect on this month's expenses if the salesperson added 55 new customers this month?

4. Assume that an assembly line can produce 120 units per hour and the material cost is $15 per unit. Suppose that a single employee, who is paid $22 per hour, can operate an assembly line. The employee works an eight-hour day and there are 20 work days in a month. In addition, the company's contribution to Social Security is 7.65 percent of employee pay, and benefits cost the company about $565 per month per employee. Maintenance on the assembly line costs $1,000 per month. What is the total cost of producing product for one month?

5. Facility rent is $2,200 per month, accounting service costs $2,600 per month, insurance is $1,100 per month, utilities such as phone and electricity cost $550 per month. The manager is paid $89,000 per year, gets benefits worth $6,500 per year, and the Social Security contribution is 7.65 percent. Given this information, what is the amount of annual fixed expense that this company has to pay?

6. Given the information in problem 6, if the profit contribution after variable expenses is $125 per unit, is the firm making a profit if it produces and sells 1,000 units per year?

7. Why do recurring revenue and commission-based firms frequently experience losses during periods of rapid sales growth?

8. If a product has variable costs of $50 per unit, fixed costs of $100,000, and revenue of $65 per unit, would it be possible for a firm to achieve a 22 percent rate of return on an investment of $2,500,000 at a sales level of 2,000 units?

9. If a firm's total material cost increases by $150,000 when the level of production increases by 6,500 units, then what is the variable cost on a per unit basis?

10. Categorize the various expenses and examine the cost behaviors of a business you now operate or plan to start in the near future.

CHAPTER

$$\boxed{6}$$

Integrated Financial Model

The previous chapters have presented a model of financial forecasting for entrepreneurial ventures. This chapter, which completes the first section of this book, integrates all of the forecasts, assumptions, goals, and objectives into a working spreadsheet model. A spreadsheet tool such as this allows the entrepreneur to adjust plans, create multiple "what-if" scenarios, and develop the beginnings of a system for the financial management of the entrepreneurial venture. By creating an inventory of assumptions and milestones, the entrepreneur is able to track and make adjustments in the forecasts "on the fly." Once completed, the financial statements that flow out of the spreadsheet can be integrated into a business plan or funding document.

THE ENTREPRENEUR'S ASPIRATIONS RECONSIDERED

As discussed in Chapter 2, any financial modeling of a new business venture should ultimately begin with the aspirations of the founders. Although an entrepreneur's aspirations can vary, clearly identifying the *financial* aspirations is the first step in building a financial model. When doing so, both the income and wealth needs of the entrepreneur should be considered. Generally speaking, the income needs of the entrepreneur should be built into the model as a fundamental assumption. Although many entrepreneurs plan to take a low salary in the early stages of a new venture, a clear set of income expectations for the entrepreneur over the first three years of the business should be established. Entrepreneurs who go into a venture with the thought that they will "get by" on whatever extra cash is created by the business are often disillusioned within a short period of time. The plan for the entrepreneur's income from the business should be as deliberate and explicit as the plan to pay rent and employee payroll. Of course, if the business does not go according to plan, it is the owner's paychecks that are the first to be deferred. However, that does not mean that the plan should not attempt to account for a reasonable salary for the owner in the forecasts and budgets.

Integrating into the plan the creation of wealth for the owner, while less precise than planning for income, is no less important. As discussed in Chapter 2, wealth for the entrepreneur is ultimately created through the ability of the business to generate a profit. Chapter 13 presents a detailed discussion of valuation for a going concern, but the "quick and dirty" method of valuation can help set profit targets in the forecasting stage of a new venture. Using the methods described in Chapter 2, a profit target can be established for the forecasting model. An important consideration is the ultimate timing of when the entrepreneur would like to take the wealth "out of the business," typically through some form of exit from the venture (Chapters 13 and 14 discuss such transitions in detail). This process is called *realization of wealth*. For example, if the entrepreneur wants to realize the wealth from a business within five years, the forecasting model should show clear and steady progress toward the profitability levels necessary to achieve this goal. Another entrepreneur may have a longer time frame in which the realization of wealth is tied to retirement in 20 years. For that entrepreneur, the pressure to build necessary profits may not be as great in the short term. The challenge for the second entrepreneur is to build a venture that can sustain profitability over a long time period. This is no small accomplishment in itself and requires a different approach to forecasting, with less concern for engineering high profitability into the new venture quickly.

Once the entrepreneur establishes the wealth and income goals for the business that will serve as the foundation of financial planning, the actual spreadsheet modeling can begin. The next section discusses how the format of the income statement can help the entrepreneur better understand the business.

CONTRIBUTION FORMAT INCOME STATEMENT

A useful tool for assessing company performance and pinpointing potential problems is the style of income statement that is generated by the templates supplied with this textbook. (The specific instructions for these templates can be found in the Appendix at the end of this chapter.) This style is called the *contribution format*. It shows the contribution from sales, also called *operating margin,* before considering the indirect costs related to general and administrative expenses. With this style one can locate the major sources of profit and, conversely, where that profit is most likely to disappear. The top of the income statement starts with revenue followed by the expenses that most professionals would consider to be direct expenses. The difference between revenues and direct expenses results in operating margin, which represents the amount available to cover indirect expenses. The balance left after indirect expenses are covered is called *Earnings Before Interest and Taxes* (EBIT).

EARNINGS BEFORE INTEREST AND TAXES (EBIT)

EBIT represents the income earned by the company before considering interest and income taxes. Interest is a result of a decision the entrepreneur made about how the business would be financed. The templates in this chapter allow the input of an interest rate for both long-term and short-term borrowings.

The templates do not attempt to provide a tax calculation because that depends on the entrepreneur's decision about how to organize the business. However, the entrepreneur needs to keep in mind the cash flow implications related to income taxes. A good rule of thumb is to assume up to 35 percent of any income generated will be needed to pay income taxes if the business is organized as a corporation and 15 to 35 percent (depending on the owner's tax bracket) if it is organized as a sole proprietorship or partnership. Therefore, when evaluating cash flows generated by the business, the entrepreneur must take this into consideration as a cash outflow.

At each subtotal stage, the entrepreneur sees the level of profit that still exists and as a result, can start to see which types of expenses have the most significant effect on reducing profit. For most firms, direct operating expenses are the most significant. Materials costs and labor costs associated with providing a product typically make up the majority of expenses for a manufacturing firm. In a service business, the salaries of those employees providing the service are usually the largest single expense. For other firms, administrative or financing costs could have the greatest effect. The main point, however, is that the operating margin allows a businessperson to see where to focus attention for continued profitability or the most likely location of a problem should the firm not be profitable.

INVENTORY OF ASSUMPTIONS

A crucial part of planning in general and raising funds from investors in particular is to list the key assumptions that the managers of the firm are making about how business will be conducted. It is not enough to make a list of assumptions—it is also important to have justifications for these assumptions. The forecasting template included with this book includes an assumption section that is a good place for beginning to determine the kind of information an entrepreneur must uncover or assume for the future.

Items about which assumptions would need to be made and justified could include:

1. The level of sales in units.
2. The selling price per unit.
3. The cost of goods sold per unit or per dollar of revenue.
4. The credit terms, if any, that the firm will offer its customers. Will all sales be made for cash, or will customers be allowed a month or two before payment is due?
5. The relationship between inventory and future sales.
6. The salaries, rent, utilities, telephone, transportation, and insurance costs that are directly related to delivering sales.
7. The administrative expenses of the business, such as managers' salaries, accounting, insurance, and so on.
8. The amount of equipment that must be purchased and how long will it last.

9. The relationship between accounts payable and expenses. Must all expenses be paid in cash or can some of them be delayed for a month or two?
10. The financing currently available to the firm. How much is borrowed funds and how much is investment by owners?
11. The interest rate the firm is expecting to pay on its debt.

Chapter 5 discusses how to make and justify the assumptions that deal with cost. The most important of all the assumptions will, of course, be the ones made about sales. To arrive at these, one must first answer the following two questions:

1. Will the product require development time, and if so, how many months will it take before the product can actually be sold to the public? During this time the firm would be operating without any revenue. To determine the length of the development period, information could be gathered from engineers, potential employees who are expected to be involved with development, or industry experts.
2. Once the product can be offered for sale, how many units can reasonably be expected to sell in the first month, the second month, and so forth? Chapter 4 provides the foundation for answering this question.

DETERMINING THE AMOUNT OF FUNDS NEEDED

A detrimental mistake for a new venture would be to not raise enough money and run out before the next funding stage. Therefore, knowing beforehand the amount of funds necessary for a company to reach its next goal or stage of development is crucial. If the necessary amount cannot be raised, then management needs to decide whether to abandon the endeavor or whether it is both possible and still feasible to change strategy and mode of operation to operate within the funding constraint.

When putting together a funding request, it is easy to add up the cost of equipment that must be purchased and the typical monthly expenses of salaries, office rent, and so on that must be paid during the initial phase of the business. What is less obvious, but just as important, is the amount of financing that is necessary to deal with working capital needs. *Working capital* refers to the current assets of a firm, such as accounts receivable and inventory. For example, inventory must typically be purchased in advance of sales. Frequently, deposits must be made for some purchases before delivery if the firm does not have a credit history with a vendor. Working capital is also needed when sales to customers are made with trade credit. The accounting effect would be to increase the level of accounts receivable as sales are booked, which by itself can cause a huge differential between net income as recorded on the income statement and the actual cash flow generated by the firm. During periods of no sales, and especially during periods of very rapidly growing sales, huge cash outflows can be caused by the need for working capital. If only direct expenditures such as equipment purchases and directly observable expenses are accounted for and not working capital needs, the firm will run out of cash and go bankrupt long before the next round of financing becomes available. The potential of an entrepreneur's idea becomes totally irrelevant once a firm finds itself unable to pay employees, purchase raw materials, or pay rent.

USING THE FORECASTING TEMPLATE TO DETERMINE THE AMOUNT OF FUNDS NEEDED

The template included in the chapter appendix can be used to determine the total amount of financing needed by the firm to get through a particular stage of development. It includes the following steps.

For the initial development stage:

Step 1: Enter all of the assumptions in the assumption section except for those concerning long-term debt and investment by owners.

Step 2: Repeat step 1 for all the months or years that correspond to this particular financing stage.

Step 3: Allow the model to recalculate and balance itself automatically on the short-term loan line.

Step 4: Go to the month of the forecasted period where the number on the short-term loan line is largest. This number is the minimum amount of financing necessary to allow the firm to survive during this time phase.

The logic of this is that because the short-term loan line has to represent the amount of funding needed to balance the balance sheet, it therefore represents the total amount of financing needed when no values are entered for other financing sources.

For any succeeding financing stage:

Step 1: Enter all of the assumptions in the assumption section, including the amounts of long-term debt and investment by owners supplied during the previous stage.

Step 2: Repeat step 1 for all the months or years that correspond to this particular financing stage.

Step 3: Allow the model to recalculate and balance itself automatically on the short-term loan line.

Step 4: Go to the month of the forecasted period where the number on the short-term loan line is largest. This number now represents the minimum amount of additional financing necessary to allow the firm to survive during this time phase.

Note that the dollar amounts from the short-term loan line represent the total minimum amount of financing needed to survive the stage of the business. If investors require an itemized list of where the funds will be used, the amount specifically needed for working capital needs can be determined by subtracting from the total financing needed the known expenditures from the assumption section, such as equipment to be purchased, salaries of employees, rent, utilities, and so on. The remaining balance represents the amount of funds that were "burned up" during this phase for working capital purposes.

TIME OUT OF CASH

A measurement that can be used for assessing progress and is sometimes asked for by potential investors is the firm's *time out of cash*. Raising money frequently requires a lead time of months, especially when a firm has to go through the investment banking process. The time out of cash is a measure of how long a current amount of cash will theoretically last. This is an especially important piece of information during the development stage when revenue is zero or close to zero. Knowing time out of cash is crucial to determining whether a firm will survive until the next round of financing. Operating cash flow from the current month's statement of cash flow is sometimes called the firm's *burn rate* because it represents the amount of cash used up that month just from running the business. When compared to the amount of cash that the business currently has on hand, the burn rate can give an entrepreneur a sense of the urgency faced by the firm similar to time out of cash.

$$\text{Time Out of Cash} = (\text{Cash /Operating Cash Outflow per Month})$$

Time out of cash represents the number of months that the firm's current cash balance would last if the firm were to continue operating in its current manner. Cash on hand is found on the balance sheet, and operating cash flow is found on the statement of cash flows. This calculation is only an approximation, however, and it is relevant only if operating cash flow is negative. If the firm were actually generating positive cash flow from its operations, it could theoretically be self-sustaining and would never need additional financing to survive.

For example, Standard Start-Up, Inc. is a recently started venture. It has $225,000 in cash from its last round of financing. Its statement of cash flows in the most recent month showed that operating cash flow was a negative $12,555, because the firm currently has operating expenses and working capital needs that exceed revenue by this amount.

$$\text{Time Out of Cash} = (\$225{,}000/\$12{,}555) = 17.9$$

Given this information, Standard Start-Up, Inc. will run out of cash in approximately 18 months unless its revenues start to exceed expenses

ASSESSMENT OF RISK/SENSITIVITY

When making financial models for a new venture it is important to look at more than one set of possible assumptions. That is, the entrepreneur should examine multiple scenarios of demand, pricing, and costs to better understand the possible situations the business may face. Among the scenarios that the entrepreneur should look at include the most likely case, the best case, and the worst case. The most-likely-case scenario would include the assumptions that are deemed most realistic and therefore the most likely to occur. The best-case scenario would include the most optimistic assumptions. The purpose of the best-case scenario is to give the investor some sense of the upside potential given the anticipated investment. The worst-case scenario, logically, would be a set of assumptions representing the situation where everything that could go wrong does go wrong. The projection from this set of assumptions would reflect the downside risk of the investment. It provides the entrepreneur the opportunity to think about the "unthinkable" and, therefore, to develop alternative strategies before things go wrong. Both the best-case and the worst-case scenarios have small probabilities of occurrence, but the point of the exercise of constructing them is to help the entrepreneur assess the range of potential outcomes to prepare the organization for the possible risks.

Assessment of various scenarios is known as *what-if analysis*. Performing these analyses in advance can be critical management tools. For example, assume an entrepreneur has made financial forecasts using a certain set of assumptions about demand and pricing of the product. If demand is not as strong as initially forecast, the entrepreneur may decide to lower prices to attract new customers. However, by reducing prices the entrepreneur may push the point of cash flow breakeven well into the future. If the implications of this decision are not fully understood, the entrepreneur may have inadvertently created a new financial model that uses up available working capital before enough cash comes in to pay the ongoing bills. If this is anticipated in advance through what-if analysis, the entrepreneur should be aware that costs must be cut to keep the business operating successfully with the lower prices.

This type of analysis can also be used when certain large contracts are pending. The entrepreneur can examine multiple scenarios that assume different contracts and timing of contracts to see the impact on profits and cash flow, which can help the entrepreneur better understand the impact of a new large customer on a business. What additional overhead will be required? How much working capital will be needed to support the timing of cash flow from the new customer? These are critical questions that need to be answered before committing to the new customer is even considered.

INTEGRATING INTO BUSINESS PLAN/FUNDING DOCUMENT

Once the financial forecasting is completed, the forecasted statements need to be built into the business plan (see Chapter 2) and other funding documents. Most often, the plan should include two years of month-by-month forecasts, with annual or quarterly statements for the next one to two years of operation. Figure 6-1 displays an example of statements generated by the template in the Appendix as they would appear in a business plan for a service company. The templates produce monthly statements for three years.

FIGURE 6-1 Year 1 Income Statement Accrual Basis

	Month 1	Month 2	Month 3	Month 4	Month 5	Month 6	Month 7	Month 8	Month 9	Month 10	Month 11	Month 12	Total
REVENUES													
Cash sales	8,800	20,000	31,200	36,800	36,800	36,800	36,800	36,800	36,800	36,800	36,800	36,800	391,200
Charge sales													
TOTAL SALES	8,800	20,000	31,200	36,800	36,800	36,800	36,800	36,800	36,800	36,800	36,800	36,800	391,200
DIRECT EXPENSES													
Direct Costs													
Salaries	4,500	9,000	13,500	13,500	13,500	13,500	13,500	13,500	13,500	13,500	13,500	13,500	148,500
Benefits	569	1,139	1,708	1,708	1,708	1,708	1,708	1,708	1,708	1,708	1,708	1,708	18,785
Rent	2,000	2,000	2,000	2,000	2,000	2,000	2,000	2,000	2,000	2,000	2,000	2,000	24,000
Utilities													
Telephone	200	200	200	200	200	200	200	200	200	200	200	200	2,400
Transportation													
Insurance													
Bad debt expense													
TOTAL DIRECT EXPENSES	7,269	12,339	17,408	17,408	17,408	17,408	17,408	17,408	17,408	17,408	17,408	17,408	193,685
OPERATING MARGIN	1,531	7,662	13,792	19,392	19,392	19,392	19,392	19,392	19,392	19,392	19,392	19,392	197,515
General & Admin. Expenses													
Salaries	4,000	4,000	4,000	4,000	4,000	4,000	4,000	4,000	4,000	4,000	4,000	4,000	48,000
Benefits	506	506	506	506	506	506	506	506	506	506	506	506	6,072
Rent													
Utilities													
Telephone													
Transportation													
Insurance													
Legal & Accounting													
Marketing													
Office supplies													
Equipment leases													
Depreciation	100	100	100	100	100	100	100	100	100	100	100	100	1,200
TOTAL G&A	4,606	4,606	4,606	4,606	4,606	4,606	4,606	4,606	4,606	4,606	4,606	4,606	55,272
EBIT	(3,075)	3,056	9,186	14,786	14,786	14,786	14,786	14,786	14,786	14,786	14,786	14,786	142,243
Interest Expense	—	57	97	107	62	—	—	—	—	—	—	—	324
NET INCOME BEFORE TAXES	(3,075)	2,999	9,089	14,679	14,725	14,786	14,786	14,786	14,786	14,786	14,786	14,786	141,919

FIGURE 6-1 Balance Sheet—Year 1 (Continued)

	Balance	Month 1	Month 2	Month 3	Month 4	Month 5	Month 6	Month 7	Month 8	Month 9	Month 10	Month 11	Month 12
Cash	—	1,000	1,000	1,000	1,000	3,577	18,402	33,288	48,174	63,060	77,947	92,833	107,719
Accounts Receivable	—	8,800	20,000	31,200	36,800	36,800	36,800	36,800	36,800	36,800	36,800	36,800	36,800
Total Current Assets	—	9,800	21,000	32,200	37,800	40,377	55,202	70,088	84,974	99,860	114,747	129,633	144,519
Land	—	—	—	—	—	—	—	—	—	—	—	—	—
Building/Equipment	—	3,600	3,600	3,600	3,600	3,600	3,600	3,600	3,600	3,600	3,600	3,600	3,600
-LESS Accum. Depreciation	—	(100)	(200)	(300)	(400)	(500)	(600)	(700)	(800)	(900)	(1,000)	(1,100)	(1,200)
Net Fixed Assets	—	3,500	3,400	3,300	3,200	3,100	3,000	2,900	2,800	2,700	2,600	2,500	2,400
TOTAL ASSETS	—	13,300	24,400	35,500	41,000	43,477	58,202	72,988	87,774	102,560	117,347	132,133	146,919
LIABILITIES													
Accounts payable	—												
Short-term loan inc. interest	—	11,375	19,477	21,488	12,309	62	0	0	0	0	0	0	0
Interest on long-term	—												
TOTAL CURRENT	—	11,375	19,477	21,488	12,309	62	0	0	0	0	0	0	0
Long-term loans	—	—	—	—	—	—	—	—	—	—	—	—	—
Total liabilities	—	11,375	19,477	21,488	12,309	62	0	0	0	0	0	0	0
OWNERS' EQUITY													
Investment by owner	—	5,000	5,000	5,000	5,000	5,000	5,000	5,000	5,000	5,000	5,000	5,000	5,000
Retained earnings(loss)	—	(3,075)	(77)	9,012	23,691	38,416	53,202	67,988	82,774	97,560	112,347	127,133	141,919
Net equity	—	1,925	4,923	14,012	28,691	43,416	58,202	72,988	87,774	102,560	117,347	132,133	146,919
TOTAL LIAB AND OWNERS' EQUITY	—	13,300	24,400	35,500	41,000	43,477	58,202	72,988	87,774	102,560	117,347	132,133	146,919

FIGURE 6-1 Cash Flow—Year 1 (Continued)

	Month 1	Month 2	Month 3	Month 4	Month 5	Month 6	Month 7	Month 8	Month 9	Month 10	Month 11	Month 12	Total
Cash flow from operations													
Receipts													
Cash sales	—	—	—	—	—	—	—	—	—	—	—	—	—
Accounts Receivable collections	—	8,800	20,000	31,200	36,800	36,800	36,800	36,800	36,800	36,800	36,800	36,800	354,400
Total receipts	—	8,800	20,000	31,200	36,800	36,800	36,800	36,800	36,800	36,800	36,800	36,800	354,400
Disbursements													
Direct expenses except bad debt	7,269	12,339	17,408	17,408	17,408	17,408	17,408	17,408	17,408	17,408	17,408	17,408	193,685
G&A except depreciation	4,506	4,506	4,506	4,506	4,506	4,506	4,506	4,506	4,506	4,506	4,506	4,506	54,072
Interest on long-term	—	—	—	—	—	—	—	—	—	—	—	—	—
Total disbursements	11,775	16,845	21,914	21,914	21,914	21,914	21,914	21,914	21,914	21,914	21,914	21,914	247,757
Net cash flow from operations	(11,775)	(8,045)	(1,914)	9,286	14,886	14,886	14,886	14,886	14,886	14,886	14,886	14,886	106,643
Cash flow from investing activities													
Purchase of Land	—	—	—	—	—	—	—	—	—	—	—	—	—
Purchase of Building/Equip.	(3,600)	—	—	—	—	—	—	—	—	—	—	—	(3,600)
Net cash flow from investing activities	(3,600)	—	—	—	—	—	—	—	—	—	—	—	(3,600)
Cash flow from financing activities													
Investment by owners	5,000	—	—	—	—	—	—	—	—	—	—	—	5,000
Long-term loan additions (payments)	—	—	—	—	—	—	—	—	—	—	—	—	—
Net cash flow from long-term financing activities	5,000	—	—	—	—	—	—	—	—	—	—	—	5,000
Net cash increase (decrease)	(10,375)	(8,045)	(1,914)	9,286	14,886	14,886	14,886	14,886	14,886	14,886	14,886	14,886	108,043
Short-term Loan increase (decrease)	11,375	8,045	1,914	(9,286)	(12,309)	(62)	(0)	(0)	(0)	(0)	(0)	(0)	(324)
Beginning cash	—	1,000	1,000	1,000	1,000	3,577	18,402	33,288	48,174	63,060	77,947	92,833	92,833
Ending cash	1,000	1,000	1,000	1,000	3,577	18,402	33,288	48,174	63,060	77,947	92,833	107,719	107,719

A business plan typically includes a most-likely-case scenario and a worst-case scenario of assumptions and the accompanying financial statements, particularly if bank financing is being pursued. The most-likely-case scenario is what the entrepreneur expects to happen during the time horizon of the business plan. The worst-case scenario usually addresses the instance where a few key assumptions are proved to be inaccurate, which may include such things as key demand assumptions for the product or service or key pricing assumptions for raw materials. Sometimes worst-case scenarios represent a much slower growth than is anticipated in the most-likely-case scenario. The inclusion of two scenarios means that a business plan will need to include two full sets of financial statement forecasts representing each of the possible scenarios.

Professionals who read many business plans, such as bankers and investors, look for consistency between the text of the business plan and the numbers in the financial statement forecasts. Specifically, the marketing plan should be consistent with the revenue forecasts and assumptions, and the operating plan should be consistent with the expense forecasts and assumptions. Also, any growth discussed within the plan, typically contained in the marketing plan and industry analysis sections, should be consistent with the trends in the financial statements over time.

SUMMARY

This chapter has presented an integrated spreadsheet model that allows the entrepreneur to place all forecasts, assumptions, goals, and objectives in a single spreadsheet. From this spreadsheet, forecasted financial statements can be created to serve both the entrepreneur and potential outside investors. The next section of this book discusses the management of a venture's financial resources once it is up and running. Monitoring the financial performance, managing the scarce resources of a new venture including cash, and using external sources of funding will be examined in Chapters 7–12.

-----------------------------**A P P E N D I X**-----------------------------

Integrated Financial Statements Template Instructions

There are two versions of the Integrated Financial Statements Template Spreadsheet in this appendix. The first version is for businesses that have inventory, for example, retail, distribution, resellers, and manufacturing. The second version is for businesses with little or no inventory, for example, service, consulting, health care, software, and engineering. The templates can be used multiple times to test different possible ventures under consideration or to test various scenarios for a single business to explore multiple assumptions.

The proper development of assumptions is key to getting the most out of the spreadsheets. Each assumption should be carefully documented and any changes in assumptions should be noted. The financial statement assumptions should be derived from the business plan assumptions, with all assumptions being consistent and clearly tied together.

Using the templates requires only a very basic understanding of computer spreadsheets. No programming is required. Simply enter data in the proper cells as instructed. Unusual errors that occur when entering data may be the result of entering a space in the assumptions worksheet instead of a zero. In troubleshooting this problem, make sure that zeros are entered in any "empty" cell.

There are two worksheets for each version of the template. One is for the assumptions, and the second is the actual financial statements worksheet. Lightly shaded cells indicate data to be entered; darkly shaded cells indicate model calculations. The worksheets will provide financial statements for three years when completed. In the actual spreadsheet, lightly shaded cells are yellow and darkly shaded cells are blue.

ProductCo Model (For a Business That Sells Inventory)

Assumptions Worksheet (see Figure 6-2)

YEAR 1, SALES

Step 1: Assumptions for sales should be derived directly from the marketing plan. Assumptions can be entered using one of two different approaches:

1. Enter the # of units sold by month.
2. Enter the average sales price/unit by month.

Or, for total budgeted sales,

1. Enter 1 in the units cell.
2. Enter the actual dollar amount of budgeted sales in the selling price cell.

Step 2: Enter the percentage of sales expected to be collected in cash. This can range from 0 percent to 100 percent, based on the nature of the business. For example, a retail business may make all sales by cash and have no sales on credit. A wholesaler may send out invoices for all of its sales, thus making 100 percent of its sales on credit. After entering the percentage of cash sales, the spreadsheet will automatically enter the balance of sales as credit sales (accounts receivable). Sales paid for with bank credit cards (VISA, MasterCard, etc.) are considered cash sales.

Step 3: If credit is extended to customers, the next assumption needed is how quickly the business will collect these receivables. This assumption is entered into the spreadsheet as follows:

1. Percent collected in the month of sale
2. Percent collected in the next 31–60 days
3. Percent collected in the next 61–90 days
4. Percent collected in the next 91–120 days
5. Percent never collected (bad debt)—this amount will show up on the income statement as bad-debt expense

An entrepreneur can obtain estimates for these percentages from other businesses

FIGURE 6-2 Year One

Lightly Shaded Cells are Input Cells
Darkly Shaded Cells will calculate-no input required

Financial Statement Assumptions	Month 1	Month 2	Month 3	Month 4	Month 5	Month 6	Month 7	Month 8	Month 9	Month 10	Month 11	Month 12
Units sold	—	—	—	—	—	—	—	—	—	—	—	—
Selling price per unit												
% sales in cash	0%	0%	0%	0%	0%	0%	0%	0%	0%	0%	0%	0%
% sales on account	100%	100%	100%	100%	100%	100%	100%	100%	100%	100%	100%	100%
Accounts Receivable Collections												
% collected in month of sale												
% collected in month following												
% collected in second month following												
% collected in third month following												
% not collected (bad debt expense)												
Cost of Goods Sold—enter % of sales by month												

Salaries	Enter amount for each month directly on the income statement worksheet	
Rent	Enter amount for each month directly on the income statement worksheet	
Utilities	Enter amount for each month directly on the income statement worksheet	
Telephone	Enter amount for each month directly on the income statement worksheet	
Transportation	Enter amount for each month directly on the income statement worksheet	
Insurance	Enter amount for each month directly on the income statement worksheet	
Benefits	Enter amount for each month directly on the income statement worksheet	

FICA	0.062	
Medicare	0.0145	
Unemp	0.01	
Health	0.05	
TOTAL	0.1365	Calculates as a % of salaries

Health Insurance
Enter %—Required coverage = 0%
  Minimum coverage = 5%
  Competitive coverage = 7–10%

INTEREST (annual rate in %)

	Month 1	Month 2
Short-term-added to loan	0%	0%
Long-term-paid month following	0%	0%

Balance Sheet Assumptions	Month 1	Month 2	Month 3	Month 4	Month 5	Month 6	Month 7	Month 8	Month 9	Month 10	Month 11	Month 12
Minimum cash	—	—	—	—	—	—	—	—	—	—	—	—
Inventory: 1–5 months supply of inventory												
Land purchase	—	—	—	—	—	—	—	—	—	—	—	—
Building/Equipment purchases	—	—	—	—	—	—	—	—	—	—	—	—
Life in months	—	—	—	—	—	—	—	—	—	—	—	—
Accounts payable												
% of current month's expenses paid next month	100%	100%	100%	100%	100%	100%	100%	100%	100%	100%	100%	100%
Balance paid in current month	—	—	—	—	—	—	—	—	—	—	—	—
Current month's inventory purchases	—	—	—	—	—	—	—	—	—	—	—	—
Long-term loan additions (payments)	—	—	—	—	—	—	—	—	—	—	—	—
Investments by owners	—	—	—	—	—	—	—	—	—	—	—	—

in the same industry, from industry trade associations, or from published financial data available in many libraries. This assumption should be entered for each month in the spreadsheet (however, the amount may be the same for each month). *The total of the percentages entered needs to equal 100 percent!*

YEAR 1, EXPENSES

Cost of goods sold: Enter the cost of the products being sold as a percent of the selling price. Enter the percent into the spreadsheet for each month (again, it can be the same if that is appropriate, or it can change if the cost goes down over time due to factors such as volume discounts).

Direct operating expenses: These are the expenses directly related to the selling and distribution of the product. They do not include general and administrative-type expenses. Enter the salaries, rent, utilities, telephone, transportation, insurance, and any other expenses directly related to delivering sales in the income statement worksheet within the spreadsheet. Several cells have been left blank to allow the entering of expenses pertinent to a particular business.

The model assumes the following percentages of salaries for benefits: 6.2 percent for FICA, 1.45 percent for Medicare, and 1 percent for unemployment taxes. A cost percentage for health care benefits will need to be entered directly into the assumptions page. If no health care or dental benefits will be offered to employees, enter 0 percent. If a minimal amount of health care will be provided (e.g., very basic health insurance, but no dental, with employees paying part of the cost), a reasonable assumption to enter is 5 percent. If more comprehensive and competitive coverage

is planned, it is reasonable to enter between 7 and 10 percent. The total percent shown multiplied by salaries will be used to calculate benefits expense on the spreadsheet.

General and administrative expenses: These are the expenses of running a business that are not directly tied to delivering sales. These indirect costs include salaries for managers, information services, and general office staff; rent for office space; utilities; supplies; marketing; accounting and legal services; outside services; equipment lease payments (monthly rentals); and depreciation related to equipment or buildings purchased. There are additional blank cells where other general and administrative expenses pertinent to a business may be inserted.

All of these categories are entered by month directly into the income statement worksheets except for benefits expense, which is calculated based on the percent entered earlier, and depreciation, which is calculated based on the assumptions entered for equipment/facilities purchases.

Interest: The model assumes that interest on short-term debt is added to the short-term loan. The amount of borrowing against the short-term line of credit is calculated based on all of the other assumptions entered into the worksheets. The interest on any long-term debt is assumed to be paid the month following the borrowing.

A rate for short-term debt *must be entered* even if the assumption is that no debt will be used (the rate can fluctuate from month to month—it is usually based on the prime rate plus a factor of 1–5 percent, depending on the risk of the business venture).

Enter a rate for long-term debt (i.e., loans to finance fixed assets). This rate is usually fixed.

BALANCE SHEET ASSUMPTIONS

Cash: Enter the minimum amount of cash to be kept on hand at month end.

Inventory: Enter the number of months of future sales that are intended to be kept on hand in inventory at cost. If inventory on hand is decreased, it should not be decreased by more than one month at a time.

Land: If land will be purchased, enter the amount to be paid for the land in the month of purchase. Enter it only once.

Building and equipment: If a building or equipment is going to be purchased, enter the dollar amount of the estimated purchase price. Also enter the number of months that the building and equipment are expected to be in use. This model assumes a minimum life of 36 months. Enter life in multiples of 12 months, and enter the amount only in the month that the asset is to be purchased. If capital assets of differing lives will be purchased, enter each purchase in a separate month.

Accounts payable: Enter the percentage of the current month's expenses that are anticipated to be paid the following month. The model will assume the remainder is paid in the current month. Some businesses try to manage cash by postponing payments, whereas others try to pay current bills in the current month. There are ethical issues concerning this, as discussed in Chapter 1.

The model will calculate current month's inventory purchases, which are assumed to be paid in the following month.

Long-term debt: Enter the amount borrowed on long-term notes (any borrowings that mature more than one year out). Also enter any payments, if applicable. (Be sure to enter payments as a negative value.)

Investments by owners: Enter the amount of any cash investments the owners plan on making in their business.

Years 2 and 3: Repeat the process above for each of the next two years on the assumption worksheet. Because inventory is based on future sales projections, enter information for the months 37–42 for sales and cost of sales.

Financial Statement Worksheet (see Figure 6-3) There is a worksheet for each of the three years. Each worksheet takes the assumptions entered and provides an income statement, balance sheet, and statement of cash flows using the direct method. Some additional data will need to be entered into the financial statement worksheets. Lightly shaded cells in the worksheet indicate data to be entered, and the darkly shaded cells indicate model calculations that are derived from the assumptions entered in the assumption worksheet. Again, in the actual spreadsheet, lightly shaded cells are yellow and darkly shaded cells are blue.

INCOME STATEMENT

Sales: The actual dollar amount and category (cash versus charge) are automatically calculated by the worksheet based on the assumptions entered in the assumption worksheet. No new data is entered here.

Cost of goods sold: The worksheet will calculate this amount based on the

FIGURE 6-3 Year 1 Income Statement Accrual Basis

	Month 1	Month 2	Month 3	Month 4	Month 5	Month 6	Month 7	Month 8	Month 9	Month 10	Month 11	Month 12	Total
REVENUES													
Cash sales													
Charge sales													
TOTAL SALES													
COST OF GOODS SOLD													
GROSS PROFIT													
Direct Expenses													
Salaries													
Benefits													
Rent													
Utilities													
Telephone													
Transportation													
Insurance													
Bad debt expense													
TOTAL DIRECT EXPENSES													
OPERATING MARGIN													
General & Admin. Expenses													
Salaries													
Benefits													
Rent													
Utilities													
Telephone													
Transportation													
Insurance													
Legal & Accounting													
Marketing													
Office supplies													
Equipment leases													
Depreciation													
TOTAL G&A													
EBIT													
Interest Expense													
NET INCOME BEFORE TAXES													

FIGURE 6-3 Balance Sheet—Year 1 (Continued)

	Balance	Month 1	Month 2	Month 3	Month 4	Month 5	Month 6	Month 7	Month 8	Month 9	Month 10	Month 11	Month 12
Cash	—	—	—	—	—	—	—	—	—	—	—	—	—
Accounts Receivable	—	—	—	—	—	—	—	—	—	—	—	—	—
Inventory	—	FALSE	FALSE	FALSE	FALSE	FALSE	FALSE	FALSE	FALSE	FALSE	FALSE	FALSE	FALSE
Total Current Assets	—	—	—	—	—	—	—	—	—	—	—	—	—
Land	—	—	—	—	—	—	—	—	—	—	—	—	—
Building/Equipment	—	—	—	—	—	—	—	—	—	—	—	—	—
-LESS Accum. Depreciation	—	—	—	—	—	—	—	—	—	—	—	—	—
Net Fixed Assets	—	—	—	—	—	—	—	—	—	—	—	—	—
TOTAL ASSETS	—	—	—	—	—	—	—	—	—	—	—	—	—
LIABILITIES													
Accounts payable	—	—	—	—	—	—	—	—	—	—	—	—	—
Short-term loan inc. interest	—	—	—	—	—	—	—	—	—	—	—	—	—
Interest on long-term	—	—	—	—	—	—	—	—	—	—	—	—	—
TOTAL CURRENT	—	—	—	—	—	—	—	—	—	—	—	—	—
Long-term loans	—	—	—	—	—	—	—	—	—	—	—	—	—
Total liabilities	—	—	—	—	—	—	—	—	—	—	—	—	—
OWNERS' EQUITY													
Investment by owner	—	—	—	—	—	—	—	—	—	—	—	—	—
Retained earnings(loss)	—	—	—	—	—	—	—	—	—	—	—	—	—
Net equity	—	—	—	—	—	—	—	—	—	—	—	—	—
TOTAL LIAB. AND OWNERS' EQUITY	—	—	—	—	—	—	—	—	—	—	—	—	—

FIGURE 6-3 Cash Flow—Year 1 (Continued)

	Month 1	Month 2	Month 3	Month 4	Month 5	Month 6	Month 7	Month 8	Month 9	Month 10	Month 11	Month 12	TOTAL
Cash flow from operations													
Receipts													
Cash sales	—	—	—	—	—	—	—	—	—	—	—	—	—
Accounts Receivable collections	—	—	—	—	—	—	—	—	—	—	—	—	—
Total receipts	—	—	—	—	—	—	—	—	—	—	—	—	—
Disbursements													
Prior month's inventory purchases	—	—	—	—	—	—	—	—	—	—	—	—	—
Direct expenses except bad debt	—	—	—	—	—	—	—	—	—	—	—	—	—
G&A except depreciation	—	—	—	—	—	—	—	—	—	—	—	—	—
Interest on long-term debt	—	—	—	—	—	—	—	—	—	—	—	—	—
Total disbursements	—	—	—	—	—	—	—	—	—	—	—	—	—
Net cash flow from operations	—	—	—	—	—	—	—	—	—	—	—	—	—
Cash flow from investing activities													
Purchase of Land	—	—	—	—	—	—	—	—	—	—	—	—	—
Purchase of Building/Equip.	—	—	—	—	—	—	—	—	—	—	—	—	—
Net cash flow from investing activities	—	—	—	—	—	—	—	—	—	—	—	—	—
Cash flow from financing activities													
Investment by owners	—	—	—	—	—	—	—	—	—	—	—	—	—
Long-term loan additions (payments)	—	—	—	—	—	—	—	—	—	—	—	—	—
Net cash flow from long-term financing activities	—	—	—	—	—	—	—	—	—	—	—	—	—
Net cash increase (decrease)	—	—	—	—	—	—	—	—	—	—	—	—	—
Short-term Loan increase (decrease)	—	—	—	—	—	—	—	—	—	—	—	—	—
Beginning cash	—	—	—	—	—	—	—	—	—	—	—	—	—
Ending cash	—	—	—	—	—	—	—	—	—	—	—	—	—

percentage entered in the assumption worksheet. No new data is entered here.

Gross profit: This represents the profit the business has made on sales after deducting the cost of the product but before any direct operating or general and administrative expenses.

Direct operating expenses

Salaries: These assumptions need to tie into the staffing portion of the business plan. Enter the gross dollar amount of payroll for nonadministrative personnel by month. As new staff are added due to growth, this number should grow. Benefits will be calculated based on the assumptions already entered in the assumption worksheet.

Rent, utilities, telephone, transportation, and insurance directly related to delivering sales should be entered by month. Enter either a dollar amount or a formula that is based on a percentage of sales.

Bad-debt expense: Calculated based on the assumptions entered in the assumption worksheet, so no new data are entered here.

Additional expenses: There are extra rows to add other expenses on the income statement worksheet. Be sure to document any assumptions behind these expenses.

Operating margin: This represents the difference between gross profit and direct operating expenses and gives the entrepreneur a picture of the profitability of the business model. In order for a business to be viable, this margin must be high enough to cover the indirect costs of the business and generate the profit required by the entrepreneur.

General and administrative expenses

Salaries: Enter the total gross salary by month for employees not directly related to production or sales. Again, be sure to tie this amount to the staffing plan assumptions in the business plan. Enter the amount by month directly on the income statement worksheet. Benefits will calculate based on the assumptions entered previously in the assumption worksheet.

For *rent, utilities, telephone, transportation, insurance, and supplies* for general and administrative activities, enter an amount by month directly on the income statement worksheet.

Legal, accounting, and marketing represent services that have been contracted for with outside vendors. Enter an amount by month. In some companies, marketing might be considered a direct expense. In those cases, it should be entered under direct operating expenses, instead.

Equipment leases: The amount for rented equipment that will go back to the vendor at the end of the lease term is entered directly on the worksheet.

Again, there are extra lines provided for expense categories that need to be added to reflect any other expenses specific to the business under consideration in this plan.

Depreciation: This will be automatically calculated based on the assumptions in the assumption worksheet. No data are entered here.

Earnings Before Interest and Taxes (EBIT): This number reflects the operating margin less general and administrative expenses.

Interest: This is calculated automatically based on the interest rates entered in the assumption worksheet. No data are entered here.

Earnings Before Taxes (EBT): This may also be referred to as income before taxes. Taxes are not considered in this model due to the many variables related to the legal form of business organization chosen by the entrepreneur.

BALANCE SHEET—*No data should be entered into the balance sheet*

Assets: All assets are calculated automatically based on assumptions entered on the assumptions worksheet.

Liabilities

Accounts payable: This represents the current month's inventory purchases and direct and general and administrative expenses (except depreciation and bad-debt expense) not paid in the current month. It is calculated based on the assumptions worksheet.

Short-term loan including interest: The short-term loan is the balancing figure to all of the assumptions. The model will automatically borrow short-term funds if cash is depleted. Any cash shortfall in the model will be reconciled with this account. It represents how much will be owed at the end of each month plus the current month's interest.

Long-term loan interest: This is the interest due on the balance of long-term debt at the end of the previous month. The model assumes it will be paid the following month.

Long-term loans: This represents the balance in long-term debt based on the assumptions entered.

Owners' Equity: This includes any cash investments by the owners based on

amounts entered on the assumptions page.

Retained earnings (loss): This is calculated by the model. It represents income (loss) since the inception of the company.

CASH FLOW STATEMENT—*No data should be entered*

This statement shows the activity in cash by month with a total for the year. It looks at cash flow from operating the business; cash flow from investments made in land, buildings, and equipment; and cash flow from financing decisions. The model borrows/pays down the short-term loan based on what is needed to maintain cash on hand at the minimum balance set on the assumptions page.

Service Co Model (For a Business That Sells Services)

Assumptions Worksheet (see Figure 6-4)

YEAR 1, SALES

Step 1: Assumptions for sales should be derived directly from the marketing plan. Assumptions can be entered using one of two different approaches:

1. Enter the # of units of service sold by month.
2. Enter the average sales price/unit by month.

Or, for total budgeted sales,

1. Enter 1 in the units cell.
2. Enter the actual dollar amount of budgeted sales in the selling price cell.

Step 2: Enter the percentage of sales expected to be collected in cash. This can range from 0 percent to 100 percent,

FIGURE 6-4 Year One

Lightly shaded Cells are Input Cells
Darkly shaded Cells will calculate—no input required

FINANCIAL STATEMENT ASSUMPTIONS

	Month 1	Month 2	Month 3	Month 4	Month 5	Month 6	Month 7	Month 8	Month 9	Month 10	Month 11	Month 12
Units sold												
Selling price per unit												
% sales in cash												
% sales on account	100%	100%	100%	100%	100%	100%	100%	100%	100%	100%	100%	100%

Accounts Receivable Collections

% collected in month of sale												
% collected in month following												
% collected in second month following	0%	0%	0%	0%	0%	0%	0%	0%	0%	0%	0%	0%
% collected in third month following												
% not collected (bad debt expense)	0%	0%	0%	0%	0%	0%	0%	0%	0%	0%	0%	0%

Direct costs as a % of sales by month

Salaries	Enter amount for each month directly on the income statement worksheet
Rent	Enter amount for each month directly on the income statement worksheet
Utilities	Enter amount for each month directly on the income statement worksheet
Telephone	Enter amount for each month directly on the income statement worksheet
Transportation	Enter amount for each month directly on the income statement worksheet
Insurance	Enter amount for each month directly on the income statement worksheet
Benefits	Enter amount for each month directly on the income statement worksheet

FICA	0.062
Medicare	0.0145
Unemp	0.01
Health	0.05
TOTAL	0.1365	Calculates as a % of salaries

Health Insurance
Enter % — Required coverage = 0%
   Minimum coverage = 5%
   Competitive coverage = 7–10%

INTEREST (annual rate in %)
Short-term-added to loan
Long-term-paid month following

Balance Sheet Assumptions

	Month 1	Month 2	Month 3	Month 4	Month 5	Month 6	Month 7	Month 8	Month 9	Month 10	Month 11	Month 12
Minimum cash												
Land purchase	—	—	—	—	—	—	—	—	—	—	—	—
Building/Equipment purchases	—	—	—	—	—	—	—	—	—	—	—	—
Life in months	—	—	—	—	—	—	—	—	—	—	—	—

Accounts payable

| % of current month's expenses paid in following month | | | | | | | | | | | | |
| Balance paid in current month | 100% | 100% | 100% | 100% | 100% | 100% | 100% | 100% | 100% | 100% | 100% | 100% |

| Long-term loan additions (payments) | — | — | — | — | — | — | — | — | — | — | — | — |
| Investments by owners | — | — | — | — | — | — | — | — | — | — | — | — |

based on the nature of the business. For example, a retail service business such as a dry cleaner may make all sales by cash and have no sales on credit. A consulting business may send out invoices for all of its sales, thus making 100 percent of its sales on credit. A medical clinic may have a combination, with 20 percent paid in cash and 80 percent on credit to insurance companies. After entering the percentage of cash sales, the spreadsheet will automatically enter the balance of sales as credit sales (accounts receivable). Sales paid for with bank credit cards (VISA, MasterCard, etc.) are considered cash sales.

Step 3: If credit is extended to customers, the next assumption needed is how quickly the business will collect these receivables. This assumption is entered into the spreadsheet as follows:

1. Percent collected in the month of sale
2. Percent collected in the next 31–60 days
3. Percent collected in the next 61–90 days
4. Percent collected in the next 91–120 days
5. Percent never collected (bad debt)—this amount will show up on the income statement as bad-debt expense

An entrepreneur can obtain estimates for these percentages from other businesses in the same industry, from industry trade associations, or from published financial data available in many libraries. This assumption should be entered for each month in the spreadsheet (however, the amount may be the same for each month). *The total of the percentages entered needs to equal 100 percent!*

YEAR 1, EXPENSES

Direct operating expenses: These are the expenses directly related to delivering the service. They do not include general and administrative-type expenses.

Direct materials: These are the material or supply costs directly related to the service the business is delivering, for example, printing, paper, supplies, and so on. Enter this as a percent of sales by month.

Other direct operating expenses: Enter the salaries, rent, utilities, telephone, transportation, insurance, and any other expenses directly related to delivering sales in the income statement worksheet within the spreadsheet. Several cells have been left blank to allow the entering of expenses pertinent to a particular business.

The model assumes the following percentages of salaries for benefits: 6.2 percent for FICA, 1.45 percent for Medicare, and 1 percentage for unemployment taxes. A cost percentage for health care benefits will need to be entered directly into the assumptions page. If no health care or dental benefits will be offered to employees, enter 0 percent. If a minimal amount of health care will be provided (e.g., very basic health insurance, but no dental, with employees paying part of the cost), a reasonable assumption to enter is 5 percent. If more comprehensive and competitive coverage is planned, it is reasonable to enter between 7 and 10 percent. The total percent shown multiplied by salaries will be used to calculate benefits expense on the spreadsheet.

General and administrative expenses: These are the expenses of running a business that are not directly tied to delivering sales. These indirect costs include salaries for managers, information services, and general office staff; rent for office space; utilities; supplies; marketing; accounting and legal services; outside services; equipment lease payments (monthly rentals); and depreciation related to equipment or buildings purchased. There are additional blank cells where other general and administrative expenses pertinent to a business may be inserted.

All of these categories are entered by month directly into the income statement worksheets except for benefits expense, which is calculated based on the percent entered earlier, and depreciation, which is calculated based on the assumptions entered for equipment/facilities purchases.

Interest: The model assumes that interest on short-term debt is added to the short-term loan. The amount of borrowing against the short-term line of credit is calculated based on all of the other assumptions entered into the worksheets. The interest on any long-term debt is assumed to be paid the month following the borrowing.

A rate for short-term debt *must be entered* even if the assumption is that no debt will be used (the rate can fluctuate from month to month—it is usually based on the prime rate plus a factor of 1–5 percent, depending on the risk of the business venture).

Enter a rate for long-term debt (i.e., loans to finance fixed assets). This rate is usually fixed.

BALANCE SHEET ASSUMPTIONS

Cash: Enter the minimum amount of cash to be kept on hand at month end.

Land: If land will be purchased, enter the amount to be paid for the land in the month of purchase. Enter it only once.

Building and equipment: If a building or equipment is going to be purchased, enter the dollar amount of the estimated purchase price. Also enter the number of months that the building/equipment are expected to be in use. This model assumes a minimum life of 36 months. Enter life in multiples of 12 months, and enter the amount only in the month that the asset is to be purchased. If capital assets of differing lives will be purchased, enter each purchase in a separate month.

Accounts payable: Enter the percentage of the current month's expenses that are expected to be paid the following month. The model will assume the remainder is paid in the current month. Some businesses try to manage cash by postponing payments, whereas others try to pay current bills in the current month. There are ethical issues concerning this, as discussed in Chapter 1.

Long-term debt: Enter the amount borrowed on long-term notes (any borrowings that mature more than a year out). Also enter any payments, if applicable. (Be sure to enter payments as a negative value.)

Investments by owners: Enter the amount of any cash investments the owners plan on making in their business.

Years 2 and 3: Repeat the process above for each of the next two years on the assumption worksheet.

Financial Statement Worksheet (see Figure 6-5) There is a worksheet for each of the three years. Each worksheet takes the assumptions entered and provides an income statement, balance sheet, and statement of cash flows using the direct method. Some additional data will also need to be entered into the financial

FIGURE 6-5 Year 1 Income Statement Accrual Basis

	Month 1	Month 2	Month 3	Month 4	Month 5	Month 6	Month 7	Month 8	Month 9	Month 10	Month 11	Month 12	Total
REVENUES													
Cash sales													
Charge sales													
TOTAL SALES													
DIRECT EXPENSES													
Direct Costs													
Salaries													
Benefits													
Rent													
Utilities													
Telephone													
Transportation													
Insurance													
Bad debt expense													
TOTAL DIRECT EXPENSES													
OPERATING MARGIN													
General & Admin. Expenses													
Salaries													
Benefits													
Rent													
Utilities													
Telephone													
Transportation													
Insurance													
Legal & Accounting													
Marketing													
Office supplies													
Equipment leases													
Depreciation													
TOTAL G&A													
EBIT													
Interest Expense													
NET INCOME BEFORE TAXES													

FIGURE 6-5 Balance Sheet—Year 1 (Continued)

	Balance	Month 1	Month 2	Month 3	Month 4	Month 5	Month 6	Month 7	Month 8	Month 9	Month 10	Month 11	Month 12
Cash	—	—	—	—	—	—	—	—	—	—	—	—	—
Accounts Receivable	—	—	—	—	—	—	—	—	—	—	—	—	—
Total Current Assets	—	—	—	—	—	—	—	—	—	—	—	—	—
Land	—	—	—	—	—	—	—	—	—	—	—	—	—
Building/Equipment	—	—	—	—	—	—	—	—	—	—	—	—	—
-LESS Accum. Depreciation	—	—	—	—	—	—	—	—	—	—	—	—	—
Net Fixed Assets	—	—	—	—	—	—	—	—	—	—	—	—	—
TOTAL ASSETS	—	—	—	—	—	—	—	—	—	—	—	—	—
LIABILITIES													
Accounts payable	—	—	—	—	—	—	—	—	—	—	—	—	—
Short-term loan inc. interest	—	—	—	—	—	—	—	—	—	—	—	—	—
Interest on long-term	—	—	—	—	—	—	—	—	—	—	—	—	—
TOTAL CURRENT	—	—	—	—	—	—	—	—	—	—	—	—	—
Long-term loans	—	—	—	—	—	—	—	—	—	—	—	—	—
Total liabilities	—	—	—	—	—	—	—	—	—	—	—	—	—
OWNERS' EQUITY													
Investment by owner	—	—	—	—	—	—	—	—	—	—	—	—	—
Retained earnings (loss)	—	—	—	—	—	—	—	—	—	—	—	—	—
Net equity	—	—	—	—	—	—	—	—	—	—	—	—	—
TOTAL LIAB. AND OWNERS' EQUITY	—	—	—	—	—	—	—	—	—	—	—	—	—

FIGURE 6-5 Cash Flow—Year 1 (Continued)

	Month 1	Month 2	Month 3	Month 4	Month 5	Month 6	Month 7	Month 8	Month 9	Month 10	Month 11	Month 12	Total
Cash flow from operations													
Receipts													
Cash sales	—	—	—	—	—	—	—	—	—	—	—	—	—
Accounts Receivable collections	—	—	—	—	—	—	—	—	—	—	—	—	—
Total receipts	—	—	—	—	—	—	—	—	—	—	—	—	—
Disbursements													
Direct expenses except bad debt	—	—	—	—	—	—	—	—	—	—	—	—	—
G&A except depreciation	—	—	—	—	—	—	—	—	—	—	—	—	—
Interest on long-term	—	—	—	—	—	—	—	—	—	—	—	—	—
Total disbursements	—	—	—	—	—	—	—	—	—	—	—	—	—
Net cash flow from operations	—	—	—	—	—	—	—	—	—	—	—	—	—
Cash flow from investing activities													
Purchase of Land	—	—	—	—	—	—	—	—	—	—	—	—	—
Purchase of Building/Equip.	—	—	—	—	—	—	—	—	—	—	—	—	—
Net cash flow from investing activities	—	—	—	—	—	—	—	—	—	—	—	—	—
Cash flow from financing activities													
Investment by owners	—	—	—	—	—	—	—	—	—	—	—	—	—
Long-term loan additions (payments)	—	—	—	—	—	—	—	—	—	—	—	—	—
Net cash flow from long-term financing activities	—	—	—	—	—	—	—	—	—	—	—	—	—
Net cash increase (decrease)	—	—	—	—	—	—	—	—	—	—	—	—	—
Short-term Loan increase (decrease)	—	—	—	—	—	—	—	—	—	—	—	—	—
Beginning cash	—	—	—	—	—	—	—	—	—	—	—	—	—
Ending cash	—	—	—	—	—	—	—	—	—	—	—	—	—

statement worksheets. Lightly shaded cells in the worksheet indicate data to be entered, and the darkly shaded cells indicate model calculations that are derived from the assumptions entered in the assumption worksheet. Once again, in the actual spreadsheet, lightly shaded cells are yellow and darkly shaded cells are blue.

INCOME STATEMENT

Sales: The actual dollar amount and category (cash versus charge) are automatically calculated by the worksheet based on the assumptions entered in the assumption worksheet. No new data are entered here.

Direct operating expenses

Direct materials: The worksheet will calculate this based on the percentage entered on the assumptions worksheet.

Salaries: These assumptions need to tie into the staffing portion of the business plan. Enter the gross dollar amount of payroll for nonadministrative personnel by month. As new staff are added due to growth, this number should grow. Benefits will be calculated based on the assumptions already entered in the assumption worksheet.

Rent, utilities, telephone, transportation, and insurance directly related to delivering sales should be entered by month. Enter either a dollar amount or a formula that is based on a percentage of sales.

Bad-debt expense: This is calculated based on the assumptions entered in the assumption worksheet, so no new data are entered here.

Additional expenses: There are extra rows to add other expenses on the income statement worksheet. Be sure to docu-

ment any assumptions behind these expenses.

Operating margin: This represents profits made on sales after deducting the direct costs of delivering the service, but before any general and administrative costs of running the business. In order for a business to be viable, this margin must be high enough to cover the indirect costs of the business and generate the profit required by the entrepreneur.

General and administrative expenses

Salaries: Enter the total gross salary by month for employees not directly related to sales. Again, be sure to tie this amount to the staffing plan assumptions in the business plan. Enter the amount by month directly on the income statement worksheet. Benefits will calculate based on the assumptions entered previously in the assumption worksheet.

For *rent, utilities, telephone, transportation, insurance, and supplies* for general and administrative activities, enter an amount by month directly on the income statement worksheet.

Legal, accounting, and marketing represent services that are contracted for with outside vendors. Enter an amount by month. In some companies, marketing might be considered a direct expense. In those cases, it should be entered under direct operating expenses, instead.

Equipment leases: The amount for rented equipment that will go back to the vendor at the end of the lease term is entered directly on the worksheet.

Again, there are extra lines provided for expense categories that need to be added to reflect any other expenses specific to the business under consideration in this plan.

Depreciation: This will be automatically calculated based on the assumptions in the assumption worksheet. No data are entered here.

Earnings Before Interest and Taxes (EBIT): This number reflects the operating margin less general and administrative expenses.

Interest: This is calculated automatically based on the interest rates entered in the assumption worksheet. No data are entered here.

Earnings Before Taxes (EBT): This may also be referred to as income before taxes. Taxes are not considered in this model due to the many variables related to the legal form of business organization chosen by the entrepreneur.

BALANCE SHEET—*No data should be entered into the balance sheet*

Assets: All assets are calculated automatically based on assumptions entered on the assumptions worksheet.

Liabilities:

Accounts payable: This represents the current month's direct and general administrative expenses (except depreciation and bad-debt expense) not paid in the current month. It is calculated based on the assumptions worksheet.

Short-term loan including interest: The short-term loan is the balancing figure to

all of the assumptions. The model will automatically borrow short-term funds if cash is depleted. Any cash shortfall in the model will be reconciled with this account. It represents how much will be owed at the end of each month plus the current month's interest.

Long-term loan interest: This is the interest due on the balance of long-term debt at the end of the previous month. The model assumes it will be paid the following month.

Long-term loans: This represents the balance in long-term debt based on the assumptions entered.

Owners' Equity: This includes any cash investments by the owners based on amounts entered on the assumptions page.

Retained earnings (loss): This is calculated by the model. It represents income (loss) since the inception of the company.

CASH FLOW STATEMENT—*No data should be entered*

This statement shows the activity in cash by month with a total for the year. It looks at cash flow from operating the business; cash flow from investments made in land, buildings, and equipment; and cash flow from financing decisions. The model borrows/pays down the short-term loan based on what is needed to maintain cash on hand at the minimum balance set on the assumptions page.

C H A P T E R

7

Monitoring Financial Performance

The first section of this book presented a model and techniques that can assist an entrepreneur in planning the financial aspects of a new venture. Once a business has actually started up and is beginning to generate revenues, a whole new set of financial challenges emerges. Chapter 8 presents a variety of tools, collectively known as *bootstrapping techniques,* that can help manage the scarce financial resources of an entrepreneurial venture. Cash flow management, discussed in Chapter 9, is critical to the survival of a new business. Finally, almost any entrepreneur is faced with raising outside funding for a growing business. The final three chapters in this section discuss debt, equity, and venture capital financing.

But first, this chapter examines how the entrepreneur can actually gain control of "the numbers" for utilization in decision making. Successful financial management requires a systematic approach. The integrated financial template presented in the previous chapter clearly demonstrated the importance of identifying and documenting key assumptions that drive financial forecasts. Developing a system for tracking and monitoring these assumptions is the first step in effective financial management in an entrepreneurial business. The model in Part I of this book assumes that the entrepreneur has established long-term personal financial goals for income and wealth that drive the financial goals of the business. The second major step in effective financial management is to establish clear milestones that can track progress toward these long-term goals.

Effective financial management requires an understanding of how to use numbers to manage and make decisions. However, this assumes that the entrepreneur understands what numbers are actually needed for the business and that those numbers are made available through the accounting systems used and the staff. Finally, entrepreneurs need to learn how to work effectively with accountants. As discussed in Chapter 1, this can be a challenge, as accountants and entrepreneurs often speak in "different languages."

TRACKING ASSUMPTIONS

All financial forecasts and projections are based on a number of assumptions. Demand for the product or service, pricing, staffing requirements, the cost of materials, rents, and so on all have to be estimated, and these estimates are based on assumptions. In Chapter 6, many assumptions were listed in the preparation of the financial statement templates. Certainly, all of these assumptions should be carefully documented and listed within the business plan, but there can be any number of additional key assumptions behind the basic assumptions listed in the template.

For example, Carlos Lopez, an entrepreneur, has made the assumption that sales of his product will grow by 10 units per month. This is based on a thorough marketing plan that clearly supports this revenue model. However, behind this critical assumption he has explicitly made several additional assumptions. He has assumed that his two salespeople can each make 30 sales calls per month to prospective customers. Of these 60 sales calls, 1 in 10 (in this case, 6) will result in a proposal being written up and submitted to the prospective customer. One-third of the 6 proposals submitted to prospective customers results in an order. This example would yield 2 orders. The average size of each order is 10 units, and each customer will order the average each month, which means these two new customers will order 20 units. Each month, one current customer will stop ordering from the company, which results in the loss of 10 units sold to that customer. Table 7-1 displays the additional assumptions behind the assumption of 10 new units sold each

TABLE 7-1 Sample List of Assumptions	
Assumption	*Measurement Technique*
Thirty sales calls per salesperson per month.	Sales staff will keep a log of sales calls with the name of the contact, the date of first contact, proposals submitted to the customer, and orders placed by this customer each month.
One in 10 sales calls results in a proposal to customer.	Sales staff will enter proposals made to each prospective client in the sales activity log.
One-third of proposals result in an order.	When a customer places an order, this will be noted in the sales log.
Each order averages 10 units.	The size of each order will be noted in the sales log.
Customers make an average of one order per month.	The date of each order is noted in the sales log.
An average of one customer will stop ordering each month.	If a customer does not place an order in a given month, the sales staff will contact to see if this client intends to place any future orders.

month. At this point, Carlos has no data for these assumptions. However, even when data become available as the business begins to grow, the assumptions should continue to be tracked, as they are key to the basic revenue growth assumptions in the financial forecast he is relying on to mange his business.

This example illustrates the importance of identifying, listing, and tracking any and all additional key assumptions that underlie the basic assumptions in the financial forecasts. It should be noted that revenue assumptions, such as those used in this example, are usually the most complex in terms of underlying assumptions. All of these additional assumptions should be added to the business plan. At some point, some of the assumptions will become known facts, such as many of the cost assumptions. These can then be removed from the assumption list, because they will no longer need to be monitored. But even with data, many assumptions will remain uncertain, subject to volatility, and worthy of close scrutiny as the business expands.

Once a comprehensive list of assumptions has been created, the entrepreneur should develop measurements for each assumption. In the preceding example, a sales log is developed, which allows for data to be gathered that can be used to measure all of the key assumptions. The second column in Table 7-1 displays how the data can be gathered to allow for measurements of these assumptions. The sales log will document all sales calls and a complete history of what has resulted from those calls, including proposals made, orders placed, and so forth.

A key step in this process is making sure that someone in the business is responsible for tracking, summarizing, and interpreting the data gathered for key assumptions. In this example, the entrepreneur has decided to take on this responsibility. Each month the sales logs will need to be reviewed to get the information needed from the raw data about the assumptions used in the business plan. If, for example, the sales log indicates that the sales staff is making only 20 sales calls per month, but all of the other assumptions seem to be fairly accurate, it can help the entrepreneur understand specifically why sales are not growing as planned. Assume that sales personnel are not making enough calls. The entrepreneur could conclude that this could be due to their lack of effort or due to unrealistic assumptions. Whatever the cause, the entrepreneur is better able to take corrective action quickly to ensure that the projections in the business plan can be realized.

ESTABLISHING MILESTONES

Financial forecasts, as discussed in Part I of this book, should be based on profit goals that are derived from, at a minimum, the income and wealth goals of the entrepreneur. The profit goals are usually longer term in nature. For example, Sally Burton, an entrepreneur, has determined her income goal from her business is to earn twice the salary that she can earn in the market as an employee in an existing business. She set this goal to compensate for the risk she is taking and to help build wealth through this business. Sally realistically assumes that it will take her three years to build the business to the point where she can draw this level of salary. In building the financial forecast, the entrepreneur has decided that she should be able to earn 50 percent of her current salary in the first year of the business, match her current salary in the second year, and reach the goal of twice her current salary in the third year. Thus, the business owner has established specific *milestones* that will help monitor the overall progress of the business.

Milestones can be based on time, as is the case in this example, or they can be based on sales growth. The entrepreneur in the example could have set milestones such as earning the equivalent of her current salary when the business reaches $500,000 in annual sales and twice her salary when the business grows to $1 million in sales. Finally, milestones may also be tied to certain events in the business's development. In the previous example the entrepreneur may set a milestone of earning her current salary when the first office is fully operational. When the second office, located in another part of town, is open and fully operational, the plan is to make twice her current salary. Whatever milestone is chosen should make sense for a given business.

Setting milestones keeps the focus on what is critically important in the growth of a business. It keeps the business plan on target for the aspirations and intentions that the entrepreneur had when first starting the new venture. Milestones can not only provide clear focus during the often chaotic growth that businesses can experience as revenues begin to build, they also allow for adjustments in plans as the business grows. In the example, assume that the entrepreneur had tied salary milestones to opening new offices. Once the business began to grow, the entrepreneur realized that the profit assumptions were overly optimistic. It would take three offices to reach the salary goal. With this information, the entrepreneur can adjust the plan to focus on growing to three offices rather than two, allowing the original personal goal still to be realized through the business.

GETTING THE NUMBERS NEEDED TO MANAGE

Monitoring the financial performance of an entrepreneurial business can take many forms; however, all methods for monitoring financial performance use some standard to compare and evaluate actual financial performance. Current year results can be compared to the results of the previous year, a budget, a competitor, the industry, or the entrepreneur's own expectations.

The specific performance metrics beyond standard financial statements are different for almost every company. Ottenheimer (1999) recommends that entrepreneurial ventures identify the activities that, when taken together, are critical for building sales and profitability. It also is important to identify measures for both short-term and long-term performance and to include some that measure cash flow. Ottenheimer recommends only about five to eight key measures, because there is a risk that the management team may lose focus if too many activities are measured. These key measures should be discussed and developed with the accountants, both internal and external, to ensure they understand the unique needs of the business and can help identify useful metrics. The key set of metrics may include daily, weekly, monthly, quarterly, and annual measures.

USING NUMBERS TO MANAGE

Most companies use several standard metrics, all of which fall into two basic categories: financial statement analysis and ratio analysis. This section provides an overview of the various performance metrics, including cash flow, using data from a medical products business. Given the importance of cash flow to entrepreneurial ventures, Chapter 9 will be devoted to covering this important topic in detail.

Financial Statement Analysis

Vertical analysis is a useful analytical technique for evaluating the income statement. In vertical analysis, items on the income statement are expressed as a percentage of total sales, which can be used to track the relationship of key expenses to sales. The technique is used to spot trends or changes in the relationship between expenses and sales in the business. At a minimum, it allows for examination of the trends in sales, gross profit, expenses, and operating margin on a monthly basis and comparing them to the current month's budget or historical figures from previous periods.

In the example displayed in Exhibit 7-1, the gross profit percentage for Medical Products, Inc. has increased by two percentage points compared to a year ago. This means it is generating 50.5 cents of gross profit for every $1 of sales, compared to 48.5 cents a year ago. If one of the goals of the company has been to increase gross profit, this is a positive trend. If, however, a new competitor is coming into the market, the company may need to decrease selling prices, which will decrease the gross profit margin. Research and development expense increased in total dollars but declined as a percentage of sales. This means that for every $1 of sales in 2000, the company spent 9.6 cents, compared to 10.1 cents a year ago. Again, this could be a positive or a negative. It may indicate a drop in the company's commitment to new product development, or the decrease in the percentage to sales may be the result of a significant sales increase. Income from operations as measured by Earnings Before Interest and Taxes (EBIT) is 4.2 cents of every $1 sold, compared to 1.1 cents a year ago. In general, this indicates that the company is getting more of its sales dollars to the bottom line.

Financial statements can also be analyzed by comparing the results this year to last year, thus analyzing the percentage increase or decrease (Exhibit 7-2). To calculate the percentage increase or decrease from month to month or year to year, the entrepreneur takes the difference between the two years and divides by the starting point. For example, taking sales from 2000, subtracting sales for 1999, and dividing the difference by the sales for 1999 will calculate the percentage change for Medical Products, Inc.

$$\frac{\text{Medical Products Sales}}{\text{Increase for 2000}} = \frac{\$10,979,000 - \$9,013,000}{\$9,013,000} = .218, \text{ or } 21.8\%$$

That is, sales for Medical Products, Inc. increased $1,966,000, or 21.8 percent. Cost of goods sold increased $796,000, or 17.1 percent. Because sales increased faster

EXHIBIT 7-1

Medical Products, Inc.
Income Statement
For the years ended December 31,
($000)

	2000		1999	
Net Sales	$10,979.0	100.0%	$9,013.0	100.0%
Cost of Goods Sold	5,440.0	49.5	4,644.0	51.5
Gross Profit	5,539.0	50.5	4,369.0	48.5
Operating Expenses				
Research and Development	1,053.0	9.6	914.0	10.1
Selling Expense	1,200.0	10.9	1,000.0	11.1
General and Administrative Expense	2,825.0	25.8	2,358.0	26.2
Total Operating Expenses	5,078.0	46.3	4,272.0	47.4
Operating Income (EBIT)	461.0	4.2	97.0	1.1
Other Income (Expense)				
Interest Expense	(146.0)	(1.3)	(95.0)	(1.1)
Interest Income	50.0	0.4	38.0	0.4
Total Other Income (Expense)	(96.0)	(0.9)	(57.0)	(0.6)
Net Income Before Taxes	365.0	3.3	40.0	0.5
Income Taxes	(124.1)	(1.1)	(13.6)	(0.2)
Net Income	$ 240.9	2.2%	$ 26.4	0.3%

than cost of goods sold, gross profit as a percent of sales increased, as mentioned, from 48.5 to 50.5 percent. Why might sales have increased faster than the cost of goods sold? There could be several reasons. Selling prices might have gone up compared to a year ago. The mix of the products sold might have changed. The cost of manufacturing the products might have declined. Selling expenses in 2000 increased $200,000, or 20%, compared to 1999. Even though sales increased 21.8 percent, selling expenses did not increase to the same degree, allowing the company to increase profits compared to a year ago.

Several issues should be considered when examining percentage changes in financial statements. First, it cannot be stated definitively that all increases are good or all decreases are bad. It depends on the facts of the situation. If gross profit percent keeps increasing because selling prices keep rising, the business may price itself out of the market. If administrative expenses increase at the same rate as sales, the business may be building an infrastructure (overhead) that cannot be supported in a downturn. If investment in research and development is declining as a percent of sales, the company may not be investing in innovations to generate future sales. Therefore, when looking at trend analysis, it is imperative to compare the results to the budget, the previous year, and competitors' or industry averages to ensure a complete understanding of the trends. Each of these comparisons can provide information for understanding current performance and for making future operating decisions.

Ratio Analysis

Another set of tools for evaluating financial performance is ratio analysis. A variety of ratios can be calculated, but most fall into one of four categories: liquidity ratios, activity ratios, profitability ratios, and solvency and coverage ratios. Liquidity ratios are used to measure a company's short-term ability to pay maturing obligations. Activity ratios are used to measure how effectively a company is managing the assets under its control. Profitability ratios measure the degree of success or failure of a company for a given period of time. Solvency and coverage ratios measure the degree of protection for long-term creditors and investors.

There is no right or wrong answer in ratio analysis. It is never advisable to simply calculate a ratio for one time period and, based on that, draw a conclusion. Indeed, it is often said that the interpretation of financial ratios is more an art than a science. Ratios should be calculated over time to determine trends. Ratios also should be compared to ratios from past periods, ratios of competitors, and industry ratios. Information on competitors or an industry may be difficult to obtain. However, there is information available from the Internet, trade journals, local chambers of commerce, trade shows, and conferences. Exhibits 7-2 and 7-3 will be used to calculate sample ratios using the results for Medical Products, Inc.

The first category of ratios is liquidity ratios. A basic measure of liquidity is the working capital of a company. Working capital equals current assets minus current liabilities. It is the lifeblood of the company. If the company has enough current assets that can be converted to cash in time to meet its current liabilities, it will not need to borrow long-term funds. Two ratios are used to measure liquidity, the current ratio and the quick ratio. The current ratio is expressed as follows:

$$\text{Current Ratio} = \text{Current Assets} / \text{Current Liabilities}$$

The current ratio for Medical Products, Inc. is calculated as follows:

2000	1999
$3,847,400/$2,838,100 = 1.36	$3,265,000/$2,004,600 = 1.63

This analysis shows that the company had $1.36 of current assets for every $1 of current liabilities in 2000, while in 1999 it had $1.63 of current assets for every $1 of current liabilities. How do we know if the current ratio is good? To answer this question, we must compare it to some benchmark. Again, the ratio can be compared to last year, the industry standard, or a competitor. The current ratio may be too high if the company's current assets include past-due accounts receivable or obsolete inventory. It could also be too high if the company is not using accounts payable as a means of financing short-term purchases. The current ratio may be too low if the company is not generating sufficient cash flow from operations to meet upcoming payments.

EXHIBIT 7-2

Medical Products, Inc.
Income Statement
For the years ended December 31,
($000)

	2000	1999	$ Increase (Decrease)	% Increase (Decrease)
Net Sales	$10,979.0	$9,013.0	1,966.0	21.8
Cost of goods sold	5,440.0	4,644.0	796.0	17.1
Gross Profit	5,539.0	4,369.0	1,170.0	26.8
Operating Expenses				
Research and Development	1,053.0	914.0	139.0	15.2
Selling Expense	1,200.0	1,000.0	200.0	20.0
General and Administrative Expense	2,825.0	2,358.0	467.0	19.8
Total Operating Expenses	5,078.0	4,272.0	806.0	18.9
Operating Income (EBIT)	461.0	97.0	364.0	375.3
Other Income (Expense)				
Interest Expense	(146.0)	(95.0)	(51.0)	53.7
Interest Income	50.0	38.0	12.0	31.6
Total Other Income (Expense)	(96.0)	(57.0)	(39.0)	68.4
Net Income Before Taxes	365.0	40.0	325.0	812.5
Income Taxes	(124.1)	(13.6)	(110.5)	812.5
Net Income	$ 240.9	$ 26.4	214.5	812.5

The quick ratio can be defined in several ways, but usually the numerator consists of all current assets listed on the balance sheet before inventories. These assets generally include cash, accounts receivable, and short-term investments, if the company has any. The denominator is current liabilities. The quick ratio is expressed as follows:

$$\text{Quick Ratio} = \frac{\text{(Cash + Accounts Receivable + Short-term Investments}}{\text{Current Liabilities}}$$

The quick ratio is also called the *acid test ratio* because it measures the ability of a company to meet the current liabilities over the next 30 to 60 days, versus the next year with the current ratio. The quick ratio for Medical Products, Inc. is

2000	1999
($799,000 + $1,572,400)/$2,838,100 = .84	($706,000 + $1,176,000)/$2,004,600 = .94

EXHIBIT 7-3

Medical Products, Inc.
Balance Sheet
December 31,
($000)

	2000	1999
ASSETS		
Current Assets		
Cash and cash equivalents	$ 799.0	$ 706.0
Accounts receivable, less allowance for doubtful accounts of $15,000 and $12,000, respectively	1,572.4	1,176.0
Inventories	1,427.0	1,310.0
Prepaid expenses	49.0	73.0
Total Current Assets	3,847.4	3,265.0
Property and Equipment		
Equipment	2,814.0	2,402.0
Office furniture, fixtures, and computers	682.0	673.0
Capitalized leases	692.0	366.0
	4,188.0	3,441.0
Less accumulated depreciation	(2,854.0)	(2,750.0)
Net Property and Equipment	1,334.0	691.0
TOTAL ASSETS	$5,181.4	$3,956.0
LIABILITIES AND SHAREHOLDERS' EQUITY		
Current Liabilities		
Note payable to bank	$1,551.0	$1,252.0
Accounts payable	437.0	383.0
Accrued expenses	668.0	334.0
Current installment of capitalized lease obligations	58.0	22.0
Income taxes payable	124.1	13.6
Total current liabilities	2,838.1	2,004.6
Long-term Liabilities		
Capitalizes lease obligations, less current installments	215.0	47.0
Total Liabilities	3,053.1	2,051.6
Shareholders' Equity		
Common stock, $.01 par value, 4,112,000 shares issued and outstanding	41.0	41.0
Additional paid-in capital	1,677.0	1,677.0
Retained earnings	410.3	186.4
Total shareholders' equity	2,128.3	1,904.4
TOTAL LIABILITIES AND SHAREHOLDERS' EQUITY	$5,181.4	$3,956.0

This analysis shows that Medical Products, Inc. had 84 cents of quick assets for every $1 of current liabilities in 2000 and 94 cents for every $1 in 1999. Is this good or bad? It depends. The company doesn't quite have enough quick assets to cover all liabilities due within a year. This may not be a problem unless all of the liabilities are due within 30 to 90 days and the receivables cannot be collected within that same time period or the company does not have availability on their line of credit.

Can liquidity ratios be too high? Yes. Is excess cash sitting around and not getting used? Are receivables high because they are not getting collected? Are there excess inventories not getting sold? Is the company not taking advantage of trade credit? If it appears that the liquidity ratios are high, a business may want to examine the makeup of current assets by looking at activity ratios or by evaluating supplier relationships.

Activity ratios look at how well assets are being managed. Two key ratios are accounts receivable turnover and inventory turnover. Accounts receivable turnover is calculated by dividing net sales for a period by the average accounts receivable during that period. This ratio measures how fast sales are being collected.

$$\text{Accounts Receivable Turnover} = \text{Sales} / \text{Average Accounts Receivable}$$

Average accounts receivable (calculated using a simple average of the current period balance and the previous period balance in this account) are used because sales are over a period of time, while the accounts receivable balance on the balance sheet is at a point in time. A turnover of 12 would indicate that accounts receivable are being collected every 30 days, or 12 times a year.

The number of days sales remaining in accounts receivable is another ratio that can be used for this purpose. It is calculated by dividing 360 days by the accounts receivable turnover ratio. This ratio is often expressed as DSO, for "days sales outstanding." A DSO of 30 would indicate that 30 days of sales are outstanding, or that accounts receivable are being collected every 30 days. If credit terms to customers are net 30, a DSO of 30 or a turnover of 12 times is good. If credit terms are net 15, the company might be having a problem collecting its accounts receivable in a timely manner. Accounts receivable turnover for Medical Products, Inc. is as follows:

2000	1999
$10,979,000/(($1,572,400 + $1,176,000)/2) = 8.0	$9,013,000/$1,100,000* = 8.2 (*Average for 1999 and 1998)

DSO (days sales outstanding) in this example is as follows:

2000	1999
360/8.0 = 45	360/8.2 = 43.9

What can be concluded about Medical Products, Inc. from these two ratios? Medical Products, Inc. is collecting its accounts receivable about 8 times a year, down slightly from 8.2 times in 1999. On average, it has 45.0 days worth of sales outstanding, which is up about 1 day from 1999. Is this good or bad? If the terms it offers its customers are net 45 days, this is good. If the terms are net 30 days, then it might want to see how it can speed up collections. As will be seen in Chapter 9, any time customers are slow to pay, they are using the entrepreneur's cash. If there is not enough cash, the entrepreneur may have to borrow from the bank until customers pay the money they owe. Any time money is borrowed, income decreases due to interest expense. The more interest paid, the less cash available. It can become a vicious circle.

Inventory turnover measures how fast the inventory is being sold. It is calculated by taking the cost of goods sold from the income statement and dividing it by the average inventory on the balance sheet. (A company providing a service would not calculate this ratio because it is not in the business of selling goods.)

$$\text{Inventory Turnover} = \text{Cost of Goods Sold} / \text{Average Inventory}$$

A turnover of 12 would indicate that the company is selling and restocking its inventory every 30 days. Inventory turnover for Medical Products, Inc. would be calculated as follows:

2000	1999
$5,440,000/(($1,427,000 + $1,310,000)/2) = 4.0	$4,644,000/$1,295,000* = 3.6 (*Average for 1999 and 1998)

Medical Products, Inc. is turning over or selling its inventory four times a year or once every three months. This is faster than in 1999. Is this good or bad? Again, it depends. If it takes Medical Products, Inc. longer than three months to replace its inventory, it might run out. However, if it takes Medical Products, Inc. only three weeks to replace its inventory, it might have too much. The more inventory on hand that is not moving, the more cash that is tied up in inventory.

Control of inventory is essential for an entrepreneur. Having enough of the right inventory on hand when a customer walks in the door must be balanced with having too much inventory. Sometimes, inventory is old because the entrepreneur is loath to mark it down or sell it at a loss. Keep in mind that inventory sitting around is not generating a return and may actually be costing more than if sold at a loss. It takes up space, has to be moved, and must be insured. The business may also be paying interest on a line of credit that could have been paid down with the proceeds of a liquidation sale.

When measuring profitability ratios, it is important to first define what numerical measures will indicate profitability for the company. One of the most common measures is return on sales. This ratio looks at how much profit is generated by every dollar of sales.

$$\text{Return on Sales} = \text{Net Income} / \text{Sales}$$

Exhibit 7-1 shows that Medical Products, Inc.'s return on sales is 2.2 percent for 2000. As discussed earlier in this chapter, this means that for every dollar sold in

2000, Medical Products earned 2.2 cents, while in 1999 the company earned only .3 cents for every dollar of sales.

2000	1999
$240,900/$10,979,000 = 2.2%	$26,400/$9,013,000 = .3%

However, because net income is influenced by capital structure and tax implications, a better measure of return on sales might be EBIT/Sales.

2000	1999
$461,000/$10,979,000 = 4.2%	$97,000/$9,013,000 = 1.1%

Using EBIT indicates the return the company is generating from its ongoing operations before taking into account interest costs and taxes.

What return on sales does not measure is the level of assets necessary to support those sales. This is measured by calculating asset turnover:

$$\text{Asset Turnover} = \text{Sales} / \text{Average Assets}$$

Medical Products, Inc.'s asset turnover is calculated as follows:

2000	1999
$10,979,000/(($5,181,400 + $3,956,000)/2) = 2.4	$9,013,000/$3,825,000* = 2.3 (*Average for 1999 and 1998)

If these two ratios were combined into one calculation, the result is the formula for return on assets (ROA), which can be measured as

$$\text{Return on Assets} = \text{EBIT} / \text{Average Assets}$$

For Medical Products, Inc., return on assets is calculated as follows:

2000	1999
$461,000/(($5,181,400 + $3,956,000)/2) = 10.1%	$97,000/($3,825,000) = 2.5%

The return on assets ratio says that Medical Products, Inc. generated 10.1 cents for every $1 invested in assets in 2000, or about a dime for every dollar. This was obviously better than in 1999, when the return was 2.5 cents for every $1 invested in assets.

By looking at the two parts of the return on assets equation, it is possible to better observe what is driving the business, a type of analysis called the *duPont model*. In the 1930s E.I. duPont de Nemours & Co. developed this model, which is an expansion of the basic ROA model:

$$\frac{\text{EBIT}}{\text{Sales}} \times \frac{\text{Sales}}{\text{Avg. Assets}} = \frac{\text{EBIT}}{\text{Avg. Assets}}$$

The significance of the duPont model is that it leads management to consider utilization of assets, including keeping investment in assets as low as feasible, as well as the income generated by sales. If the asset level is too high, the company may be borrowing money to pay for the assets before enough cash is generated internally. In turn, this increases interest expense, which reduces net income.

For Medical Products, Inc., the 2000 ratio would appear as

$$\frac{\$461,000}{\$10,979,000} \times \frac{\$10,979,000}{(\$5,181,400 + \$3,956,000)/2}$$

$$4.2\% \quad \times \quad 2.4 = 10.1\%$$

For 1999, the ratio would be

$$\frac{\$97,000}{\$9,013,000} \times \frac{\$9,013,000}{\$3,825,000}$$

$$1.1\% \quad \times \quad 2.3 \quad = \quad 2.5\%$$

The lower ROA in 1999 was not due to asset turnover as much as it was the lack of return on the sales generated. The owners and management may not be satisfied with the 2000 return and may wish to increase it. With the duPont equation, they can evaluate the impact of increasing the profit margin versus trying to increase sales without adding additional assets, versus reducing assets without harming sales, and so on. For example, in 2000, just reducing average assets by $200,000 would improve asset turnover to 2.5, which would improve return on assets to 10.5 percent. Such an analysis is important in helping give entrepreneurs a more objective evaluation of the return they are receiving from the investments they have made in their businesses. The duPont ratio can also be calculated using net income instead of EBIT.

Many lenders will look at solvency and coverage ratios in evaluating whether to extend long-term credit to a company. One solvency ratio is debt to equity, a ratio that measures the relationship between the amount financed by the creditors of the company and by the owners. If this ratio is greater than 1, then the creditors have a greater claim against the assets than do the owners. Again, there is no right number for this ratio, but lenders may use it to evaluate the riskiness of making a loan (see Chapter 10).

$$\text{Debt to Equity} = \text{Total Liabilities} / \text{Owners' Equity}$$

2000	1999
$\dfrac{\$3,053,100}{\$2,128,300} = 1.4$	$\dfrac{\$2,051,600}{\$1,904,400} = 1.1$

For Medical Products, Inc. this ratio indicates that in 2000 the creditors had a claim that was 1.4 times what the owners had. This is an increase compared to 1.1 in 1999. Is this good or bad? Again, it depends. If the company borrowed money to expand or to purchase equipment to increase its efficiency, it might be good. However, if the ratio increased only due to borrowing additional money to fund negative cash flow, then the increase would not be positive.

A similar ratio is the debt ratio, which measures the level of assets against which creditors have a claim. A debt ratio greater than 50 percent means the creditors have a claim against more of the assets than the owners do. A lender will usually use only one of the two ratios.

$$\text{Debt Ratio} = \text{Total Liabilities} / \text{Total Assets}$$

For Medical Products, Inc., the debt ratio is as follows:

2000	1999
$\dfrac{\$3,053,100}{\$5,181,400} = 58.9\%$	$\dfrac{\$2,051,600}{\$3,956,000} = 51.9\%$

Creditors had a claim against almost 60 percent of Medical Products, Inc.'s assets in 2000, compared to just over 50 percent in 1999. Again, one would have to determine why Medical Products, Inc.'s liabilities had increased faster than its assets in order to evaluate whether this is good or bad.

Another ratio most lenders use is interest coverage or times interest earned. Times interest earned measures how many times income before interest and taxes (EBIT) exceeds interest expense. Lenders use this metric to measure the level of risk that they will not be paid their interest (see Chapter 10).

$$\text{Times Interest Earned} = \text{EBIT} / \text{Interest Expense}$$

The higher the number, the more likely the lender will be paid. Sometimes a lender will require the company to maintain a minimum number in order to meet debt covenants, usually at least 2.0 and sometimes much higher.

For Medical Products, Inc., the ratios are as follows:

2000	1999
$\dfrac{\$461,000}{\$146,000} = 3.2$	$\dfrac{\$97,000}{\$95,000} = 1.0$

Although Medical Products, Inc. has increased its debt and therefore increased interest expense, income has also increased, resulting in higher interest coverage than a year ago.

WORKING WITH ACCOUNTANTS

Entrepreneurs typically work with two types of accountants. The first type are the staff accountants and bookkeepers. Accountants are trained to follow certain basic procedures in keeping a company's financial records. Their technical training can create the kind of "language barriers" between the entrepreneur and accountants described in Chapter 1. Overcoming these barriers requires that both parties take action. The entrepreneur needs to learn the "language" of accounting to effectively manage his business. He should also become familiar with the policies and procedures used by accounting and bookkeeping staff that are guided by their professional training and ethics. In their turn, the staff accountants and bookkeepers should take time to get to know the business and to learn what the different departments and functional areas do for the business so that they can effectively tailor what they do as accountants to fit the needs of the company.

It is important for the entrepreneur to understand the functions the internal accounting staff can perform. Many businesses start with a *bookkeeper*. A bookkeeper's primary responsibility is to keep accurate basic financial records, which will serve as the basis for the preparation of financial statements and tax returns for the company. Almost all businesses use computer-based accounting software to enter and record financial transactions. The bookkeeper also provides basic accounts payable and accounts receivable management. As a business grows, there may come a time when a *controller* is needed. In addition to the types of activities that a bookkeeper performs, the controller can generate custom financial reports on a weekly or monthly basis that provide better data for decision making. The controller also can manage the day-to-day cash flow in most businesses. Some businesses eventually need a *chief financial officer* (CFO), who can structure complex financing, generate complex financial projections, and manage the relationship with bankers and other sources of financing while also performing all the usual duties of a controller.

External accountants are used to generate business tax returns and, for some companies, to perform a review or an annual audit. In the book *The Entrepreneur's Guide to Business Law*, Bagley and Dauchy (1998) provide a useful guide to hiring and working with attorneys that also applies to hiring and working with outside accountants. When hiring an accounting firm, the entrepreneur should collect referrals from other professionals and entrepreneurs and choose two or three firms to interview. During the interview, the accounting firm's culture and even the personality of its staff should be carefully evaluated to ensure a good fit. This includes making sure the accounting firm staff will be compatible with the internal accounting staff, as they will need to work together very closely. It can be beneficial to hire an accounting firm that understands the industry in which the business operates; such specific knowledge can make the firm's work more efficient and more effective. It is advisable to gain a clear understanding of billing policies and to be clear about whatever cost constraints may be in the budget for outside accounting services. Some firms are too expensive for smaller businesses. However, lower cost does not necessarily mean inferior service. Some firms are better equipped to handle the needs of smaller businesses more efficiently without losing any quality.

After an accounting firm is chosen, there are ways to ensure a good working relationship. Entrepreneurs should take the time to prepare for meetings with their accountants in advance. The accounting firm and the entrepreneur should reach an understanding as to what tasks can be performed by the internal accounting staff to help keep the cost of external accounting services to a minimum. External accountants should be kept apprised of any significant developments in the company, because such events may have an impact on the tax or audit situation of the business. It is beneficial to give the outside accounting firm permission to challenge decisions and assumptions made by the entrepreneur. An outside perspective from someone knowledgeable about the business can often be invaluable to a growing venture.

SUMMARY

This chapter examined how the entrepreneur can actually gain control of "the numbers" for utilization in decision making. With this in mind, a system for tracking and monitoring key assumptions should be developed in every company. The entrepreneur should establish clear milestones to track progress toward long-term goals. Furthermore, every owner/manager has different needs for information; the key is to identify what a specific business needs to assess and then find a way to get that information. Important information required by the entrepreneur may be different from what the bank needs or what the accountants normally prepare. It is up to the entrepreneur to work closely with the accountant, using accounting language, to develop the reports required. This assumes that the entrepreneur understands which numbers are actually needed to follow the activity of the business and that those numbers can be generated through the accounting systems and staff. This chapter also discussed the importance of recruiting and working with accountants who know the business and get along well with the internal staff. The next chapter will explore bootstrapping techniques, which can create more efficient means for managing the finances of an entrepreneurial venture.

DISCUSSION QUESTIONS

1. Why are lenders interested in a company's liquidity and solvency ratios?
2. What is DSO, and why is it important to an entrepreneur?
3. Why should an entrepreneur monitor inventory turnover? What could the issues be with a low turnover? A high turnover?
4. How do you plan to accomplish the accounting for your business? What steps will you take to make sure your accountant understands your business and you understand your financial statements?
5. What other types of metrics could an entrepreneur use?
6. How would you determine what should be measured?

OPPORTUNITIES FOR APPLICATION

1. Using the financial statements you generated in Chapter 6, calculate the following, if appropriate:
   Current ratio
   Quick ratio

    DSO
    Inventory turnover
    Debt ratio
    Debt to equity
    Times interest earned
    Return on assets using the duPont ratio

What areas do you think a lender would be concerned about? What areas are you concerned about?

2. Using the financial statements you obtained in Chapter 3, repeat the process in problem 1.

3. What other metrics would be important to have for your company?

4. Interview a small CPA firm. Ask how it approaches a new client. How does it get to know the business? What types of services does it offer? How does it bill a company?

5. Interview some accounting students at your school. Ask if they plan to work with entrepreneurs. Ask how they would approach working in a new business. Ask why they decided to major in accounting.

6. Contact a local bank or Small Business Administration office, and ask for an interview with a loan officer. Is there a minimum set of reporting requirements from companies they do business with? What are the biggest issues they see with small businesses? What do they look for in the numbers when evaluating a small business? What do they look for outside of the numbers?

REFERENCES

Bagley, C., and Dauchy, C. (1998). *The Entrepreneur's Guide to Business Law*. New York: West.

Fraser, J. (1998, January). Hire finance. *Inc.,* p. 87.

McGrath, R., and MacMillan, I. (1995, July–August). Discovery-driven planning. *Harvard Business Review,* pp. 4–12.

Ottenheimer, J. (1999, February). How are we doing? *Journal of Accountancy,* pp. 35–37.

Internal Sources of Funds: Bootstrapping Techniques

Not only did Michael Knowles start his security-guard company in the guest room of his house in Tallahassee, Fla., but he didn't relocate to larger quarters for two years. . . . Borrowing $1,000 from a buddy, he founded Seven Hills Security Inc. . . . Knowles shared the house with his wife, Evelyn, who served as de facto receptionist, and his cocker spaniel, whose enthusiastic yelps in the background often interrupted business calls. But unlike some home-based entrepreneurs, Knowles never pretended to be anywhere else. . . . His frugality paid off. Seven Hills is now situated in a 20-room suite in a contemporary office complex in Tallahassee, employs 130 people full-time, and last year produced $2.1 million in revenues.
                    —D. FENN (1999).

Raising external funding is a major goal for many entrepreneurs. There are numerous sources of external funding that can be used to capitalize a business, ranging from venture capitalists with their untold billions of investment dollars looking for the next Microsoft to family members willing to invest part of their life savings often based on nothing more than blind faith. The various means of debt and equity financing will be discussed in Chapters 10–12. However, before pursuing *external* funds, the entrepreneur should consider how the business could be managed in a way that reduces the external funding required. One way is to learn how to manage the cash flow of the business better, discussed in Chapter 9. Another way is by using what is commonly known as *bootstrapping,* introduced in Chapter 5. This chapter will present a variety of bootstrapping techniques that can help an entrepreneur achieve success without needing to raise a large amount of start-up capital.

WHY BOOTSTRAP?

In Chapter 5 bootstrapping was described as a means of starting a business using very limited resources. Some entrepreneurs bootstrap because they do not have access to large amounts of cash to start their businesses and it may be the only way that their businesses can actually get started. Many younger entrepreneurs often bootstrap because they have not had many years of high salaries in the business world and have not been able to save money that can be invested in their own start-ups. It also is common to observe bootstrapping being used by entrepreneurs in places that do not normally attract investment monies, such as the inner city or poor rural areas.

More recently, however, bootstrapping techniques have become more widely used by entrepreneurs of all types, regardless of their financial means. For these entrepreneurs, bootstrapping techniques help them preserve more income and build more wealth; that is, they have a desire to keep control of their business (Bhide, 1992). Many successful companies were started and built with bootstrapping techniques. Logo Athletic, for example, was started with only $250. By 1994, it had grown to over $230 million in revenues. The founder of Yankee Candle started his business with only $20 that he borrowed from a friend. Within seven years, Yankee Candle grew to over $30 million in revenues.

As will be discussed in later chapters, external funds are generated through either debt or equity. In using equity financing, the entrepreneur gives up a percentage of ownership in the business in exchange for cash, which can then be used to start or to grow the business. People who invest cash in a business in exchange for equity become shareholders or partners with the entrepreneur. However, equity financing may decrease the amount of income the entrepreneur will receive from the business and the wealth that the entrepreneur can accumulate in the business. *Dilution* is the term for this reduction in income and wealth due to the use of equity financing. Any cash that is available to the entrepreneur due to profits or the sale of the business must now be shared with the new owners who have invested in it. Thus, the amount available to the entrepreneur has been diluted over more shareholders or partners. The intent of equity financing is that through the extra cash received from investors, the business will grow larger than it could otherwise. But there is growing evidence that this is not always the case.

As an example of the impact of raising external funds, assume an entrepreneur wants to build a business that creates $1 million in wealth. To achieve this goal, the entrepreneur decides to sell stock in the business and is able to raise $500,000 by doing so. The investors receive 50 percent of the stock in the company in return. To achieve the goal of creating $1 million in wealth, the entrepreneur must build a business worth $2 million, because the equity investors now own half of the company due to dilution.

$2 Million in Total Value
$\times$ 50% Ownership
_____
$1 Million Diluted Value to the Entrepreneur

Now assume a second entrepreneur has the same financial goal, $1 million in wealth. To reach this goal, this entrepreneur decides to raise the $500,000 through borrowing the money (debt). Just as the value of a home to the owner is worth the market value less any mortgage owed, so too does debt reduce the value of a business to its owner. The entrepreneur who borrowed the funds will need to build the business to a value of $1.5 million to realize the goal of building a business that creates $1 million in wealth. Thus, debt financing can have an effect similar to using equity.

$1.5 Million Total Value
– $0.5 Million Owed to the Bank
$1 Million Net Value to the Entrepreneur

A third entrepreneur with the same $1 million wealth goal decides to build a business without using debt *or* equity, but to use bootstrapping techniques instead to build the business without external funds. To achieve the $1 million goal, the entrepreneur will only need to build a business worth $1 million. But if the business becomes worth $1.5 million or $2 million, the entire value belongs to the entrepreneur. The value is neither diluted by other shareholders nor reduced by paying off loans.

If an entrepreneur is able to build a business using less equity and/or debt financing, or even by using no outside financing at all, the impact on wealth and income for that entrepreneur can be significant. Rather than beginning the entrepreneurial process by raising as much money as possible, bootstrapping provides a variety of management techniques that reduce the amount of necessary funding. Thus, these techniques become an *internal* source of funding for the business. Every dollar saved by using these internal sources reduces the need of external funding by that same dollar. Bootstrap marketing techniques will be discussed first, as marketing is one of the first areas requiring the attention of an entrepreneur in a new venture.

BOOTSTRAP MARKETING

In a new venture the entrepreneur must find the right product or service for the right customer group at the right price. That is, the entrepreneur must be effective at marketing. The goal of bootstrap marketing is to achieve the same desired impact on customers, getting them to buy a product or service, by using the least possible amount of resources. Levinson and Godin (1994) identify several basic principles that guide bootstrap marketing, including:

1. *Know the customer:* To effectively and efficiently market to their customers, entrepreneurs should seek to understand their customers' needs and expectations, and how they make decisions to purchase.

2. *Focus on the impact of the message, not volume:* Larger corporations have budgets that allow for mass promotion and advertising of their products. Advertising campaigns reach many people who are not, and never will be, customers. But these large companies understand this is just a cost of doing business. Entrepreneurs cannot afford to waste their message on those it is not intended for, if that can be avoided.

BOX 8-1

When Chuck Miller listens, his customers talk. The owner of Aztec Tents and Events in Torrance, California, routinely sends out survey forms to customers of his party-equipment rental firm. He wants to know everything from how the employees behaved to the quality of the equipment.

And when the responses are bad, Miller personally calls to get more details. . . . As a result, he gets back 80 percent of the surveys, each loaded with information and worth its weight in gold.

S. Godin (1998)

---

3. *Focus on benefits the product/service brings to the customer*: In many cases, special benefits offered by the product, how the product is delivered to the customer, and services that go with the product are the entrepreneur's strongest competitive advantage. Although entrepreneurs cannot match dollar-for-dollar the advertising spent by larger competitors, they can provide a product in a way that will attract and keep customers.

4. *Understand the market niche*: Many entrepreneurs have discovered the significant advantage of gaining control of a small, often undiscovered or underserved segment (niche) in the market. The ultimate goal of the market niche strategy is not to be noticed, therefore not attract competition. For example, an entrepreneur recognized that all of the charter boats operating on a local lake were focused on large groups of 50 or more people. His research revealed there were many smaller groups of 10 to 15 people who wanted to book a charter boat that were not being served in this market. The entrepreneur recognized this unserved market and began what became a successful charter business designed for these smaller groups.

5. *Spend marketing dollars wisely*: At times it may be possible to achieve remarkable results while spending little or no money. Other times, as will be seen in the following discussion of bootstrap marketing techniques, it is essential to spend enough money to get the quality needed to be effective. A careful plan can help avoid wasted resources.

6. *Marketing is a process, not an event*: Many entrepreneurs concentrate on marketing their businesses only during the start-up and when revenues slow down. To be cost-effective, marketing should be a continuous part of doing business.

THE BASIC BOOTSTRAP MARKETING TOOLS

A single chapter cannot capture all of the creative tools and techniques that entrepreneurs have developed to help market their businesses to their customers, so the focus here will be on the more commonly used tools and techniques. This section will highlight the basic tools and techniques that are most effective for bootstrapping.

The Power of the Business Card

One of the most important, and often one of the first, marketing tools for any entrepreneur is the business card. In larger companies, a box of business cards often just appears on a manager's desk. The company has a predetermined design, and the employee's name and contact information are inserted on the standard card. The entrepreneur must decide on the design, the paper, the colors, and the content. Because the business card often provides the first contact and the first impression, these decisions are important. Following is a list of considerations for creating a business card:

1. *Design:* Experts tend to agree that a professional designer should do the design of a business card. Although this may cost several hundred dollars, it is money well spent given the importance of first impressions. A professional designer can provide valuable input into decisions regarding logos, white space, font, and so forth.

2. *Include all critical data, but only if it is useful:* Business cards should include all important contact information. For example, if clients will only contact a business by phone, it may not be necessary to include such things as e-mail addresses or fax numbers. Or an entrepreneur may prefer that mailings be sent to a post office box. If clients will also be visiting the business in person, it is necessary to include both the box number and the street address on a business card.

3. *Paper:* Top-quality paper is important. A card printed from a home computer on perforated paper tends to make the business appear as if it is not permanent or even a "real" business. A professional printer using the best paper that the entrepreneur can afford should do the printing. This is another example of when it is important to spend money, but spend it wisely.

4. *Color:* Colored ink can make a card stand out. Most experts suggest using at least two colors of ink. Additional colors are more expensive, and it is questionable how much benefit is gained by adding a third and fourth color. Standard colors are much less expensive than custom-blended colors, so it may be advisable to try to stick to standard colors offered by the printer.

5. *Include description or slogan:* Most cards have room to include a brief description of the business or a slogan. Because cards may be one of the only forms of advertising for a new business, it is recommended that such information be included on the card.

6. *Remember, it has two sides:* If getting more content onto the business card is important, it is possible to include additional information on the back side. This may include non-contact-related information such as pricing, a map with directions, or a photo of the product. Slogans and descriptions of the business also can be moved to the back if necessary.

7. *Make a Rolodex card:* If an entrepreneur can determine that most customers still use a Rolodex card system for their contacts, it may be beneficial to print some business cards in a Rolodex card format that can be inserted directly into a Rolodex card holder.

Brochures

Brochures can be an inexpensive means of providing a visual presentation of the business. This is another tool that requires understanding the bootstrap marketing principles of spending wisely and knowing the customers' expectations. It is easy to both underspend and overspend on design and production. In an example of overspending, a health care entrepreneur spent thousands of dollars to design and produce a full-color, glossy brochure only to find that the customers thought that the brochure communicated all style and no substance regarding the entrepreneur's new clinic. The customers would have been much more attracted to a simpler brochure that highlighted the factual details of the clinic's programs. On the other hand, an entrepreneur with a new commercial cleaning business made a handwritten brochure and copied it at a neighborhood copy store. The other cleaners she was competing against were distributing professionally printed brochures. The entrepreneur's brochure was not effective because it was handmade and did not meet the basic standards set by her competitors.

If a brochure makes sense for a business or is a standard practice for that type of business, Levinson and Godin (1994) identify two important marketing advantages that a properly designed brochure can provide. First, having a brochure can immediately increase credibility for a new entrepreneur. The brochure gives the impression that the entrepreneur has created a legitimate business that has a past and a future. Second, a brochure can decrease the immediate pressure on customers to make a decision. It gives customers information that can be evaluated when they are ready to consider it, while still capturing the basic sales pitch.

Several design features should be considered in creating a brochure. By working on this basic information before meeting with a designer or printer, the entrepreneur can realize significant savings on the design costs of the brochure:

1. As discussed earlier, be sure to tailor the brochure to the customers' expectations. Collect as many competitors' brochures as possible for comparison, and if possible talk with a few customers to get their reaction to some of the more common designs.
2. Include a clear headline on the brochure. This should be more than the company name; it should clarify what business the company is in.
3. Brochures should be visually appealing. If not, customers are less likely to read them. This requires considering visual features such as graphics, white space, logos, and photographs.
4. The brochure should tell the company's story and make a good sales pitch.
5. If possible, it may be helpful to include a list of customers and testimonials.
6. Just as with a business card, a brochure should include useful contact information, including such things as a map if the customer will be coming to the place of business.
7. Order forms or information request forms can help increase the likelihood of action by the customer.

The digital age has created new media that moves information off the printed page to various digital formats. Video brochures can create a much stronger visual presentation of a product or service. For example, a small private boarding school that specialized in teaching troubled children needed to reassure parents of potential students that the school was a safe and nurturing environment. Students came to this school from across the United States, so the owner wanted to be able to communicate this message visually to parents who might not be able to visit the school before they enrolled their children. A video brochure, sent only to parents who had inquired about the school to help keep costs in line, proved to be very effective. A video brochure developed by Select Comfort, a manufacturer of air-filled mattresses, had two goals. The first was to show visually that their product was a real mattress and not an air mattress used by campers under their sleeping bags. The second was to demonstrate the ease of setting up the mattress, an issue that previously caused resistance to buying the product. Again, the video brochure was only sent to interested potential customers to keep costs down. This video brochure also proved to be effective.

Businesses are beginning to experiment with brochures in digital formats, such as CD-ROM, that can include much more information than a printed brochure. Due to enhanced digital imaging it is possible to create virtual tours or virtual demonstrations on a CD that can be inserted in most personal computers. Some CD-ROM brochures are now shaped like a business card, which may be a novel innovation. However, people may not always be willing to use such formats. Production costs for CD-ROM brochures can be relatively high, so it is important to make sure that the target customers will be willing to take the time to put the CD in their computer and view the content.

Web pages are another digital medium that may replace or enhance the traditional printed brochure. In the 1990s, businesses were in a panic to get Web pages set up quickly. The common wisdom was that every business had to have a Web page or would surely face disastrous business consequences. It is now clear that Web pages are just one possible tool for a business to use in communicating with its customers. Applying the bootstrapping principles from earlier in this chapter, a few general rules of thumb regarding Web pages have emerged. First, make sure customers will use a Web page to get information about the product, to make a purchase decision, or to make the actual purchase. Second, if the Web page is used to attract *new* customers, it is a wise use of resources to tie the Web page to major search engines. Search engines direct Web users to new Websites, and they make their revenues by charging businesses a fee to get identified in searches. If the Web page is useful only as a tool for existing customers, the fees to tie to search engines are not worthwhile. Also, the Web page must be in a format that is easy for existing customers to use and download quickly. If customers will use the Web page for information about the product or the business itself, to make purchases, to contact staff, and so forth, then those features must be built into the page within the resources available. It may not be possible to include all features due to cost, so the relative importance of each feature to the customer must be understood. Finally, to make the investment in a Web page a wise use of resources it is important to budget for *Web page maintenance,* the process of keeping all information on the page up-to-date. Such maintenance can be costly in terms of both time and money. For example, pricing, product lines, special offers, and staff rosters all change frequently, and those changes should be reflected in the Web page to keep it useful for the customer.

Banners, Signs, and Trade Show Displays

Entrepreneurs can use a variety of banners and signs to bring attention to their businesses. Banners and signs can help draw attention to the business location, promote special offers, highlight new products, and so forth. Such tools are typically used in businesses, such as retail, where the customer comes directly to the place of business. Banners and signs can also be used by service companies to highlight jobs that these businesses are currently doing, for example, lawn signs used by home repair companies or signs on the trucks and equipment of a landscaping business that are parked at a job site. When designing banners and signs, a business owner must carefully proofread all text. Although banners and signs are relatively inexpensive, it is wise to use materials that will last with normal use and be visually attractive to customers.

Trade shows are a good opportunity for business-to-business marketing. These shows typically feature tabletop or floor displays that are used to attract the attention of potential customers. Because many businesses are competing for the attention of the attendees, it is important to have a display that is at least comparable in appearance. Before purchasing a display, entrepreneurs should determine whether or not it will get enough use to justify the cost—it should not be a one-time-use marketing tool—and they can save part of the development cost of the display by creating some of the visual items themselves. Lighting is important for the display, as trade shows are often held in large, poorly lit facilities, such as convention centers.

Newsletters

Another basic marketing tool is a customer newsletter. Most newsletters are sent out routinely, usually quarterly. There are various formats for newsletters, but most range from one to eight pages in length. To increase the likelihood that the newsletter is read by the customer, it should be made interesting, informative, and educational. The content can be a mix of articles related to the entrepreneur's industry and some that highlight the company itself. When possible, a good idea is to highlight customers in the newsletter. It is important to proofread carefully and to keep the content tightly written. A top-quality design will increase readership, and the design should be kept consistent over time, as should the focus and type of content. Some industries have newsletters in template form with industry articles provided. The company name is inserted at the top, and there is room for the company to write an article or two of its own. Finally, once a business starts a newsletter, there should be a commitment to continue it over time. Customers can become disaffected when a newsletter that they have grown to anticipate stops arriving in the mail.

Other Basic Marketing Tools

Entrepreneurs can employ a wide variety of other basic, inexpensive tools to bootstrap their marketing efforts. Information about an entrepreneur's business can be distributed through "take-one" boxes, circulars, door hangers, and so forth. In all of these types of marketing tools a professional-quality appearance is important to communicate legitimacy. Valuable offers, such as discount coupons, help move the customer to action. It is also critical to distribute these items in a place and manner that will lead potential customers to read the marketing message.

BOOTSTRAP TARGET MARKETING TECHNIQUES

Target marketing is the use of marketing tools that go directly to known customers or those who are likely to become customers. Target marketing techniques are tied to several of the basic principles of bootstrap marketing outlined earlier in this chapter. Target marketing requires a strong relationship with the customer. It tends to be an efficient use of scarce marketing dollars, for its goal is to have high impact on the market niche, with a focus on the specific benefits the customer will receive. This section will examine direct mailing, which is the most common form of target marketing used by entrepreneurs. Other methods of bootstrap target marketing will also be reviewed.

Direct Mailing/E-Mailing

Mailing lists are a means of contacting existing and potential customers using a variety of techniques. Mailings can be done through traditional postal services or through electronic means. Coupons or other special offers can be mailed that encourage potential customers to try the business. For example, a new commercial cleaning service offered one week of office cleaning through a direct mailing to potential customers. From this mailing, several new customers were created. The entrepreneur was able to demonstrate the quality and reliability of his service. Mailing lists of existing customers are used to help keep the loyalty of these customers by sending items such as:

- Greeting cards at holidays
- Customer "gifts" (usually trinkets with company information printed on the item, such as magnets, calendars, etc.)
- Copies of articles that may interest the customer (usually related to the type of products or services offered by the entrepreneur)
- Thank-you notes for large orders or referrals
- Newsletters
- Special promotions only for existing customers
- Special announcements (new hire, new product)

Information to build a direct mail/e-mail database can be gathered from a variety of sources. Many entrepreneurs find it most effective to begin building the database at the start-up of the business. Information can be added on new contacts as the business grows. Data is also gathered to keep names and contact information as current as possible. Such database maintenance is best achieved by having a specific employee responsible for continuously updating the database as new names and new contact information for existing names are collected. Sources of information for the direct mail/e-mail database include:

- A basic form that is used to collect contact information on everyone who comes in contact with the business
- Fishbowl contests, where business cards are put in a bowl to win prizes or free products/services at trade shows, events, or at the point of customer contact
- Suggestion boxes
- Special offers, such as free newsletters or contests, that require people to fill out a form
- Yellow pages, phone books, or other free lists

Some entrepreneurs find that it is not possible to generate the kind of mailing list needed for their marketing efforts. In these situations, mailing/e-mailing lists can be purchased. To keep the costs as low as possible, the requested list should be very focused so that it contains only likely customers. List providers can achieve this by limiting the lists to certain customer types, zip codes, demographics, and so on. Lists are usually paid for each time they are used, so it is beneficial to test the effectiveness of the list by making special offers only through the mailing and tracking how many new customers were created through these offers.

Other Bootstrap Target Marketing Tools

There are other techniques that allow the entrepreneur to target marketing efforts to likely potential customers. Newspaper inserts or inserts in the mailings of larger businesses can be tailored to specific delivery areas. Mailbox inserts can be effective, and most cities have brokers that specialize in this type of delivery. Catalogues are a time-tested method of target marketing. The cost associated with catalogues can be high, due to special production and printing, postage, and order handling. Also, catalogues require frequent updates to reflect current pricing and product offerings. Rather than producing their own catalogue and incurring all the costs themselves, many businesses bootstrap by placing their products in catalogues that offer products from a variety of businesses that share a common type of customer. For example, a small manufacturer of a specialty product for horses placed a product in two catalogues that offer a wide variety of products for horse owners and enthusiasts and thereby gained access to a large number of new customers that helped get his business off the ground.

BOOTSTRAP ADVERTISING

More traditional methods of advertising also can be effective for entrepreneurs trying to bootstrap their companies. Start-up advertising agencies are eager to work for more reasonable rates than established agencies. Levison and Godin (1994) offer two rules of thumb for bootstrap advertising:

1. ***One-shot ads are rarely effective:*** Most advertising experts stress the importance of repeated exposure to an advertising message for it to be effective. For example, several dot-com start-ups spent their entire advertising budget to produce and run an ad one time during the 2000 Super Bowl. These businesses found little or no benefit from these expensive one-time ads. Repeated exposure to ads increases brand or name recognition and retention.

2. ***Quality of production is important:*** Following the principle of using resources wisely, it is important to have ads that are produced with a level of quality comparable to the competition's. Some advertising firms specialize in working with smaller companies. These firms understand limited budgets and are able to achieve high-quality production standards at a reasonable cost.

Yellow Pages

Smaller businesses commonly use the yellow pages for advertising. However, just as not all businesses need a Web page, not all need to be listed in the yellow pages. Once again, the entrepreneur must understand customers well enough to know where they will go to find information on the entrepreneur's type of business. There can even be differences within a specific type of business; for example, many full-service restaurants find the yellow pages a very effective form of advertising. When potential customers want to find a new restaurant, many will look through the yellow pages for ideas on where to eat. However, fast-food restaurants find that most of their customers do not choose their restaurants through such ads.

Especially in larger cities, yellow pages advertising can be expensive. Therefore, the entrepreneur should take an active role in designing the ad (remember, the representatives from the phone company get paid a commission, so they may try to sell the most expensive ad possible). A good starting point is to study the yellow pages carefully. Make note of the size, content, and design of competitors' ads. Also note how many sections in the yellow pages the competitors' ads run. For example, an entrepreneur with a new yard irrigation business discovered that competitors were running ads under "irrigation systems," "landscape equipment," and "sprinklers—lawn & garden." This entrepreneur did an informal survey and found that most people would look under "sprinklers—lawn & garden" first when looking for a business to install a new system for their homes. Therefore, he only ran the ad in that one section. The phone company representative tried to sell him ads in all three sections, but he knew where potential customers would most likely look to find his type of business.

The yellow pages ad itself should be of comparable size to the competition and should include similar content. The ad should stress reliability, integrity, and trustworthiness. The ad should also make clear the scope of the services or products offered. Finally, if customers will be coming to the place of business, the address and clear directions should be included. The use of a second color and illustrations in the ad can help draw attention, which may be important if there are many competitors advertising. However, these all add significantly to the cost of the ad.

Yellow pages are normally printed just once a year. Timing can therefore be critical. For example, an entrepreneur planned on starting a charter boat business on a lake in Minnesota in the summer of 2000. His research revealed that much of his business would be coming from yellow pages advertising. However, the yellow pages that would be used by customers in the summer of 2000 would be printed in the fall of 1999! Therefore, to be placed in the correct year's yellow pages he needed to pay for a phone number and yellow pages advertising six months before his business actually began offering cruises.

A large number of private yellow pages and on-line yellow pages are now being produced as well. Many experts warn that these publications are not very effective, because most people refer to the yellow pages printed by the local phone company and throw away or simply ignore the rest.

Newspaper and Magazine Ads

Advertising in newspapers, especially in larger cities, can be quite costly. Placement within the newspaper is important. Ads for tire stores are much more effective in the sports section than in the food section. Coupons can lead customers to try the business and at the same time give the entrepreneur some idea of the ad's benefit in bringing in new business. Repeating ads on a regular basis increases their effectiveness. Magazine advertising is even more expensive, so care should be taken to ensure that it actually can create new business.

Radio

Advertising on the radio can be highly targeted because stations cater to fairly narrow demographic categories. It is best to use only one or two stations whose listeners match the demographic category of the business running the ads. Stations will barter or negotiate pricing and often will offer remnant airtime. Remnant ads run when advertising slots are not sold or extra time is available. A business can never be certain when or how often the ads will run, but the cost is significantly lower. Remnant ads can be a good way to test the effectiveness of radio advertising.

Television

Although national television ads can be extremely expensive, the cost of local ads can be comparable to other local advertising media, particularly so when local ads run on cable television. Television also offers remnant ad times, which, like radio, offer a low-cost alternative that can be used to test the effectiveness of this medium for a particular business.

PUBLICITY

Publicity is, in effect, free advertising. Therefore, finding ways to get stories run in the paper, on radio, or on television can be an effective means of bootstrap marketing. Most stories about businesses start with a press release sent to various media outlets; that is, much of the news written about businesses is written by those very businesses in their news releases. Although public relations firms can be hired to write and distribute news releases, many entrepreneurs are successful at creating publicity on their own. It may be necessary to build a relationship or educate people in the media to get their attention before sending news releases about the business. Once a news release is sent, a follow-up phone call to answer any questions can help increase interest in running the story.

HUMAN RESOURCE MANAGEMENT

Employee expenses are often the largest single expense category in new and growing ventures. Although the temptation is to hire people early enough so that they are in place when they are actually needed, this is a luxury that many start-ups cannot afford due to cash flow constraints. A basic principle is to insist on periods of "stretching," in which new hiring is always delayed as long as possible and current employees carry an added workload until the business's cash flow can support additional staff. It is important to make sure that newly hired staff members understand the way growing businesses need to operate. Spreading tasks among several employees, with each doing a few extra hours, can reduce the impact of stretching on individual employees. Clear milestones should be established when new staff will be hired, and those promises should be kept. When new staff is brought on, it is advisable to offer extra time off to the employees who have been carrying the extra workload. Another bootstrapping principle is that it is usually cheaper to develop management talent within the company rather than hire from the outside. There are several other more specific methods of bootstrapping employee costs that can also be employed by new and growing companies.

Independent Contractors

Many smaller companies use independent contractors to keep employee expenses lower. Independent contractors do not have to be covered under workers' compensation insurance or employee benefits, and the company does not have to pay the employer portion of Social Security and Medicare taxes. However, in recent years the Internal Revenue Service and the courts have established much stricter guidelines on independent contractors. The status of independent contractor versus employee is not governed by a specific law, but by a series of court cases. There is no simple checklist, but rather a growing list of criteria that help determine independent contractor status. Therefore, a certified public accountant or an attorney should be consulted to help ensure that a business is in compliance with the current interpretation of this area of tax law.

Employee Leasing and Temporary Employees

Entrepreneurs can reduce employment costs by subcontracting with firms that provide employees for short-term needs through employee lease or temporary employment contracts. This avoids the problems that can arise by hiring permanent employees for what are really only short-term workload needs. Using such firms can also keep administrative overhead lower, as these firms perform all of the human resources functions for these employees. It is now possible to bring in executive-level employees through such arrangements. Small companies can gain the expertise of a part-time, temporary CEO or controller to help them navigate through a specific, complex issue or a particularly difficult time in the company's growth.

Student Interns

A growing number of businesses are taking advantage of a relatively underutilized workforce—students. Students in high schools may wish to gain more significant work experience than they can get through traditional teen-aged job categories. University students are eager to work in internships in business so they can list such work experience on their resumes. Smaller businesses are beginning to take advantage of this pool of workers, which in the past was mainly used by large corporations. Student interns are willing to work for relatively low pay in exchange for the experience that can be gained by such work, and most are seeking part-time rather than full-time positions.

Equity Compensation

Entrepreneurs are able to offer lower salaries by offering various equity compensation programs to key employees. Many employees are willing to work for less salary now with the hope of earning much more through sharing in future profits or in the proceeds of a business sale or taking a business public. Employees who join the company near the time of the start-up may be issued actual stock in the company. *Stock options* are another vehicle for employee equity compensation. With stock options the employees have the right to purchase a set number of shares of stock in the company at a predetermined price (usually at a slight discount of the value of the shares when the stock is issued). If the company becomes highly profitable, the employee can purchase the stock (known as *exercising an option*) and receive the benefits of those profits. Or, if the business is sold, the employee can purchase the stock at the discounted price and immediately sell it as the business is sold. *Phantom stock* is a type of bonus compensation for employees in which the employee does not actually receive stock or the promise of stock through options. Instead, the employee is given a written promise of a bonus whenever profits are distributed to owners or a lump sum if the company is ever sold. The bonus amount is based on what they would have received if they had actually owned stock.

Nonmonetary Benefits

Smaller companies can offer nonmonetary benefits that are not available in a larger company. Many employees are willing to work for a little less salary in exchange for these nonmonetary benefits. Smaller companies can offer more flexibility because they usually have not developed a large number of formalized policies, for example, flexibility on hours or even workdays. Smaller businesses often have a more positive work environment and a stronger sense of team and feeling of "family." Employees also may see better professional growth potential because a growing company offers the opportunity for rapid advancement. Finally, participating in a start-up can be as fun and exciting for employees as for the entrepreneur.

ADMINISTRATIVE OVERHEAD

Although the importance of administrative staff and systems grows as a business grows, the costs associated with these functions can create a significant financial burden for a new or growing venture. Administrative overhead includes expenses such as bookkeeping, accounts receivable, accounts payable, sales and marketing, human resources, information systems, and the general management of the business. Overhead includes expenses that are not directly related to making the product or providing a service. The functions represented in overhead are required by most businesses if they are to operate effectively. However, an entrepreneur trying to grow a business through bootstrapping quickly learns that these are expenses that must be carefully managed.

It is not uncommon to find entrepreneurs who successfully raise a large amount of external funding, only to commit to large amounts of expenses that are tied to administrative overhead and not to producing goods or providing services. For example, a new venture was started in the 1990s with millions of dollars of external funds to manufacture a new, high-end motorcycle. Before a single motorcycle was produced, the entrepreneurs had committed to a large, highly paid administrative team and had built a state-of-the-art office complex, next to a state-of-the-art manufacturing facility, to house this team of administrators. The company ran out of cash before any significant sales could be generated, due in large part to the overhead expenses that had been created. The business was forced into bankruptcy.

Chapter 5 discussed the concept of breakeven. In the preceding example, the fixed overhead costs were so high that the breakeven became impossible to attain before the business ran out of cash. Bootstrapping overhead can help lower the point of breakeven effectively and thus reduce the amount of cash required to start a business. This section will examine common methods for reducing overhead expenses without necessarily sacrificing the company's ability to perform the administrative functions it needs to operate.

Space

The start-up locations of many businesses have become legend. Hewlett Packard and Apple Computer were literally started in the owners' garages. Businesses have been started in bedrooms, basements, garages, dining rooms, kitchens, and barns. All of these entrepreneurs were able to eliminate a major overhead expense item, rent

BOX 8-2

When Allen Shatto started his consulting firm in 1988, renting office space was out of the question. He worked from his house in Bel Air, Md. When he could no longer shoulder the workload, he hired four engineers and a scientist, who worked from <u>their</u> houses. . . . Shatto added an "adjunct staff" of 15 freelancers who worked out of <u>their</u> homes.

J. Finegan (1995)

for space, until the business could afford to pay for it through operating profits. New businesses today can create "virtual offices" through copy centers and mail service centers that rent conference rooms and even offices on an as-needed basis.

Other entrepreneurs are able to get free space from companies that have unused space, particularly if these larger companies have an interest in seeing the new business succeed. For example, a large mental health clinic allowed psychologists just starting in practice to use space in their facility with the hope that as the psychologists became successful they would refer patients to the clinic for its specialized programs. Other entrepreneurs can sometimes barter their services in exchange for temporary space. Once a business can afford to move into space, locating areas with higher vacancy rates can save money through lower rents.

Furnishings and Office Equipment

Many entrepreneurs find that forgoing brand-new furnishings and equipment can reduce overhead expenses. Certain dealers specialize in high-quality used furnishings, and some also refurbish their merchandise. Even more cash can be saved by buying at auctions or by finding businesses closing or moving that are willing to sell furnishings at a drastic discount.

The digital economy comes with the potential to use up significant amounts of the entrepreneur's scarce financial resources. Even with falling prices, computers, copiers, printers, and so forth come with hefty price tags. The entrepreneur needs to understand clearly what equipment is really needed and when it is needed. Instead of purchasing all the equipment that might be useful, entrepreneurs can use copy centers, which offer highly sophisticated equipment that can be used as needed. One information technology consultant observed that well over 50 percent of computers and other equipment sits idle at any one time in the smaller businesses in which she consults.

Telephone costs are a hidden expense that entrepreneurs do not always plan for accurately in their forecasts. Although phone systems can be quite expensive, the entrepreneur can easily install many smaller systems. Each additional line the company carries is a new fixed cost; therefore, someone should monitor phone line usage during the day to make sure that the business has enough, but not too many, phone lines. Cell phones should not always be standard equipment for any employee who works off-site.

Administrative Salaries

Employee expenses are often the largest single component of overhead costs. Each new staff employee adds salary and benefits expenses, as well as the cost of support (furniture, phones, business cards, computers, etc.). In smaller companies, administrative staff must be able to perform a variety of functions. Many entrepreneurs serve as their own bookkeeper, receptionist, salesperson, and janitor. New staff must be able to assume a broad range of responsibilities. Some functions, such as payroll, can be outsourced for less cost than when done in-house, even when there are only a few employees.

PRODUCTION, OPERATIONS, AND INVENTORY BOOTSTRAPPING

Several techniques are available to help bootstrap businesses that manufacture products. At the beginning, it may be possible to outsource production until there is enough cash flow to support bringing production in-house. Once production is brought in-house, it is possible to realize significant savings by buying equipment through auctions, from business closings, from other businesses that have outgrown their smaller machinery, and even from salvage companies or junkyards. For example, a start-up box manufacturing company was able to find all the machinery it needed for its first two years of operation by buying equipment that another company was ready to send to salvage. Once it had been painted and basic maintenance performed, the equipment was in good enough condition to operate reliably for several more years. The cost of buying, transporting, and restoring this equipment was less than 20 percent of the cost of buying comparable new equipment. In addition, the company that sold the machinery allowed payment over two years with no interest.

Manufacturing companies can also use inventory management to bootstrap their businesses. Inventories comprise both raw materials used to manufacture the product and finished goods that are waiting to be shipped to customers. Poorly managed inventories of both types can tie up large amounts of cash. *Just-in-time* is one method of inventory management that keeps on hand only inventory that is needed for the current jobs being processed. To successfully implement just-in-time, the entrepreneur must have the cooperation of suppliers (raw material inventory) and customers (finished goods inventory) to ensure product will be delivered as needed. In addition, the business must develop four key elements:

- A continuous inventory update system to ensure that inventories are always at the proper level to meet immediate production and shipping schedules
- High standards for on-time shipping to minimize the cost of back orders and keep raw materials at proper levels
- A tracking system for the time to fill back orders from suppliers when they occur and communicating data to suppliers to facilitate improved performance
- Tracking customer complaints as a percentage of orders shipped to monitor timeliness and quality of finished goods

---

BOX 8-3

Buschman had little money, but he was clever with machinery. Keeping his regular job—and using $500 in overtime pay—he scrounged in junkyards for materials to construct a little factory in his basement. "There's a feeling you need tons of money and bank financing and all kinds of crapola to start a business. . . . If I needed a tow motor, I'd find something at a junkyard, change the engine and transmission, and rebuild it."

C. Caggiano and J. Finegan (1995)

Even small companies need to use cost accounting to better manage inventories (see Chapter 5). Accurate knowledge of the costs associated with manufacturing each product the company makes will help ensure acceptable return on investment for the cash that is invested in inventory. Smaller companies can benefit from keeping their inventories simple. For example, a small printing company realized it had colors and grades of paper that were almost never used. It aggressively trimmed inventory to only the more popular colors and grades, with no negative reaction from the customers. This example also illustrates the importance of tracking the usage, or turnover, of each item in inventory (see Chapter 7). It is important to communicate inventory reports to all key managers (finance, production, and sales) and to analyze them frequently.

There also are opportunities to bootstrap a service company. A method that has proven to be successful in keeping costs down for service businesses is to create a so-called *virtual company*. The story described in Box 8-2 is a good example. During the start-up, Allen Shatto's staff all operated out of their own home offices, thus avoiding the need to rent space. In setting up a virtual service company, communication and coordination are two of the biggest challenges. The entrepreneur should establish daily communication as one of the major priorities. Telephones, e-mail, and even Internet instant messaging can be used as the communication system, and all employees should be trained on the proper use of such systems. As a company grows, some elements of the virtual company may be continued by having some staff engage in telecommuting, which has proven to be popular with many employees and has actually improved recruitment of new staff.

THE ETHICS OF BOOTSTRAPPING

In a study of start-up ventures, Winborg and Landstrom (1997) identify entrepreneurs who bootstrap using delaying techniques. That is, these entrepreneurs delay payment to vendors and other creditors as a management practice in their businesses. This approach to bootstrapping, used by entrepreneurs who are desperate and some who are not so desperate, has been generally criticized in the entrepreneurship literature. These entrepreneurs are using other peoples' resources, most often without their permission or consent, to offset their own lack of resources.

Certainly, many entrepreneurs find themselves in times of limited cash flow, which may require that difficult decisions be made. (The next chapter will discuss techniques and issues related to the management of day-to-day cash flow in more detail). However, to intentionally choose delay of payment as a bootstrapping technique creates serious ethical and moral issues. In some cases it creates situations in which entrepreneurs are using something that is not their own, cash flow and other resources, without permission. In others, it creates an exchange, for example inventory for account receivable, in which the entrepreneurs have no intention in meeting the terms of that exchange (i.e., payment within the agreed-upon time period). Such behavior can even become standard practice for some entrepreneurs, which can create a climate of unethical and immoral actions.

Bootstrapping should not be practiced in such a way that it intentionally harms other businesses. If delays in payment become necessary due to circumstances outside an entrepreneur's control, creditors should be approached in an open and honest manner about payments due. If problems in making payments are anticipated, creditors should be made aware so that they can consent to working with the entrepreneur, if they so choose, to help get through the difficult time.

SUMMARY

This chapter has explored a variety of tools and techniques—collectively known as bootstrapping—that can significantly reduce expenses and cash flow requirements in entrepreneurial ventures. Bootstrap marketing allows a company to be highly effective at reaching the customer while keeping marketing expenses much lower than those of traditional marketing methods. Bootstrapping also can be applied to better manage the expenses associated with staffing, administrative functions, and the operations of the business. The next chapter will examine the process of managing and forecasting day-to-day cash flow in a business. With bootstrapping techniques implemented and cash flow well managed, the amount of outside funding required can be significantly reduced. However, many businesses will still need to raise external funding. Chapters 10–12 will present the various sources of external funding and their uses.

DISCUSSION QUESTIONS

1. Discuss the potential advantages and disadvantages of bootstrapping a new business venture.
2. What are the principles behind bootstrap marketing? Give examples of why each principle is important.
3. What are the ethical concerns that apply to the various bootstrapping techniques discussed in this chapter?
4. Why is it critical to examine overhead expenses carefully in a new business venture with limited resources?
5. What are the advantages and disadvantages of equity compensation methods?

OPPORTUNITIES FOR APPLICATION

1. Interview entrepreneurs to find examples of bootstrapping techniques they have used in their businesses.
2. Develop a bootstrap marketing plan for a new business idea you currently have under development.
3. Design a business card, brochure, and Web page for your new business idea.

REFERENCES

Bhide, A. (1992, November–December). Bootstrap finance: The art of start-ups. *Harvard Business Review*. pp. 109–117.

Caggiano, C., and Finegan, J. (1995, August). Bootstrapping: Great companies started with less than a thousand dollars. *Inc.* p. 38.

Fenn, D. (1999, August). Grand plans. *Inc.* p. 24.

Godin, S. (1998). *The Bootstrapper's Bible*. Chicago: Upstart Publishing.

Larson, K. (1999). Don't leave home without it. *http:www.aquentmagazine.com.*

Levinson, J., and Godin, S. (1994). *The Guerrilla Marketing Handbook*. Boston: Houghton Mifflin.

Winborg, J., and Landstom, H. (1997). Financial bootstrapping in small businesses—A resource-based view on small business finance. In P. D. Reynolds et al. (eds.). *Frontiers of Entrepreneurship Research.* Babson Park, MA: Babson Center for Entrepreneurial Studies, pp. 471–485.

CHAPTER

Day-to-Day Cash Flow Management and Forecasting

Most experts agree that effective cash flow management is one of the most important areas of financial management for entrepreneurial ventures. The National Federation of Independent Business (NFIB) Education Foundation recently did a survey of small business owners about cash flow. The survey found that one out of five small business owners experienced "continuing" cash flow problems. Fifty percent of the businesses suffered from cash flow problems, but not on a continuous basis. Only one in three said they "never" experienced cash flow difficulties. The primary reason cited for cash flow problems was the difficulty in collecting monies owed, the second was seasonality of sales, and the third was unexpected variations in sales.

The inability to manage cash can destroy an otherwise promising venture. The entrepreneur should consider both the technical and the emotional side of cash flow management. An entrepreneur should also know the answers to several important questions when developing a business plan: Why is cash flow different from net income? How is cash flow measured? Why is cash flow management important? This chapter will examine each of these technical questions in detail, as well as explore the emotional burden that cash flow problems can place on an entrepreneur.

WHY IS CASH FLOW DIFFERENT FROM NET INCOME?

Generally accepted accounting principles (GAAP) require companies to recognize revenues when earned and expenses when incurred regardless of when cash exchanges hands. This results in net income on an accrual basis on the income statement. Accrual accounting means that expenses and revenues are recognized when the activities associated with them occur rather than when cash is received or expended. The statement of cash flows is used to reconcile and explain what happened to cash during the current period. To an entrepreneur, the statement of cash flows is second in importance only to the income statement. Yet many entrepreneurs do not receive this statement from their accountants on a regular basis, and many who do have no understanding of its importance for managing their businesses.

Several examples show the differences that arise due to the practice of accrual accounting versus actual cash flow in the business. Depreciation is an example of an expense on the income statement that does not use up cash; the cash is used when the equipment is purchased. Sales are recognized on the income statement when the product or service is delivered; however, the cash may not show up until the following month, or even later. Employees have worked through the end of the month, but they may not receive the paycheck for those hours until the following month. The income statement recognizes the wages expense in the month worked, not the month paid.

HOW IS CASH FLOW MEASURED?

There are three parts to a statement of cash flows that represent the three major functions an entrepreneur must manage to gain optimal cash flow:

1. *Cash Flow from Operating Activities.*   This is the cash inflow and outflow from the company's day-to-day operations. Cash inflows would include cash sales to customers, collection of customer accounts receivable, customer down payments, and interest received on investments. Cash outflows occur as a result of payments for wages, office supplies, inventory, advertising costs, travel, and so on.

2. *Cash Flow from Investing Activities.*   This is the cash inflow and outflow related to purchasing or selling property, plant, and equipment, or investments in marketable securities or other nonoperating assets. Examples include cash receipts from the sale of land, equipment, buildings, or marketable securities. Cash outflows would include payments for equipment, buildings, and land or to purchase another company or stock as an investment.

3. *Cash Flow from Financing Activities.*   Cash flow from financing activities relates to the cash flow from debt holders and shareholders. Cash receipts come from borrowings or the sale of company stock. Cash payments include repayment of debt, dividends, or withdrawals by the owner.

Although entrepreneurs do not usually receive the statement of cash flows, they should ask to have it included with regular financial statements and should begin to understand what it is telling them. Entrepreneurs also need to monitor cash flow projections on a regular basis to avoid an unexpected phone call from the bank telling them they are overdrawn and at the end of their line of credit.

There are two methods of presenting cash flow statements, which differ mainly in the presentation of the operating cash flows. The indirect method starts with net income on an accrual basis and adjusts it to show what net income would have been on a cash basis. The advantage of this method is that it directly ties net income to cash flow, allowing the entrepreneur to see why the company may be showing a profit but using up cash and vice versa. However, this method is not as user-friendly as the direct method. The direct method actually spells out where the operating cash came from (e.g., collections from customers) and where it went (e.g., payment for inventory). Most software packages generate a cash flow statement using the indirect method. However, an accountant should be able to generate the cash flow statement using the direct method. Entrepreneurs should keep in mind it is their responsibility to understand their cash flows to make sure they are receiving the cash flow statements they need to make appropriate decisions.

To illustrate the cash flow statement, we will return to the example of The Company from Chapter 3. The transactions that occurred within the cash account will be examined first. Then each of these transactions will be placed into the cash flow statement using the direct method.

The transactions that involve the cash account and how they will be entered into the cash flow statement are summarized as follows (refer to Table 9-1):

A. This represents the entrepreneur's initial investment in the business. This $100,000 would show up under financing activities, because it was a means of financing the new company.
B. The company then used $36,000 of the cash to buy a piece of equipment. This represents an investment in the company in that the equipment will enable the company to carry out its business. Therefore, this is an investing activity, and because it is a cash outflow, it shows up as a negative.
C. The $15,000 borrowed from the bank is another type of financing activity. It is another source of funds to finance the company's business operation. When The Company repays the loan, it will show up as a negative amount and represent a cash outflow.
D. The payment for rent represents an operating activity. Rent is a cost of operating a business.
E. The collection of $10,000 from a customer who purchased merchandise for $35,000 on account represents a cash inflow. This is also an operating activity. Note that the income statement shows sales on an accrual basis of $35,000 but the cash flow shows only $10,000 because that is all that was collected in the current month.
F. $20,000 represents the amount of cash paid for the inventory that was purchased earlier. The total cost of the inventory was $40,000, but only $20,000 has been paid. Again, this is an operating activity because it is part of the business's day-to-day operations. The balance remains in accounts payable. Note that the income statement reflects an expense of just $10,000 because that is the only portion of the inventory sold. The remainder is an asset on the balance sheet waiting to be sold in the future.
G. The last cash payment for the month is the $100 for interest paid on the note. This is an operating activity. If a business borrows money, it must pay interest and the interest shows up as expense on the income statement.

TABLE 9-1

	Cash	+ Accounts Receivable	+ Inventory	+ Equipment	− Accum. Deprec.	=	Notes Payable	+ Accounts Payable	+ Wages Payable	+ Common Stock	+ Retained Earnings	+ Revenues	− Expenses
A.	100,000					=				100,000			
B.	(36,000)			36,000		=							
C.	15,000					=	15,000						
			40,000			=		40,000					
		35,000				=						35,000	
			(10,000)			=							(10,000)
D.	(10,000)					=							(10,000)
E.	10,000	(10,000)				=							
						=		2,000					(2,000)
F.	(20,000)					=		(20,000)					
						=			5,000				(5,000)
					(1,000)	=							(1,000)
G.	(100)					=							(100)
Balance	58,900	25,000	30,000	36,000	(1,000)	=	15,000	22,000	5,000	100,000		35,000	(28,100)

Assets = *Liabilities* + *Owners' Equity*

EXHIBIT 9-1	

The Company
Statement of Cash Flows
Month ended April 30, 2002

Cash Flow from Operating Activities:	
Collections from customers	$ 10,000
Payment for inventory	(20,000)
Payment for operating expenses	(10,000)
Payment of interest	(100)
Net Cash Flow from Operating Activities	$(20,100)
Cash Flow from Investing Activities:	
Purchase of equipment	$(36,000)
Cash Flow from Financing Activities:	
Issuance of common stock	$100,000
Proceeds from note payable	15,000
Net Cash Flow from Financing Activities	$115,000
Net Cash Increase (Decrease)	$ 58,900
Beginning Cash	0
Ending Cash	$ 58,900

Exhibit 9-1 is the statement of cash flows for The Company based on these transactions.

INTERPRETING A STATEMENT OF CASH FLOWS

Exhibit 9-2 displays a cash flow statement for the example company used in Chapter 7, Medical Products, Inc. This statement has been prepared using the direct method. Medical Products, Inc. generated $354,000 in cash flow from operating activities in 2000 compared to $438,000 in 1999. First of all, this means that the company is generating positive cash flow from its day-to-day activities. Why did operating cash flow decrease in 2000? Two reasons stand out. First, the company spent $5,503,000 for inventory this year compared to $4,500,000 one year ago. Is this good or bad? It depends. If the company is growing, that is, sales are increasing, it is probably good. However, if inventory turnover (see Chapter 7) is decreasing, it may mean inventories are building up or are obsolete. Payments for operating expenses have also increased, from $4,000,000 in 1999 to $4,616,000 in 2000. To evaluate whether this is good or bad requires examination of where the money was spent and whether the growth of the company justified it. Cash flow from operating activities will often be negative during the start-up phase of a company. However, if this period continues too long or at least beyond what was expected, the cash already raised will be used up and other sources of cash must be found.

EXHIBIT 9-2

Medical Products, Inc.
Statement of Cash Flows (Direct Method)
For the years ended December 31
($000)

	2000	*1999*
Cash Flows from Operating Activities:		
Collections from customers	10,582.6	9,000.0
Interest received	50.0	38.0
Payments for inventories	(5,503.0)	(4,500.0)
Payments for operating expenses	(4,616.0)	(4,000.0)
Payments for taxes	(13.6)	(5.0)
Payments for interest	(146.0)	(95.0)
Net cash provided by operating activities	354.0	438.0
Cash Flows from Investing Activities:		
Purchases of property and equipment	(747.0)	(525.0)
Net cash used in investing activities	(747.0)	(525.0)
Cash Flows from Financing Activities:		
Net change in capital lease obligations	204.0	10.0
Borrowings on note payable to bank	299.0	100.0
Dividends paid	(17.0)	(15.0)
Net cash provided by financing activities	486.0	95.0
Net increase (decrease) in cash and cash equivalents	93.0	8.0
Cash and cash equivalents, beginning of year	706.0	698.0
Cash and cash equivalents, end of year	799.0	706.0

Cash flows from investing activities are usually negative because the company is continuously investing in new equipment or systems. Cash flow related to the acquisition of another company would also be shown here. Medical Products purchased $747,000 of property and equipment in the year 2000 compared to $525,000 in 1999. Later in the chapter we will discuss ways to make this investment without upfront cash outflow.

Cash flows from financing activities describe where the cash is raised. In the case of Medical Products, Inc., it utilized capital leases to fund some of its equipment purchases and borrowed money from the bank. The payments it made on these capital leases are netted out of the total shown. Medical Products also paid out dividends to its owners.

The net change in cash for Medical Products for 2000 was an increase of $93,000, which when added to the cash at the beginning of the year, $706,000 (found on the balance sheet for the year ended 1999), results in cash at the end of the year of $799,000. (This number is also found on the balance sheet for the year ended 2000.)

The cash flow statement explains where the cash came into the business and where it flowed out. Thus the entrepreneur can start to determine what needs to be done to improve cash flow or better invest the cash that is coming in. The cash flow statement in Exhibit 9-1 shows the results for one year. The template in Chapter 6 projects cash flow month-by-month for up to three years.

STATEMENT OF CASH FLOWS—INDIRECT METHOD

When comparing the cash flow statement prepared under the direct method (Exhibit 9-2) and the cash flow statement prepared under the indirect method (Exhibit 9-3), you see that the major difference is the presentation of the cash flow from operating activities. The indirect method starts with net income (on an accrual basis) and reconciles it to cash flow—in effect, net income on a cash basis. Depreciation is added back because it is an expense for which no cash exchanges hands, as discussed earlier in the chapter. The cash outflow for equipment, buildings, and so on happens when they are purchased.

The $396,400 change in accounts receivable indicates a reduction in cash flow. This is because the company sold more on credit than it collected in the current year. Under accrual accounting, all sales are recorded when delivered; in this case, more sales were recorded than were collected in the same year. Therefore, an increase in the balance of the accounts receivable account represents a reduction in cash flow.

Accounts receivable 12/31/99	$ 1,176,000
Sales during 2000	10,979,000
Less: Accounts receivable 12/31/00	1,572,400
Cash collections	$10,582,600

Cash collections were $396,400 less than sales. Therefore, when we start with net income and work to convert it to cash flow, we need to back out the $396,400, as seen in Exhibit 9-3. In 1999, the company actually collected more in accounts receivable than it sold. In other words, the collections from prior year's receivables and the current year's receivables exceeded the sales for the current year. So in 1999, we add $177,600 to net income to come to cash flow from sales. Inventories work the same way. In 2000, the company purchased $117,000 more in inventory than it sold. Since the cost of goods sold reflected in net income only reflects what was sold, the cash outflow related to inventories is higher than the cost of goods sold. In effect, when current assets increase during the year, cash flow is decreased. When current assets decrease during the year, cash flow is increased.

Changes in current liabilities work the opposite way. As current liabilities increase, cash flow is increased; in effect, the company is using someone else's money. In other words, the company has recorded more expenses (which reduce

EXHIBIT 9-3

Medical Products, Inc.
Statement of Cash Flows (Indirect Method)
For the years ended December 31
($000)

	2000	1999
Cash Flows from Operating Activities:		
Net income	240.9	26.4
Adjustments to reconcile net income to net cash provided by operating activities:		
Depreciation	104.0	100.0
Changes in operating assets and liabilities:		
Accounts receivable	(396.4)	177.6
Inventories	(117.0)	(125.0)
Prepaid expenses	24.0	(10.0)
Accounts payable	54.0	40.0
Accrued expenses	334.0	224.0
Income taxes payable	110.5	5.0
Net cash provided by operating activities	354.0	438.0
Cash Flows from Investing Activities:		
Purchases of property and equipment	(747.0)	(525.0)
Net cash used in investing activities	(747.0)	(525.0)
Cash Flows from Financing Activities:		
Net change in capital lease obligations	204.0	10.0
Borrowings on note payable to bank	299.0	100.0
Dividends paid	(17.0)	(15.0)
Net cash provided by financing activities	486.0	95.0
Net increase (decrease) in cash and cash equivalents	93.0	8.0
Cash and cash equivalents, beginning of year	706.0	698.0
Cash and cash equivalents, end of year	799.0	706.0

net income) than it has paid out. If current liabilities decrease between years, the company has paid out more in the current year than it has recorded as expense.

Entrepreneurs do not necessarily need to know how to prepare the cash flow statement. However, they do need to know how to read it and how to ask for the information they need in a format they can use to make decisions. EBITDA (Earnings Before Interest, Taxes, Depreciation, and Amortization) is often used as a quick measure of cash flow. For many companies, depreciation expense is the largest difference between income on an accrual basis and cash flow from operating activities. For Medical Products, Inc., EBITDA can be calculated as

	2000	*1999*
EBIT	$461,000	$ 97,000
Depreciation expense	104,000	100,000
EBITDA	$565,000	$197,000

Although EBITDA does not equal cash flow from operating activities, it does give the amount of cash the operation is generating before considering the cyclical changes in accounts receivable, inventory, accounts payable, and other working capital balances.

INVESTORS' AND CREDITORS' USE OF THE CASH FLOW STATEMENT

Investors' and creditors' primary concern when evaluating a company is often whether a company is generating cash from operations. If cash is being generated simply by selling off investments and long-term assets or by borrowing in order to meet cash requirements, this will raise significant concerns, particularly with bankers. Investors and creditors also want to know where the company is spending its cash. They want to know how the company is coming up with cash if it is not generating it from its operating activities. They want to know why net income is different from operating cash flow.

Negative operating cash flow cannot be sustained over the long term without forcing a company to sell off assets or try to raise additional cash. Investors and creditors become nervous about engaging in a relationship with a business if its operating cash flow is negative, unless it is a start-up company or a company going through expansion. Long-term negative operating cash flows can be evidence of impending bankruptcy. Investors and creditors look to see what other sources of cash the company is using. They will look to see how much debt the company is adding and when it has to be paid back. Investors will look to see if their investment is being diluted because the company has to sell more stock to raise cash. If the company is selling off pieces of its operating units in order to raise cash, this will raise concerns about what the company will do when it runs out of assets to sell. Usually a company doesn't sell off significant assets unless it is reorganizing or is unable to raise cash from other sources.

When forming a relationship with bankers and investors, it is important to establish the amount of cash needed to fund the business from the very beginning. If an entrepreneur has to come back to ask for more cash, lenders and investors become concerned that there may be something seriously wrong with the company. They want to know why the business needs more cash. What was not foreseen in the assumptions behind the original projections? What has gone wrong? If the business cannot come up with cash when it is needed, the company may be forced to liquidate even if it is profitable!

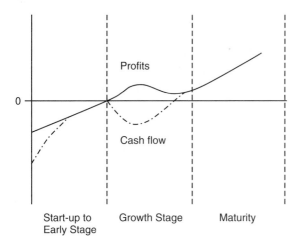

0

Profits

Cash flow

Start-up to   Growth Stage   Maturity
Early Stage

Figure 9-1   Example of Cash Flow Cycle over the Life Cycle of a Business

Even as a business moves out of the early periods of negative cash flow experienced by most start-ups, it is important to keep in mind that periods of negative cash flow can arise again as a business grows. This is particularly true during periods of rapid growth, when the company needs money to buy inventory, hire employees, expand facilities, fund growing accounts receivable, and buy new equipment. Time after time, entrepreneurs report how surprised they are that cash flow management challenges are not just a one-time event during start-up. Figure 9-1 is a graph that shows how a typical entrepreneurial venture can experience negative cash flow both during start-up and during growth, even with profits remaining positive after the initial start-up period. These trends can often be predicted during forecasting and can be used to communicate well in advance with bankers and investors about future cash needs as the business grows. When the business reaches a second period of negative cash flow due to the demands of preparing for growth, the sources of funding will not be surprised and should understand this as a planned part of the business's growth needs.

EFFECTIVE CASH MANAGEMENT

As cited in the NFIB survey, the primary reason given for cash flow problems is the difficulty in collecting receivables. This would indicate the need to carefully manage the credit extended to customers. Explicit credit policies should be established for any business and should include payment terms and possibly cash discounts for timely payment. The terms of payment tell the customer when payment is expected, such as "balance due in full within 30 days of invoice." Credit policies need to be tight enough to maintain cash flow without losing good customers. In situations where a project requires large cash outlays up front, it is not unreasonable for a business to consider asking the customer for an up-front deposit. Needless to say, timely and accurate billing of work performed is also important.

Seasonality of sales is the second reason given for cash flow problems. Diversifying the offering of products and services can help. For example, many ski resorts have converted parts of their land to golf courses. This not only helps to keep rooms filled more months out of the year but also generates cash flow from an entirely new product. Some vendors are willing to modify payment plans to seasonal businesses, particularly if this is a common issue among many of their customers. This can include negotiating dating (extended payment terms) or cash discounts.

The third most common reason cited for cash shortages is unexpected variation in sales. This is often related to the entrepreneur's inability to develop an accurate sales forecast. As discussed in Chapter 4, accurate revenue forecasting requires thorough and careful consideration of all assumptions underlying sales. A cash forecast should always include at least two scenarios: most likely and worst case. With the worst-case scenario, the entrepreneur can be proactive about how to fund any cash shortfall, rather than getting caught by surprise.

There are other issues beyond the three cited by entrepreneurs in the NFIB survey that affect cash management on a day-to-day basis. Policies on how payments are made to suppliers affect cash flow. A company may choose to pay vendors on a 60-day cycle. This is good for cash flow but it can cause problems if the vendor holds shipments because invoices are not paid promptly. Large expenditures up front for customer projects or capital projects may also use up cash in the short term, resulting in a cash shortage. Payments to suppliers can be delayed, but it is critical to call the vendor in advance and negotiate longer terms. Most vendors are willing to work with a good customer on a short-term basis if they understand the issue and are kept informed. Just withholding payment or refusing to take their phone calls can badly damage a business's reputation and reduce future cooperation from suppliers.

Ineffective inventory management is another major source of cash flow problems. Inventory on hand should be reviewed on a regular schedule. If it is obsolete and just sitting around, it is using cash. Even if the excess inventory has to be sold at a loss, that can result in more cash flow into the business. Dead inventory, which will likely go unsold unless offered at a deep discount, is a sunk cost that takes up space and hurts cash flow. Inventory purchasing policies are another tool for cash management. Many companies will order extra because it reduces the price per item. However, this again uses cash. If the business will be holding those inventories for a while, the actual cost will be higher than what has been paid. What are these additional costs? If a company is in a borrowing position with the bank, then interest is being paid on the purchase of this excess inventory. If space is being rented to store inventory, the additional rent needed to house the extra inventory should be considered. If the inventory is getting in the way of production workers due to ineffective storage or lack of space, there are likely inefficiencies in production. If the inventory sits around too long, damage or even obsolescence becomes a significant factor.

During extremely difficult cash flow periods, it may even be possible to delay the payment of commissions or bonuses. Employees may agree if they understand the issues and are warned in advance; however, this should be a last resort and done only with their knowledge. Banks may be willing to offer flexibility on delaying or reducing interest payments until cash flow improves. However, it is *never* advisable to delay payroll tax payments. Although this may be a temptation, as these payments are usually due right after payroll is paid when cash might be especially tight, the government does not hesitate to close down companies that fall behind in their payroll taxes. The employer is the legal liaison between the employee and the government in that it collects this money on behalf of the employee. It is *not* the business's cash and therefore should never be treated as such.

One early stage entrepreneur in the video rental business fell behind on all of his bills including his payroll taxes. As the notices came from the government, he just put them in a drawer and ignored them. Then came the notice that authorities would lock the doors if he did not pay in a certain number of days. A consultant brought in to help turn the business around attempted to negotiate time for payment. However, because the situation had gone on so long, the only thing that saved the video store operator was an emergency influx of cash from his brother. The payroll taxes themselves were not the biggest issue. The Internal Revenue Service charges huge penalties and interest for late payers. These are difficult to negotiate away. Another business, a restaurant, actually had government authorities show up during the breakfast hour, take the cash from the register, and shut it down for failure to pay taxes.

In Chapter 7 we discussed developing methods to monitor a company's performance. One overall measure that also should be used by entrepreneurs is the relationship of operating cash flows to sales. This metric tells how much cash is being generated for every $1 of sales. The formula is

$$\frac{\text{Operating Cash Flow}}{\text{Sales}}$$

In the example of Medical Products, Inc., these results were

2000	*1999*
$\dfrac{\$354,000}{\$10,979,000} = 3.2\%$	$\dfrac{\$438,000}{\$9,013,000} = 4.9\%$

In 2000, Medical Products generated 3.2 cents in cash flow for every $1 of sales. This was down from 4.9 cents per $1 of sales the year before. As with other metrics discussed thus far, there is no wrong or right answer to this metric. More important are the trends, the entrepreneur's expectations, and business's cash situation.

Another measurement that helps the entrepreneur plan is a calculation of the cash conversion cycle. Simply stated, the cash conversion cycle measures the length of time it takes between incurring a cash expenditure (e.g., inventory) and the receipt of cash from the sale of goods or services. The shorter the conversion cycle, the more liquid the firm. This measurement can be calculated as follows:

Number of days inventory on hand
+ Days in accounts receivable (DSO)
− Days in payables

Referring to Chapter 7, we determined that inventory was turning over 4.0 times in 2000. To convert this to days inventory on hand, we divide 360 days in a year by the turnover, $360/4.0 = 90$ days. DSO for 2000 was 45. Days in payables can be calculated in several ways. Days in payables represents how long it is taking to pay for the inventory sold (cost of goods sold) and some operating expenses. Because the accounts payable for companies that sell inventory consist mostly of inventory purchases, we can get a good measure by taking cost of goods sold/average accounts payable to get accounts payable turnover. For Medical Products, Inc., this turnover in 2000 was $5,440,000/(($437,000 + 383,000)/2)$, which equals 13.3 times. To convert this to days in payables, we divide 360 by 13.3, which equals 27 days in payables. For Medical Products, Inc., the cash conversion cycle equals

Average days sales outstanding	45
Days inventory on hand	91
Total days in operating cycle	136
Less: days in payables	−27
Cash conversion cycle	109

The company's operating cycle means that it takes 136 days from the time raw materials are purchased and converted into inventory until the inventory is sold and collected. Suppliers provide 27 days of credit but the remaining 109 days must come from working capital. The shorter this cycle, the higher the liquidity, the greater the cash flow.

THE EMOTIONAL SIDE OF CASH FLOW MANAGEMENT

The NFIB survey cited at the beginning of this chapter found that two-thirds of entrepreneurs reported at least some problems with cash flow in their businesses. The stress created by cash flow management can take a toll on an entrepreneur. Cash is expected to be tight during start-up, but it can become emotionally wearing when the expected cash shortfall goes on longer than planned. Some businesses find that although they had overcome the start-up cash shortage, the problems only arise again and can even become worse during periods of rapid growth. Cash flow once more becomes negative as the business adds new staff and overhead and as accounts receivable balloon while revenues expand. Some cash flow problems

---

BOX 9-1

Entrepreneurs and the Emotional Side of Cash Flow

I remember waking up, night after night, at 3:00 A.M. I kept going through spreadsheets in my head. . . . How could I move cash around to make payroll? What could I cut to end this mess? All I wanted was enough relief from the constant worry to get one good night's rest.

It was the worst day of my life. It had become clear that we had to cut about ten percent of our expenses. In our business, all I could cut was people, so I spent a day and a half going from office to office, letting people go. Thirty people all together had to be laid off. They cried, they yelled at me, they asked me how I could do this to them. Some of them were pretty nice, though. They seemed to understand what I was going through.

The hardest part was coming home and telling my wife that we weren't going to get paid again. We had spent all of our savings and cashed in our retirement funds, so we were barely able to make ends meet. She handled it real well, but I felt like I had failed her and failed our family.

I felt completely paralyzed. I didn't know what to do next.

---

are short term and may simply be part of the transition that every business must endure as it grows.

Other cash flow problems, on the other hand, are more systemic, requiring a complete rethinking of the business model. The business plan that was the original guide for the new venture might need to be abandoned to keep the business afloat. When the business plan shifts to survival, growth and expansion are put on hold and staffing is cut back. The source of systemic cash flow problems might arise from overly ambitious plans or market changes. But no matter what the cause, the psyche of the entrepreneur can certainly be challenged. Systemic cash flow problems often cut to the core of the entrepreneur's ego, leading to self-doubt and a crisis of self-confidence. The stress of cash flow can challenge the relationship between partners, family members and other business stakeholders. Box 9-1 displays several quotes from entrepreneurs regarding the emotional strains created by cash flow crises in their businesses.

SUMMARY

This chapter discussed the technical aspects of cash flow management. Effective cash flow management requires careful monitoring, effective planning and forecasting, and judicious day-to-day policies. The entrepreneur also faces the emotional side of cash flow management, which can create great stress and strained relationships if not effectively managed. The next three chapters will discuss the various methods of generating external funding for an entrepreneurial venture, which can also be critical factors in developing methods for more effective long-term cash management.

DISCUSSION QUESTIONS

1. Why is cash flow different from net income?
2. Is it important to track both net income and cash flow? Why?
3. What does EBITDA measure?
4. How would you increase cash flow if you found out your bank would not loan you any more money and you had a payroll due at the end of the week?
5. Why is it not a good idea to delay payroll tax payments to the government?
6. What does the cash conversion cycle measure? Why is it important?
7. Can you ever have too much cash?

OPPORTUNITIES FOR APPLICATION

1. Using the statements you prepared in Chapter 6, answer the following questions.
   a. What month will you have borrowed the most cash?
   b. How long is your cash conversion cycle?
   c. What is EBITDA for your company for the first year?
   d. How long does it take you to achieve positive operating cash flow?
2. Find a recent article on cash flow in a business magazine or on the Internet. What recommendations are made to improve cash flow?
3. Interview a local entrepreneur. How does he or she manage cash? Has he or she ever run out of cash? What did the entrepreneur do?

REFERENCE

Dennis, W. Jr., ed. (2001). *The Cash Flow Problem.* NFIB Education Foundation Series, Volume I, Issue 3.

CHAPTER

10

External Sources
of Funds: Debt

Almost every business uses some form of debt in a variety of ways and from a variety of sources. Businesses use debt to support day-to-day operations and also to purchase long-term assets such as land, buildings, and equipment. Debt can be created simply by buying raw materials from a supplier on credit. On the other hand, debt also can include extremely complex instruments that finance business expansion through acquisitions. It is important to create a plan for the use of debt in any business. Typically, this will involve the use of several different types of debt from several different sources.

Accountants recognize two basic categories of debt or liabilities: short-term and long-term.[1] Many different types of liabilities fall into these categories. However, for the purposes of debt planning, these liabilities share a fundamental characteristic: timing of the repayment. This chapter provides an overview of the various types of debt and will examine how each works and for what it is best used.

SHORT-TERM DEBT

Any liabilities that are expected to be paid within one year are considered short-term debt. Examples include outstanding invoices from a supplier, wages that are payable to employees for hours already worked between paydays, lines of credit from banks, and payroll taxes that will be due within a few days after payroll is paid.

Typically, short-term liabilities arise in the day-to-day operations of a business and often reflect the timing differences between business activities and cash flow. For example, an entrepreneur needing to purchase inventory for a retail store would contact the supplier and place an order. If the entrepreneur has established credit with the supplier, that supplier may be willing to ship the inventory with the understanding that the goods will be paid for within a short period of time, usually under 30 days. In another example, a computer consulting business has credit established with a bank. This credit may be used from time to time to cover payroll

---

[1]The terms *debt* and *liabilities* are basically synonymous and will be used interchangeably throughout this chapter.

because it may take until the completion of a consulting job for the entrepreneur to get paid by the customer. The bank, in this example, would lend the money to cover payroll, expecting the entrepreneur to pay the borrowed money back once the payment for the consulting job is received. Again, this is a liability that will be paid back within a few days, weeks, or months.

Trade Credit

The type of debt most commonly used by entrepreneurs is called *trade credit,* which is debt that arises from credit extended by suppliers and other vendors. For example, an entrepreneur first starting a business may determine that business cards are needed, and so places an order with a local printer. When picking up the order, the entrepreneur is surprised that the printer wants immediate payment. Assuming that a bill would be sent and the cards could be paid for when checks are run at the end of the week, the entrepreneur inquires why other business owners seem to be able to pick up their printing orders without immediate payment. But the printer does not budge. What the entrepreneur has not considered is that expecting the printer to send an invoice for the business cards is incurring debt. The entrepreneur must establish credit worthiness, as the printer is taking a risk by extending credit. It is not personal; it is just business.

It is not unusual for entrepreneurs to have difficulty establishing trade credit with suppliers and vendors, particularly early in the life of a new business. Even service providers, such as accountants and lawyers, may require payment in advance. The entrepreneur must establish a trust that the business is sound and will be able to pay its bills. This may take time. The entrepreneur will need to build relationships with vendors before most will consider extending even very short-term credit for inventory, supplies, or services. It is important to address this in a business plan. Entrepreneurs often fail to understand that for many new ventures building relationships with suppliers and vendors can be just as important as building relationships with the customers (see Box 10-1). This may require sharing information, which the entrepreneur may at first resist, such as a basic business plan, financial statements, credit references, letters of credit, and even personal financial information. Once credit is established, the vendors and suppliers will monitor payment history to determine if they are willing to continue extending credit to the entrepreneur.

Trade credit is normally extended for only a few days or at most a few weeks. Sometimes a business will need to finance operations over a longer period of time. Cash flow coming into businesses can often be anything but steady. Cash may come in only during certain times of the year or periodically throughout the year due to any number of factors. For example, retail stores are often highly seasonal businesses that sell 80 percent of their goods during the Christmas rush that may last only six weeks. These retailers will still need to build and maintain inventory, pay rent, employees, payroll taxes, the light bill, and so forth throughout the year. However suppliers, employees, landlords, and the Internal Revenue Service are not willing to wait for payment until the cash starts coming in during the Christmas

BOX 10-1

In Their Own Words . . . A Supplier

Establishing trade credit with suppliers is not as automatic a process, as is assumed by many new entrepreneurs. Here is a description of what a small manufacturer looks for when working with entrepreneurs *in his own words:*

Establishing trade credit with a supplier can be a very long task, especially to new businesses. It can take anywhere from six months to four or five years. The main thing suppliers want to know before working with a small business, is what the business's cash flow is so they know that it can afford to pay them for their supplies. In order to take in account if a smaller company can foot the bill, we look at all sorts of things such as: tax reports, statements of how long it has been in business, and number of employees in the company in relationship to the sales generated. We will also look at an entrepreneur's business plan to make sure that he isn't just flying by the seat of his pants. We find with many entrepreneurs that they don't have business plans. They have a great idea that has just kind of grown. This is great at the present time, but we want to know their plan for the future. We want to know how they are going to keep their sales up so they can afford to buy from us. Another point about establishing trade credit with a company that some entrepreneurs don't realize, involves how many orders a year they place. If a small business only orders once a year it will take that business several years to build up trade credit versus a company that orders twice a week.

The best advice for a small business that is having problems obtaining credit from a company is to continue to buy from the company. The small business will have to do this on a cash-only basis. They will then start to build a history with the company, which should make it easier to gain credit with that supplier in the future.

If a small business ever gets in trouble and can't pay their supplier, I suggest that they immediately sit down with not only their supplier but also with their banker. The small business should first sit down with their banker and figure out a plan. They should then sit down with their supplier and let them know the plan that was figured out at the bank, and start to form their own plan with the supplier.

Interview with Robert Cornwall, former president, Rotocast Plastics Products, Inc., Miami, Florida.

buying rush. Therefore, these retailers will need to use a different type of short-term liability to finance this part of their day-to-day operations, that is, to help cash coming in match the cash that must go out of the business. Typically, this cash will come from bankers and other institutional creditors.

Institutional Creditors

Institutional creditors, including banks, require a more formalized credit relationship. Sources of short-term debt to manage cash flow include banks, asset lenders, and factors. Each of these types of creditors will be willing to take differing levels of risk on the businesses they will fund. With more risk, the cost of financing can increase significantly. Therefore, it is important for the entrepreneur to take care to use the lowest-cost creditor possible given the risk that the business presents to the creditor.

To a creditor, *credit risk* is their assessment of the probability that a client can and will repay borrowed money and interest owed on that money. Credit risk is assessed based on several objective and subjective criteria. Although these criteria may vary from creditor to creditor, there are basic factors that most creditors will assess.

The most basic objective criterion is the ability of the business to generate cash to repay the money borrowed. Creditors will determine the history of cash flow generated and used by the business and future cash flow that will be generated by current customers. Having long-term relationships with customers and contracts in hand for future orders reduces credit risk. Objective criteria also include the amount of assets that can be quickly turned into cash, such as accounts receivable and finished inventory. Accounts receivable from large, creditworthy customers reduce credit risk. Creditors also will examine the personal assets of the entrepreneur. If the entrepreneur has personal wealth that could easily be turned into cash, such as publicly traded stocks, this may also reduce credit risk if the entrepreneur is willing to pledge those assets against business liabilities. Most banks require pledging personal assets, which will be discussed later in this chapter. Finally, the amount of debt already incurred is another key objective factor used to evaluate the overall credit risk of a business.

There also are more subjective criteria that creditors will assess to determine the degree of credit risk of a business. Most of these criteria are based on perceptions of the creditor rather than on hard financial data. The reputation and history of both the entrepreneur and the entrepreneur's business will be assessed. An entrepreneur who has started successful business ventures in the past will have less credit risk, as will a business with a profitable operating history. A sound business plan also can reduce the perception of credit risk. Doing business in a thriving industry is another positive factor considered by some creditors. On the other hand, a business in an industry that is experiencing general decline may actually increase the perception of credit risk even if other factors are all positive.

If a business is initially evaluated as a poor credit risk, there are actions that can be taken to alleviate the problem. For example, an entrepreneur may be able to obtain letters of commitment for future business from customers to reduce some of the perceived risk. The entrepreneur may be able to have family members with sound financial records guarantee debt if the entrepreneur and the business are unable to repay the loans. Establishing credibility with creditors may require several interactions that provide additional documentation and evidence to support the creditworthiness of the business.

The most common types of institutional creditors and the role each can play in creating a financing plan for the entrepreneur are discussed next.

Banks

The institutional creditor that is generally willing to take the least credit risk even on short-term lending is a bank. Banks face strict regulation and must meet demanding credit standards imposed by federal regulators. Over time, banks will take on slightly more or less credit risk based primarily on the overall strength of the economy. However, the range of risk-taking for all banks during any given economic climate is firmly rooted on the conservative side of institutional creditors.

Some banks—sometimes referred to as *aggressive banks*—are generally more willing to work with entrepreneurs than others. These banks have a reputation for working effectively with entrepreneurs and will often focus much of their marketing efforts toward attracting small and growing businesses. Often, small, locally owned, community banks are most interested in working with entrepreneurial ventures (Lange, Warhuus, and Levie, 1998). Because these banks are rarely able to compete for larger corporate business, they try to match their own small business culture with small businesses in the community. These banks can generally handle the size of the smaller loans needed by the entrepreneur.

Banks are best suited for certain types of short-term credit. Lines of credit, for example, are among the most common types of loans banks can offer to entrepreneurs for the short-term cash flow needs of their businesses. A *line of credit* is a loan that is used to help smooth out cash flow. The money is loaned against accounts receivable that are expected to be collected in the near future; it may also be loaned against inventory that is likely to be sold in the near future. A line of credit is negotiated for a maximum amount, or credit limit, that can be borrowed by the entrepreneur as the need arises. Because the loan is already approved, it provides quick and easy access to cash for the entrepreneur. A phone call to the loan officer can provide funds from the line of credit often on the same day that the request is made. As described previously in this chapter, the entrepreneur will have already incurred expenses associated with business activity (e.g., payroll, rent, raw materials), and the line of credit helps provide cash until the payment for goods and services is actually received from the customer.

The bank typically will charge interest on a line of credit that is based on its *prime rate*, which is the rate charged to its best corporate customers. The bank will set a rate that reflects the level of risk it perceives it is taking with the loan. A very low risk line of credit to an entrepreneur may be priced only slightly above the bank's prime rate, possibly only a fraction of a percent higher. Higher credit risks, but ones that still fall within the bank's comfort level, may be charged up to several percentage points higher than the bank's prime rate.

A bank will require that certain conditions be met or maintained by the business as part of the loan agreement. The bank will often ask to receive monthly verification of accounts receivable and/or inventory balances to make sure that the assets that secure the loan are at an adequate level. Assume, for example, a bank has issued a line of credit to a business for up to $50,000. The loan agreement states that the bank is lending this against 70 percent of the accounts receivable that are under 90 days old. If the entrepreneur submits a report that indicates that 70 percent of the accounts receivable under 90 days old is actually only $42,000, the bank will not lend the full amount of the line of credit, but only up to $42,000. If the entrepreneur has already borrowed more than $42,000, the bank can, and likely will, require the entrepreneur to pay the principal balance down to $42,000.

Banks place such limits on lines of credit to manage their credit risk. Bankers have learned that not all accounts receivable will be collected, thus the 70 percent limit in this example. They also know that older accounts receivable are the most difficult to collect, thus the 90-day-old limit on receivables. In addition, banks will often require that the principal of a line of credit be paid in full at least once during the year and may require that the principal be zero for at least 30 consecutive days at least once a year. This helps assure the bank that the line of credit is really being used to fund temporary timing issues in cash flow. The topic of how entrepreneurs effectively work with bankers will be discussed in more detail a little later in this chapter.

Asset-Based Lenders

Institutional creditors that can take a higher level of credit risk on short-term lending are commonly referred to as *asset-based lenders*. These lenders are not banks, although bank holding companies may own this type of entity. Asset-based lenders also lend money against accounts receivable and sometimes against inventory. Asset-based lenders do not face the same regulatory constraints as a bank. However, since they work with businesses that have a higher risk of defaulting on the loan, they will often charge much higher interest rates than a bank—sometimes 6 to 10 percentage points above the prime rate charged by a bank. Unlike banks, asset-based lenders do not examine as many other factors when lending money (see Box 10-2). They are primarily concerned with the value of the assets they are lending money against. Therefore, these lenders are more likely to quickly seize the assets they back if the loan becomes at all distressed (i.e., late payments). Many asset-based lenders view their role as a temporary one, providing financing until a business is able to secure bank financing. They will work with start-ups more readily than most banks. They also will work with businesses that banks are no longer willing to serve due to poor financial performance.

Factors

A final source of short-term financing is not really a lender of funds at all. It is a form of "financing," called *factoring*, used by entrepreneurs who have an extremely high level of credit risk. A factor does not lend against assets, as does a bank or an asset-based lender, but actually will purchase certain accounts receivable from the entrepreneur. Factors are used by businesses that are considered too much of a credit risk for either bankers or asset-based lenders.

Using a factor requires that both the entrepreneur and the customers agree to the sale of these receivables. Factors are used by high-risk businesses, and such a sale can cause a strain in the relationship between the entrepreneur and the customers because there can be a perception, often correct, that the future of the entrepreneur's business is questionable. Some customers will cut back on or even stop doing business with a company that uses a factor to advance money. Therefore, it is important for entrepreneurs to communicate directly with their

---

BOX 10-2

In Their Own Words . . . An Asset-Based Lender

Asset-based lenders can offer an alternative for entrepreneurial ventures that may not be "bankable" under normal criteria for bank lending. Here is a description of what an asset-based lender looks for when working with entrepreneurs *in his own words:*

The customer that we see typically is experiencing some sort of financial distress, but this is not always the case. As an example, often owners of privately held companies will take out substantial sums of money, leaving the company in a highly leveraged position. Highly leveraged companies are not a good fit for a traditional bank lending arrangement, but do present an opportunity for asset-based lenders. When a company transitions to an asset-based lender, there is significantly more structure to their transaction and it will generally cost them more. Our structure would include reporting as frequently as daily, quarterly collateral audits and advance rates typically lower than what traditional banks would offer. Generally speaking, the closer we are to cash, the happier we are. Advance rates tend to decline as the time it takes to convert the asset to cash increases. Prior to issuing a proposal we will conduct an audit of the company's records and procedures. Advance rates for accounts receivable are set with consideration of the audit findings concerning billing practices, aging stratification, concentrations, dilution, contras, and other factors. Inventory advance rates are often set based on appraised forced liquidation value or in consideration of type and category, turns, price and test count results and prior liquidation results. Advances against fixed assets are typically tied to some percentage of appraised value with much shorter loan amortizations than what would be available from a traditional bank lender. Depending on the size and complexity of a transaction, rates can vary from slightly below prime to 7 or 8 over prime.

Interview with Terry Jackson, Vice President, Wells Fargo Business Credit, Minneapolis, Minnesota.

---

customers about why they are using a factor and what the long-term outlook actually is expected to be for the business.

Factors are a very costly source of funding. Depending on the risk they perceive in a business, they will charge between 4 to 7 percent of the accounts receivable they purchase. That is, a $10,000 receivable from a customer may only result in an advance of $9,300 to the entrepreneur. The highest-risk businesses may face even further limitations and charges from factors. Although the 4 to 7 percent fee may not at first seem to be that high, it is actually the equivalent of a bank charging an annual rate of 50–85% on a line of credit! Given the high cost and problems that can be created in customer relations, factors are generally a funding source of last resort that should only be used for a short period of time and, in many cases, only as an emergency source of funding for a business that will likely not survive without a quick infusion of cash (see Box 10-3). The entrepreneur should develop a plan to make a transition from the factor to an asset-based lender or even a bank.

BOX 10-3

In Their Own Words ... A Factor

Although factors are sometimes thought of as a financial last resort for desperate businesses, factors view themselves as key lifelines for new or struggling businesses. Here is a description of how a factor views his role *in his own words:*

> Cash is key in a business. We, as factors, mainly work with businesses that are new, growing, or that have run into trouble by providing them with cash for their receivables. We can give them tomorrow's money today so they can concentrate on selling their product and turning their operating cycle more quickly to become profitable.
>
> Most businesses that choose to work with a factor work with us on a short-term basis. Most factors in the field generally require a minimum of 6 months to a year agreement and a $10,000 a month minimum of a company's receivables before we'll work with them. When it comes to an issue of who will qualify for financing, we can usually work with most businesses as long as they have bona fide commercial receivables that can be collected. Some exceptions to this rule, however, would be

> if the business doesn't have a creditworthy customer, if the business doesn't have enough receivables, or if the business only has one customer. These are all situations in which we might turn down working with a business.
>
> A lot of people have questions about what happens to a receivable that doesn't get paid. Factors will either buy receivables with recourse or without recourse. When a factor buys a receivable with recourse that means if the receivable is not collected it will be returned to the business. Buying without recourse means that if the receivable is not paid it is the factor's responsibility. Some factors are reluctant about buying without recourse because they want to be able to collect the receivable and will usually only do this for very creditworthy customers.
>
> The bottom line for deciding if factoring is an option for you is if you need immediate cash because you are a start-up business or you have gotten into a difficult situation or for some other reason you need cash fast; we can give you the money you need and get it to you immediately.

Interview with Rick Yunger, President, GreenBridge Finance, Minneapolis, Minnesota.

LONG-TERM DEBT

Any liabilities that a business expects to be paid off in a time frame beyond one year are considered long-term debts. Long-term debt is most often used to fund assets that are to be purchased and used over a long period of time and not consumed in the course of day-to-day business, such as is the case with assets like inventory or office supplies. Known as *fixed assets,* these assets will remain with the company for more than one year, and often for an indefinite period of time. Examples of fixed assets include equipment, automobiles and other vehicles, land and buildings, and finishing work such as walls and so forth in rented space with a multiyear lease.

Credit risk is a critical issue with long-term debt, just as it was with short-term debt. In fact, it can become an even greater issue because the money is being lent over a much longer period of time. Therefore, the lender may place much more severe restrictions and conditions on such loans. Also, just as with short-term lenders, there are various types of long-term lenders. Long-term lenders also vary by the types of lending they will engage in, ranging from a generalist such as a bank that will lend against a variety of assets to a specialist that may lend only against one type of asset, such as real estate.

Banks

Banks face the same basic restrictions and limitations in long-term lending as they do in short-term lending. Because banks limit their credit risk, they again offer among the lowest costs for this type of lending. The type of loan that a bank uses to finance long-term assets is called a *term loan*. A term loan agreement is written so that it is paid back over a specified period of time, known as the *term*. Typically, the term is no longer than, and often less than, the expected useful life of the asset being financed. For example, land and buildings loans may have a fairly long term for payback, 10 to 30 years, whereas loans to purchase computers will likely be made for only a 2- to 3-year term due to their short useful life. The specific assets being funded are used to secure the term loan. However, bank term loans are generally subject to additional conditions and restrictions that protect the bank, as will be discussed later in this chapter.

Some term loans will be structured with a *balloon payment,* which gives the bank the option of ending the term loan before the actual number of years used to structure the payments. For example, a bank may offer a term loan for a building that is amortized over a period of 15 years. However, the actual term of the loan is only 3 years. At the end of the 3 years, the loan shows the entire remaining balance due in a balloon payment. If the company is doing well, the bank will likely renew the loan for another period of time. However, if conditions for the business have changed and the credit risk is no longer acceptable to the bank, the balloon allows the bank to get out of the loan by not renewing it at that point in time. A business with a very low credit risk may be able to negotiate a no balloon payment, but such clauses are a common technique used by bankers to reduce their credit risk.

Leasing Companies

Almost any asset can be leased, and leasing should be considered as just one more option for financing asset purchases. Leasing is often used for equipment purchases, especially equipment that has a limited useful life, such as computers. Ownership of the asset is maintained by the company leasing it to the business. However, the obligation for the lease is with the entrepreneur for the life of the contracted period.

Real Estate Lenders

The purchase of land and buildings can be funded through real estate lenders. Real estate lenders can be stand-alone companies that specialize in this type of loan, or they can be the investment departments of insurance companies or pension funds.

These lenders can be very competitive with banks if the credit risk is low, but they also are able to lend money to much higher risk entrepreneurial ventures than can a bank. Therefore, the terms and conditions of loans from real estate lenders are as varied as the customers they serve.

FORMS OF DEBT OVERLOOKED BY ENTREPRENEURS

There are liabilities that a business will incur that may be overlooked by an entrepreneur and may not even show up as specific items on internal financial statements. Nevertheless, these are liabilities that the business owes and that will affect the overall credit risk of a business. For example, property leases for office space, warehouses, or manufacturing space are liabilities for the business. Although notations may be made about such leases on an audited financial statement, these liabilities generally do not show up on a standard balance sheet. However, such leases are often entered into for several years and create large liabilities for the business over that period of time. For example, assume a service business leases office space at a rate of $3,000 per month on a five-year lease. That business has effectively created a long-term commitment of $36,000 per year for five years, or a total of $180,000.

Another business activity that can create a liability is an employee contract. For example, some employment contracts guarantee payment even if the employee is terminated, while others have guaranteed severance packages for termination. Such contracts create liabilities for the company that also may not show up on standard financial statements. Credit card debt is also sometimes not carried "on the books" of an entrepreneurial start-up, but may obligate the entrepreneur to significant, and often expensive, debt.

GOVERNMENT FUNDING THROUGH SBA

Many entrepreneurs are able to secure debt financing through loans guaranteed by the Small Business Administration, or SBA, an agency of the federal government. The SBA does not itself provide funding or grants to businesses. Rather, the entrepreneur works with a traditional lender, usually a local bank, to apply for an SBA guarantee of a loan issued by the bank. Many banks have loan officers or even lending departments that focus on SBA-guaranteed loans. These lenders work with entrepreneurs to complete all the necessary forms.

The SBA has two basic types of loan programs. In addition, it has equity programs, which will be discussed in Chapter 11. The 7(a) Loan Guarantee Program is the most commonly used SBA program. Through 7(a) loans, the SBA will guarantee up to $1 million.[2] SBA loans require that the entrepreneurs also make an equity contribution. For smaller loans, under $150,000, the SBA will guarantee

---

[2]The actual loan amount can be up to $2 million.

85 percent. For loans over that amount, the SBA will guarantee 75 percent. The 7(a) loans must be used for business purposes, including land and buildings to house operations of a business, renovations of the business facilities, furnishings and fixtures, machinery and equipment, inventory, and working capital to support cash flow fluctuations.

A second loan program offered by the SBA is the Certified Development Company (504). A Certified Development Company (CDC) is a nonprofit corporation set up to support economic development in a region. There are almost 300 CDCs nationwide.[3] The 504 loans fund land and buildings for a small business venture with the specific purpose of creating or retaining jobs. In fact, the proposal must demonstrate that one job will be created or retained for every $35,000 guaranteed by the SBA. In a typical 504 loan, the bank will issue a loan that covers 50 percent of the project, the entrepreneur must contribute equity equal to 10 percent, and the CDC will lend 40 percent. The SBA only guarantees the CDC's portion of the project; it does not guarantee the bank's loan to the entrepreneur in the 504 program.

The SBA has established certain eligibility criteria for its loan programs. The business must operate for profit, do business in the United States, have reasonable equity invested by the owners of the business, and use other types of financing, including personal assets of the entrepreneurs (see Box 10-4). The SBA also has certain size requirements to qualify for its programs, which are displayed in Table 10-1. The size requirements include not only an upper limit but also a lower limit as well. For smaller businesses, the SBA has the MicroLoan Program, ranging from $100 to $25,000. The SBA makes funds available for MicroLoans through nonprofit economic development agencies. MicroLoans generally require only that the assets funded be used as collateral and that the owners personally guarantee the loans. There are some types of business that are ineligible for SBA loans, including real estate investment companies, companies engaged in lending activities, companies in the gambling industry, pyramid sales companies, or businesses engaged in any illegal activities. The SBA has a fully developed Web site (http://www.sba.gov) that provides complete information on all of its programs and services.

TABLE 10-1 SBA Size Standards

Industry	Size
Retail and service	$3.5 to $13.5 million in annual revenues
Construction	$7.0 to $17.0 million in annual revenues
Agriculture	$0.5 to $ 3.5 million in annual revenues
Wholesale	No more than 100 full-time employees (or full-time equivalent)
Manufacturing	500 to 1,500 full-time employees (or full-time equivalent)

---

[3]See the Small Business Development Web site at http://www.sba.gov to find specific CDC locations.

BOX 10-4

In Their Own Words . . . An SBA Lender

Loans using the Small Business Administration's programs are a common tool of emerging and growing entrepreneurial ventures. Here is a description of what an SBA lender looks for when working with entrepreneurs *in her own words:*

> SBA loans are for entrepreneurs who have financing needs that cannot be met by conventional bank financing. My advice to them is to go to their bank and request a small business loan. If the request is turned down, they should ask for an SBA loan.
>
> I can't stress enough that prior to applying for an SBA loan the entrepreneur should have a business plan that includes financial projections that they understand and can explain. I like to review all aspects of the plan and in particular the business's financial projections with them. Sometimes they will underestimate the costs of operating the business and overestimate revenue growth. They will also underestimate their cash flow needs. They don't take into account the relationship between expenses and income that typically results in a cash shortfall. This is particularly important for start-up businesses because in my experience entrepreneurs often fail to fully understand their financial needs. If they do have a need for more cash and they have an existing SBA loan they can request that the bank increase their loan, or they can consider applying for a new SBA loan.
>
> Although the business plan is important, the most critical factor affecting a loan approval is the entrepreneur's personal credit history. Personal credit must be clean for the bank and the SBA to approve a loan request.
>
> Prior to applying for an SBA loan some people think it is necessary to go to a loan packager, who would put the loan documents together. However, this is not a requirement of the bank. The fact is entrepreneurs simply need to make sure their loan application forms are accurately completed. If they do need assistance with the loan package or with developing a business plan there are a number of organizations that can help: SCORE, Small Business Development Centers, etc.
>
> Entrepreneurs should realize one thing: The SBA and the bank want to help their businesses to succeed, they just have to take the right steps to get the loan.

Interview with Tammy Hambrook, Assistant Vice President, SBA Portfolio Banker, Wells Fargo Bank, Minneapolis, Minnesota.

WORKING WITH BANKERS

One of the most important relationships that an entrepreneur can have is the one they have with their banker. Bankers can be a source of critical financing at several key junctures in the growth of a business and for several types of both short-term and long-term financing. Therefore, understanding how banks make business loans and how to establish and nurture a good relationship with the banker should be part of the entrepreneur's financing plans (see Box 10-5).

BOX 10-5

In Their Own Words ... A Banker

Although financial data are critically important to bankers, there are other factors and characteristics that can become important. Here is a description of what two community bankers look for when working with entrepreneurs *in their own words:*

(A) key aspect we look for is how long the entrepreneur has kept his key employees. If the employees working with the company have been working there for 10 or 15 years, the person must be a pretty good manager. This would lead us to be more willing to work with them. If the entrepreneur is willing to take more risk than the bank, such as in risking their house, this tells the bank how dedicated an entrepreneur is, therefore improving their chances of getting a loan. The interview with the banker is very important for an entrepreneur. I find that when people meet with a banker they often tend to be a little defensive, not because they don't like the bank but because they are in an uncomfortable situation and that comes across. To alleviate this, don't come into an interview with a banker with any preconceived notions. Come into the meeting thinking of it as a financial partnership. This can get rid of some of the defensiveness. Also, in these interviews it is the little things that count. Be on time and be organized. Have all of the tax returns, financial statements, and your business plan ready. No one reason leads us to not work with entrepreneurs. If we don't work with one, it may be because the deal itself didn't make sense, lack of collateral, or the individual is not prepared. If an entrepreneur comes into a meeting with a banker and he isn't prepared, chances are his business is not prepared. We are not only getting the feel for you in this interview as a person but also we are getting a feel for how the business might operate. Usually the two are one and the same. Within meetings with a banker it is a lot of the small things that in the course of a half-hour interview stay with you other than the numbers.

Interview with Robert Vogel, President, and Daniel Ringstad, Vice President, New Market Bank, Lakeville, Minnesota.

A myth held by first-time entrepreneurs is that bankers lend based on collateral. That is, if the business has assets to pledge, the banker will lend money without any question. Nothing could be further from the truth. The ability of the business to generate enough cash flow each month to easily make payments of interest and principal is the primary factor that a bank will use to determine if they are willing to make a business loan (Petty, Upton, and Griggs, 1997). That is why banks are generally not willing to lend money to a true start-up venture. A history of positive cash flow is a fundamental condition for most bank loans.

Next, the banker will evaluate the entrepreneur's ability to personally pay back the loan if the business fails. One study found that 96 percent of bankers consider personal guarantees of business loans a requirement of lending to entrepreneurs (Petty, Upton, and Griggs, 1997). The bank may eventually lift this requirement, but only after the business reaches a point where the positive cash flow is so substantial that the business no longer carries significant credit risk. The banker will ask for personal financial statements from all shareholders in the business. This will include a personal balance sheet, which shows personal assets and liabilities, and a personal income statement or tax return. The bank will focus primarily on what it considers liquid assets, such as cash and marketable securities, and free cash flow from each shareholder. The bank needs this information, as it will almost always require that the entrepreneurs and their spouses personally guarantee the business loans. That is, if the business fails, the bank will want a legal right to pursue full payment of the loan from the entrepreneurs and their spouses. Even if the business enters bankruptcy and closes its doors, the banks want the ability to pursue repayment from the guarantors.

The final primary consideration is assets to serve as collateral to back the loan. Bankers have no interest in taking over distressed businesses and even less interest in selling assets they can seize to pay off defaulted loans. Even if a business has valuable assets, for example, a building and land that is owned without any encumbrance of debt, most banks will not lend money unless the business is profitable and generating strong cash flow. Most banks will pursue repayment from the shareholders rather than seize the assets of the business, if at all possible.

If the primary criteria are met, the bank also will evaluate secondary criteria before committing to a loan. Secondary factors that may be considered include character of the entrepreneurs, management capability, and the entrepreneurs' own personal funds invested as equity in the business. Loans issued with SBA guarantees must meet these same primary and secondary criteria.

The relationship with a bank involves not just the activities surrounding the securing of a loan. Before a bank makes a loan, certain information will need to be shared. And after a bank makes a loan, the relationship with the banker must be managed properly to ensure a good, long-term relationship (see Box 10-5). There are three phases of a relationship with a bank.

Initial Contact with Bankers

First impressions *do* count when making contact with a banker. Even though financial analyses are the primary criteria used by bankers, their perception of the character and professionalism of the entrepreneur does come into their evaluation. The entrepreneur should be fully prepared to provide all of the information needed to make a lending decision even at the initial meeting. The banker will be evaluating the entrepreneur's own understanding of the financial data and the assumptions used in generating projected financial statements. Bankers prefer relationships with entrepreneurs who have been referred by someone they know and trust, such as an accountant, attorney, or successful entrepreneur with whom they already work (Hutt and Van Hook, 1987).

It is important for the entrepreneur to actively manage the relationship with the banker from the very beginning. Many entrepreneurs become frustrated by the banker's seemingly cold, analytical approach. One entrepreneur said, "I always take the time to tell my story before I give one piece of financial information to a prospective banker. If the banker is not interested in hearing my story first, I move on to the next banker because to me it is important for the banker to be excited about my business as a business. There's a bank on every corner."

Banks will sometimes give preference to certain industries or types of businesses. This is guided by their experience with these industries. If they have had favorable experiences with other companies in an industry, their perception reduces the credit risk of the next company in that industry. Conversely, if the bank is relatively unfamiliar with an industry, this may increase their perception of credit risk. Information and experience reduce uncertainty for banks. Therefore, it is advisable for an entrepreneur to research which banks currently lend money to businesses in the same industry because the chances of a favorable response may be higher.

Preparation of Key Loan Documents

Loan Proposal

The first document generated by the bank is often a loan proposal, also referred to as a *commitment letter*. The loan proposal is a letter of commitment that outlines the general terms and conditions of the loan. This is the time when the entrepreneur can try to negotiate certain items in the proposal. The loan proposal will include a variety of terms and conditions, including loan amount and interest rate, purpose of the loan, payment schedule, fees, collateral, conditions to be met before loan closing, restrictions and reporting expectations, loan guarantees, and events that are considered to be a default of the loan. An officer of the bank, officer(s) of the company, and the guarantors of the loan are usually all asked to sign the loan proposal.

Loan Document

Once the loan proposal is agreed to by both parties and fully executed, the bank will create the actual loan document, which is the legal documentation of the loan. It will contain all of the general terms, conditions, restrictions, and performance requirements agreed to in the loan proposal. The loan document may also contain additional terms and conditions that the entrepreneur should carefully evaluate. Although there is a real hesitancy to change the standard format of a loan document, there can be negotiation at this point as well, even over the standard contract language on the back of any standard form the bank uses. Every aspect of the loan document should be carefully considered, as it may have a significant impact on the operation of the business going forward. For example, a loan agreement may include a standard clause that prohibits a company from buying any assets over $50,000 without written permission of the bank. Given the cost of even some office equipment and vehicles, this restriction could become a significant constraint to doing everyday business.

Personal Guarantees

As discussed earlier, most loans made to entrepreneurial ventures will require that the shareholders or owners and their spouses personally guarantee the loans. The document that creates this personal obligation is called the *personal guarantee.* In most cases, the guarantee will be what is called a *joint and several guarantee,* which means that all shareholders are responsible for their share of the loan (several liability) and that each shareholder can be held responsible for the entire loan (joint liability). In some cases, the bank may allow only several liability, in which case each shareholder is responsible for only his or her share of the liability based on percentage of ownership in the company. The personal guarantee may allow the bank to go straight to the guarantors to pay off a loan if concerns arise about increasing credit risk, even if the loan payments are being made on a regular and timely basis and without any notice. Also, all beneficiaries can be held to the guarantee if the entrepreneur should die before the loan is paid. All collection and attorney fees incurred in collecting money from guarantors can be added to the loan balance that is due. Fortunately, very few guarantors are called upon to pay off a loan.

Ongoing Communication After the Loan Is Made

There is an old adage that says, "Bankers hate surprises." Loans are made to an entrepreneurial venture based on future performance, which is reflected in its projected financial statements. As was discussed in Chapters 4 and 5, projected financial statements are created in large part by generating any number of assumptions regarding both revenues and costs. It is the entrepreneur's responsibility to provide information to the banker on progress toward the projected financial performance. Banks will require certain financial statements at predetermined intervals of time (i.e., monthly, quarterly, annually). To assist the banker in understanding the actual financial statements, the entrepreneur should also provide updates on the key assumptions behind the projected financial statements so that any variances can be understood.

If assumptions prove to be significantly wrong or certain factors require assumptions to be changed, the entrepreneur should inform the bank as soon as possible about the changing conditions, their impact on the business, and any steps the business is taking to adjust for changing conditions. For example, one group of entrepreneurs faced a market in which their three largest customers merged within a period of six months. The newly merged customer, now representing 80 percent of the entrepreneurs' revenues, was able to demand significant price concessions from the entrepreneurs. The entrepreneurs contacted their banker about the change in projected revenues from this event, the short-term impact on profitability, and steps that were already underway to cut costs and return the business to its targeted profitability. All of this information was provided before the bank would receive the financial statements that reflected the actual impact of these events. Although the bankers paid closer attention to this business during the next few months, the bank considered this communication to be an indication of the strength of management and the relationship remained strong. Had the entrepreneurs not provided the information when they did, the bank would have received financial statements showing much lower profits without an understanding of why this occurred and what was being done to alleviate the situation. In situations such as this, bankers also may be able to provide valuable assistance, such as help in finding new customers, management advice, or even contacts with other sources of capital should it become necessary. Regular communication with the banker may take both written and verbal forms. Such updates can provide the banker with a better understanding of the variations in performance that inevitably occur (Binks and Ennew, 1997).

THE DOWNSIDE OF DEBT

Debt is certainly critical to almost any business venture. However, there are some risks and concerns that debt can create that should always be taken into account. If a business has relied heavily on debt to finance the operation, it can become much more susceptible to downturns in the economy. If a downturn occurs and profits decline, large payments on loans can become difficult or impossible to meet. A similar business with less debt will have more excess cash flow, without the large debt payments, to cushion the blow of declining revenues and profits.

When a business is sold, the buyer may not be willing to assume all, or even any, of the debts of the business. This will require that the entrepreneur pay off all debts before any money can be distributed to the owners. Because taxes owed on the proceeds of a sale are typically calculated without consideration of any debt that must be paid off, entrepreneurs who have relied heavily on debt can have little or no money left after the sale of their businesses. The exit process will be discussed in more detail in Part III of this book.

Lenders, particularly bankers, can impose many restrictions on a company as part of the terms of the loan. These restrictions may limit the entrepreneur's freedom to make some decisions on major issues affecting the business, such as expansion, payment of dividends to shareholders, or compensation of management.

Finally, as some forms of debt require personal guarantees by both the entrepreneur and his or her spouse, increasing use of debt can create tension or conflict in the entrepreneur's family. Guarantees of debt may not be a significant issue when a business is young and the entrepreneur has little real wealth, but as the business grows and succeeds, the entrepreneur can amass real wealth that is at risk if the business suddenly begins to falter.

SUMMARY

This chapter has discussed debt as a source of funding for entrepreneurial ventures. Sources of short-term debt include trade debt, bank debt, asset-based lenders, and factors. Sources of long-term debt include banks, real estate lenders, and leasing companies. The Small Business Administration can guarantee bank loans for some small business uses. Entrepreneurs must learn to develop a good working relationship with their bankers and create a strategy that can include an array of sources of debt funding. Finally, debt, although used by almost all businesses to some degree, requires prudent and careful planning. The next two chapters will examine equity sources of funds for entrepreneurial ventures.

DISCUSSION QUESTIONS

1. Discuss the various types of short-term credit. What are the best uses for each type? What should an entrepreneur do to establish each form of short-term credit?
2. How can entrepreneurs manage their own business's credit risk?
3. Discuss the various types of long-term credit. What are the best uses for each type? What should an entrepreneur do to establish each form of long-term credit?
4. What are the roles of bankers and the government in the SBA lending process?
5. Discuss the advantages and disadvantages of debt financing for entrepreneurial ventures.

OPPORTUNITIES FOR APPLICATION

1. Choose one form of debt financing, and conduct two interviews: the first with a person who is a source of such financing; the second with an entrepreneur who used such financing. Describe the form of debt financing from both the source's and the entrepreneur's point of view.
2. Write a plan to build relationships with various sources of debt financing (bankers, suppliers, etc.) for a new business venture you are developing.

REFERENCE

Blechman, B., and Levinson, J. (1991).
  Guerrilla Financing. Boston: Houghton
  Mifflin. http://www.sba.gov/financing

CHAPTER
11

External Sources
of Funds: Equity

The previous chapter discussed using debt to generate funding for an entrepreneurial venture. Debt financing involves a contractual, temporary use of funding provided by an outside person or entity. Debt creates an obligation to repay the funding provided to the business. Equity financing, on the other hand, creates a more permanent relationship in which ownership interests are transferred to the person or entity providing funds.

Equity in a business reflects the owners' investment in a business. This investment comes from capital invested by the owners and through profits generated by the business, less any distribution of profits taken by the owners. In the accounting equation (see Chapter 3), equity equals assets minus liabilities. From a financing perspective, equity also can refer to the actual market value of a business if it were to be sold to new owners on the open market. *Equity funding* of a business is the exchange of a share of ownership in return for a capital investment, which an entrepreneur may use during the start-up of a business. But it also can be a source of funding to support the growth of business during periods of significant expansion.

Equity funding is generally an investment that is made with the expectation of a return on that investment. Such returns can come from future cash flows from the business, selling the business, taking a business public, or from the repurchase of stock. Equity investors generally hope to realize a certain return from their investment, but because the investment is in equity and is fully at risk, no formal expectation of a return can be provided.

This chapter examines the basic approaches to equity financing, including investment by the entrepreneur, friends and family, strategic partners, angels, private placements, and SBICs. Discussion will include how each equity strategy works and the best uses for each approach. Venture capital financing, which is also a form of equity funding generally reserved for use with high-growth ventures, will be discussed in detail in Chapter 12.

FUNDING FROM THE ENTREPRENEUR

The initial source of equity funding is the investment made by the entrepreneur(s) who founded the business. Entrepreneurs will often use personal assets—such as savings accounts, investments, retirement accounts, and cash value of life insurance—to fund their business ventures during start-up. Entrepreneurs also may incur personal debt, through second mortgages and personal lines of credit, to create cash that can be invested in their businesses. While there are many stories of entrepreneurs using credit card debt to fund their businesses, this is an expensive source of money and is not recommended by most experts. In addition, using personal credit cards to fund a business is explicitly prohibited in most credit card contracts. As discussed in Chapter 10, personal investment in the business by the entrepreneur is considered important by many debt-funding sources. This also is true with many equity investors, who want to see the entrepreneurs personally sharing in the business risk.

There is another form of "investment" in a business that can be made by the entrepreneur. This investment is the time and effort put into the business for which the entrepreneur is not compensated with true market salary, or possibly any salary at all. Such an investment is referred to as *sweat equity*. Although sweat equity is not reflected on the balance sheet, the entrepreneur is willing to work for below-market compensation in the belief that it will help build the market value of the business. It is advisable to attempt to keep track of sweat equity, as both sources of debt and equity funding may be willing to consider sweat equity as evidence of the entrepreneur's commitment to the business. Although only a subjective estimate, it may help build the case for raising outside funding. The entrepreneur should not view such an investment as an "IOU," as this diminishes the "equity" nature of the sweat equity. Also, investors will want their funds to go toward growing the business and not toward paying off informal debts to the entrepreneur.

FAMILY AND FRIENDS

Friends, family members, and even business associates are some of the most common sources of financing for entrepreneurial ventures. Sometimes this source of funding may be considered a loan. However, in other situations the funding may be made as an investment. In either case, it is advisable to avoid the temptation to keep the transaction informal. Creating written documentation may seem awkward, but such documents can prevent any misunderstandings in the future. If the money is given as a loan, the terms of the loan should be made explicit in the document. If the funding is made as an equity investment, an attorney should be retained to make certain that all legal requirements are met. It is important that the entrepreneur fully understand the expectations of family and friends who invest in the business. And it is also important to provide family and friends with full, accurate, and honest information about the business. The potential for a downturn in the business, or even business failure, should be part of the exchange of information *before* funding is provided to avoid potential conflicts. Once a loan or an investment is made, it is important to keep the business and personal relationships as distinct as possible. Many a friendship has been ruined, and many a family has been torn apart, by business problems that arose due to poor planning or inaccurate information.

STRATEGIC PARTNERS

Certain businesses may be interested in providing equity financing to entrepreneurs because of their close business relationships or the potential for mutually beneficial working relationships in the future. Businesses with such close relationships are known as *strategic partners* or *strategic alliances.* Strategic partners can be suppliers, customers, or other businesses operating in the same industry. For example, a supplier may decide to invest in a new company that can help get its products distributed into a new market. Another example of a strategic partner is a large manufacturing company that invests in small local suppliers of raw materials or packaging. Yet another example would be a large company in the same industry investing in a start-up company that has a completely new product or service. This is quite common in the pharmaceutical industry.

Most strategic partners have lower expectations for financial returns than investors such as angels (discussed in the next section). These firms expect a closer relationship if the venture begins to succeed, which will create market advantages. For example, many of the pharmaceutical companies that invest in start-ups may plan to purchase the business if it succeeds, or at least have the ability to market any new drugs that are developed, which can create a long-term profit for the larger company. Clearly, an advantage of a strategic partner is that it knows the business and can make a quick decision with less development work. The costs associated with strategic partner investments are often quite a bit lower than other forms of equity investment.

Most strategic partners are companies with which the entrepreneur is already doing business, so initiating contact is rather simple. If the potential strategic partner is a new contact for the entrepreneur, it is relatively easy for both sides to learn more about the other through industry contacts. It is important for both sides to take the time to determine their level of comfort with the new possible relationship as business partners. The corporate cultures of the two businesses should be evaluated to determine if they might clash, creating difficulty in working together over the long term. Also, it is important to understand expectations of both sides for governance and control. Some strategic partners play a very hands-off, passive role in companies in which they invest, whereas others will expect a seat on the board of directors or other significant roles in decision making. The exit plan should be clearly discussed to prevent avoidable surprises in the future.

ANGEL INVESTORS

Angels are individuals who invest directly in entrepreneurial ventures. Angels have enough personal wealth to invest part of their personal portfolios, typically between 1 to 10 percent, in riskier investments in start-up or growing companies. Angels have acquired their wealth from any number of sources and could be professionals, such as physicians, attorneys, accountants, executives in large corporations, or successful entrepreneurs. Still others may have acquired their wealth through an inheritance. What angels share is a desire to invest directly in companies that have the potential for a higher rate of return than traditional equity investments in public companies. Most angels can be considered sophisticated investors who understand the risks they are assuming with this type of investment.

Most angels are interested in a deal size between $10,000 and $1 million. Larger deals will attract only a small number of angels—to fund a $1 million deal typically suggests a net worth of up to $100 million. Also, angels often are involved in multiple ventures, so the investment in any one deal will not reflect the total funding they are willing to put into entrepreneurial ventures. Most angels are looking for a payoff within three to seven years. They do not desire year-to-year distribution of profits, and in fact may view such a distribution negatively because they generally want profits to be retained to fund growth. In the end, they hope to realize an approximate 20–50 percent annual return, depending primarily on the level of risk the angel perceives in the entrepreneurial investment.

For example, assume an angel is interested in investing $100,000 in a fairly new venture that has growth potential. This angel is willing to leave the money in this business for about five years and is hoping for an annual rate of return of about 30 percent. A quick estimate of what the angel hopes to see in five years is

$$\$100,000 \times 1.3^5 = \$371,293$$

The angel will want to see an exit strategy that will allow for cashing out of the investment within five years. This can occur though the sale of the business, the repurchase of the angel's stock by the company, second-stage investment by a venture capital firm, or a public offering of the company. The angel also will try to determine an estimate of the value of the business in five years in order to negotiate enough ownership in the business to realize the desired return. Assume that, based on the business plan, a reasonable estimate of the value of the business in five years is $3 million. The angel investor will probably want a percentage of ownership based on the following:

$$\$371,293 \text{ Desired Return} / \$3 \text{ Million Estimated Value} = 12.38\% \text{ Ownership}$$

Much of this calculation is based on estimates and assumptions, so the angel may try to negotiate for a number of shares of stock that roughly reflects that percentage of ownership. Some angels may insist on more sophisticated valuations, but many are willing to use simple methods due to the high degree of uncertainty in any multiyear estimate of an entrepreneurial venture. (The exit process and valuation will be discussed in more detail in Chapters 13–14).

Angels are generally willing to provide seed funding for start-ups or second-stage funding that will help an existing business grow. Angels generally do not like retail businesses unless they have the potential to grow into multiunit operations. Some angels tend to specialize in an industry that they have knowledge about or experience in for their investments. Others may look for opportunities in a "hot industry." For example, it was relatively easier to find angel investors in the health care industry during the late 1980s and early 1990s; by the later 1990s, technology was the favored industry.

Finding angel investors can be a challenge. As one angel said, "You're not going to find me in the Yellow Pages." In fact, many angels closely guard their privacy to avoid being overwhelmed by entrepreneurs looking for funding. To illustrate, one of the authors of this book was interviewed by a local newspaper for a story on angel investors. Only one brief quote was used for the article, but that quote generated dozens of calls from entrepreneurs asking for help finding investors. So where and how are angels found? First, many angels work through their attorneys, accountants, bankers, or other professional advisors to help identify possible investment opportunities. Therefore, entrepreneurs must develop a network that will help gain visibility in this group of intermediaries in their local community. These intermediaries may then be willing to make a referral, which is the preferred method of contact for most angel investors (Kelly and Hay, 1996). Second, many programs for connecting entrepreneurs and angels are sponsored by universities or other neutral institutions. Third, some business brokers or smaller investment bankers specialize in connecting angels with entrepreneurs. However, this approach can require large fees that will add to the cost of finding an investor. Finally, some entrepreneurs find angels though matchmaking Web sites and magazines that present profiles of businesses for angels to review. One matchmaking source is ACE-Net, which is a nonprofit supported by the Small Business Administration set up to help entrepreneurs and qualified investors network with each other over the Internet. Generally, the entrepreneur will have to pay a fee, either directly or indirectly, to get the business profiled by any of these matchmakers.

Once contact is established between a potential angel investor and an entrepreneur, an initial meeting will be set up to help both sides begin to gauge the fit between the angel and the entrepreneur and the business (see Box 11-1). Most angels report that these initial meetings are primarily to help them evaluate the entrepreneur more than the business. As one angel said, "I invest in people, not in businesses." Entrepreneurs also must understand that this is their opportunity to assess the angel as a person. The angel, if he or she invests in the business, will become one of the owners: The angel is a new partner. The same angel advised entrepreneurs to consider that "angels are not just a source of cash like a bank. The entrepreneur should make sure that the angel is someone they want to be in business with."

If initial meetings generate continued interest by both sides, more detailed discussions can ensue about the business itself and the angel's expectations. This leads to an attempt to develop a general agreement on a deal structure for the investment. The structure of any deal varies based on type of business, but many

BOX 11-1

In Their Own Words . . . An Angel Investor

Although they have been around for as long as there have been entrepreneurs with opportunities but little of their own capital, angel investors recently have become more widely recognized as a source of equity financing. Here is a description of what an angel investor looks for when working with entrepreneurs *in his own words:*

> When an entrepreneur is deciding to work with an angel he should make sure that their strategy is the same: when to get in, how to run the business, and when to exit. Deciding on the exit strategy beforehand is crucial. I have seen many times the entrepreneur wanting to build the business beyond what the angel wants. This should all be resolved in the beginning.
>
> Angels are looking to make a substantial return in a potentially risky investment. One thing entrepreneurs imagine about angels is that they have so much money that their investments don't matter to them. This couldn't be farther from the truth. We care a lot about who and what we invest in. We want to work with

someone who has a well-thought-out plan and understands what it is going to take to become successful. One of the biggest mistakes entrepreneurs make is in their presentation to an angel investor. Most entrepreneurs when they come and do a presentation (you will get about a 30-minute attention span from an angel) make the mistake of spending 25 of those minutes talking about how good their widget is and the other 5 minutes talking about the financial implications. What the entrepreneur should do is concentrate his time on what the investment is, what the person is going to get out of it, what the return is going to be in a certain period of time. He should then spend the rest of the five minutes on proving how great his product is. If entrepreneurs do it the other way around, the angel's mind begins to wander because he has no idea what he has to put in, what the returns are going to be, and what he is going to get out of it. You have to remember angels are out to make a risk–reward return. They don't fall in love with a widget; they are investing in a product and expect a return for their money.

Interview with John M. Morrison, angel investor, Minneapolis, Minnesota.

angels will want preferred stock if possible to provide a little more protection for their investment. Some angels will want to have a position on the board of directors, or at least have some decision-making role, such as veto power over major decisions. Communication is an important part of the relationship with an angel, and specific expectations for information may actually be formalized in the deal itself. In almost all situations, the angel will not want to be involved in day-to-day operations. As one angel put it, "I want to own the restaurant, but I don't want to flip hamburgers." Generally, angels will provide a much quicker decision about their investment than other equity sources. The final steps involve the angel conducting due diligence on the investment (i.e., verifying all of the key information supplied by the company) and the entrepreneur's attorney creating all of the legal documents needed to complete the investment.

PRIVATE PLACEMENT

Individual or small groups of investment angels may not always be an option for an entrepreneurial venture. In such situations, it may be necessary to offer equity investments to a wider group of people who would consider making smaller individual investments in the firm. It is possible to raise equity capital through a process of offering unregistered securities to a certain type of investor. This form of equity financing is known as a *private placement* or a *private offering*. Any placement that goes beyond the regulatory and legal limits of a private offering must follow the full registration process for public offerings. The registration process is costly and leads to significant public reporting requirements from the company for as long as it is considered a publicly held business.

The Securities and Exchange Commission (SEC) has set specific limitations on private stock offerings. Private placements usually have lower expectations of return on investment than some other forms of equity financing, particularly venture capital, and therefore will result in less dilution of the entrepreneur's equity. In other words, venture capitalists often require high equity stakes in a business to be able to realize the high returns that they expect from their investments. Transaction costs in private placements tend to be among the highest of all forms of equity financing due to legal compliance requirements, and the relative time to raise funds can be quite lengthy.

A private offering can only be made to what is known as either a *qualified* or an *accredited investor*. Qualified investors must be able to demonstrate knowledge, financial strength, and investment experience that prove they can tolerate the risk of such an investment. For example, a health care company was established in a southeastern state to build a contracting network for health care providers wanting to contract with large insurance companies and self-insured employers. The company needed to raise about $800,000, which was to be used to pay for professional management and staff to build the network and develop software systems. Potential investors for this venture included individual physicians and health care companies, such as labs, clinics, and hospitals in the region. All of the investors were wealthy, experienced investors and had a good understanding of the industry.

An accredited investor must be one of the following:

1. Any national bank
2. Any corporation or business trust with assets in excess of $5 million
3. Any insider of the issuing company (officer, director, or owner)
4. Any individual with income over $200,000 or couple with income over $300,000 (two years of income at these levels and reasonable expectations for the continuation of this level of income)
5. Any individual with net worth in excess of $1 million

The amount of capital that can be raised through a private placement varies based on the number and mix of investors. These restrictions are spelled out in what are known as safe-harbor exemptions. SEC Rule 504 applies to offerings up to $1 million dollars. Under this rule, the restrictions of the private placement are the most flexible. Under Rule 505, private offerings can be up to $5 million, but they must meet more restrictive requirements to still be exempt from registration. Under Rule 506, it is possible to raise more than $5 million, but again the requirements are even more specific and restrictive. Under all of these exemptions, no public advertising is allowed. Other exceptions to stock registration allow for offerings over the Internet and offerings to employees, all of which have very specific limitations and requirements. All exemptions have specific reporting requirements to the SEC to ensure compliance with the various rules.

Because advertising and formal promotion of private offerings is prohibited, potential investors are generally found through personal networking, which can be a very time-consuming process of building referral upon referral. The entrepreneur initially supplies basic information on the business to determine the general comfort level and fit of each potential investor. If interest seems significant, additional information is supplied, which must comply with any formal requirements of a private placement. It should be made clear to the investors how they will be represented on the board of directors and what routine communication will be supplied to shareholders.

The primary disadvantage of this strategy is the complexity it can create for the entrepreneur. Even a fairly limited private offering can create a large number of shareholders to whom the entrepreneur is now accountable as fellow owners of the business. Because the transfer of stock is usually restricted, any shareholder problems will be long term, for a disgruntled investor cannot simply dispose of the stock, as is the case in a publicly traded company. Management of the board becomes a much more formal, complex, and even political process that can take up much of the entrepreneur's valuable time. The founder of the health care company in the earlier example reported that he spent as much as one to two days a week just on shareholder and board-related issues during the first two years of operation.

SBICS

A Small Business Investment Company (SBIC) is a privately owned and managed investment company that is licensed by the SBA. SBICs can provide a combination of equity investments and long-term loans to small businesses (see Box 11-2). Because the funding is, in part, backed by the federal government, the risk is much lower to the investors in the SBIC. Therefore, the rate of return expected by the SBIC is much lower than angel, private placements, or venture capital investment. This opens SBIC funding up to much smaller businesses with more limited growth potential. The SBA provides up to three times the capital invested in the SBIC through guaranteed notes to leverage the funding to help more small businesses. The limitations and restrictions on the small businesses supported through the SBIC are similar to those found in SBA loan programs (see Chapter 10).

BOX 11-2

In Their Own Words . . . An SBIC Leveraged Fund

In addition to SBA loan programs, the Small Business Administration supports another program known as SBIC. Here is a description of what an SBIC licensee looks for when working with entrepreneurs *in his own words:*

Some venture capitalists are able to qualify for a SBIC license, which allows them to use SBIC leverage to increase the amount of capital under management. Usually, the SBIC leverage is two times the private capital, so $25 million of private capital can become a $75 million venture fund with 2:1 leverage from the SBA. Entrepreneurs often have some misconceptions about SBIC leverage funds. Some entrepreneurs think that there are lower hurdles or different hurdles to get money out of an SBIC leverage fund compared to a venture capitalist. This is just not true. The companies have to have the same potential as if they were going to a normal venture capitalist. The only difference is a portion of our funding is from SBIC leverage rather than traditional limited partners. The SBA does, however, put some restrictions on the types of businesses that are eligible investments. The investment hurdles such as market size, management, valuations, intellectual property, etc., are the same as all other investment opportunities.

When I meet with an entrepreneur about possibly investing in their business, the most important thing is for them to give me a very concise message. The first 10 to 15 minutes of a presentation needs to convey why this idea is so compelling I have to invest; this is really hard for some people. We look at a lot of opportunities and if you don't get me excited within the first 10 minutes about learning more during a presentation, then I have a hard time getting interested. It sounds harsh, but the reality is you have to be able to express why this is an exciting technology or idea and why investors would be interested in it. If you can't do this, you'll lose my interest and my investment. Bottom line: SBIC leverage funds are venture capitalists, they just get part of their money from a different source. My advice is to be as prepared with them as you are with any traditional venture fund or any other equity investors.

Interview with Buzz Benson, Piper Jaffray Healthcare Capital, L.P., Minneapolis, Minnesota.

THE DOWNSIDE OF EQUITY FINANCING

Equity financing can be an effective source of funding for entrepreneurial ventures. This is particularly true for businesses that cannot meet the funding requirements to use only debt financing or that need more capital than can realistically be raised through debt. However, there are some cautions that should be understood about equity financing before an entrepreneur decides to raise money using this method of funding.

A common concern with equity financing is dilution, which was discussed previously in this chapter. Equity financing reduces the ownership percentage of the founding entrepreneurs, thus reducing their share of any profits and any wealth created through the venture. The business must get that much larger for them to reach the financial goals that they established for their business. However, they may need to create a much bigger pie to have any chance at all of reaching the entrepreneur's personal goals. Therefore, dilution may be a necessary aspect of their business and financing models.

Some entrepreneurs who are desperate to raise money for their businesses end up taking equity funding from less than scrupulous individuals, sometimes called *sharks*. Sensing the entrepreneur's vulnerability, these investors will demand much more of an ownership stake than the deal actually requires, based on their investment. For example, one entrepreneur had developed a process to turn corn waste products into fuel pellets. Eager to start the business, he rushed into a financing arrangement with a small group that demanded 90 percent ownership in the venture. However, if the typical rate of return for such an angel investor were applied, the entrepreneur should have given up no more than 30 or at the very most 40 percent ownership to these investors. Also, the investors had voting control of the company and within six months fired the entrepreneur from his own company. By the time he sought advice from his local Small Business Development Center, it was already too late for him to save his interest in the company. Unfortunately, analysis of the original deal showed that this was a fundable deal with more reasonable terms if only the entrepreneur had more fully understood financing and had been more patient to find the right investors.

When using equity funding strategies, the entrepreneur is adding on new partners or shareholders in the business. Even if the original ownership structure had more than one owner, adding on more can create interesting dynamics. Many entrepreneurs report that partnership relationships can be as complex as a marriage. The commitment is long term and, in reality, indefinite. It also involves sharing something, the venture, which can elicit strong emotional reactions from the founding entrepreneurs. For example, a group of three entrepreneurs had been in business together for several years. Although their relationship had been at times quite volatile, they had matured into a strong working partnership. The opportunity for significant growth had led them to bring in an angel investor. "The balance that the three of us had developed in our working relationship was instantly torn apart," reported one of the entrepreneurs. "Although the investor was a great guy, it created a whole new set of relationships among the four of us to be worked out, even though he was not very active in day-to-day operations. It took us several more years to reestablish the trust and positive relationships that the three of us had developed before our new partner came in."

WORKING WITH OUTSIDE INVESTORS

Standard procedures are typically followed when working with debt financing. For example, although each bank may have different forms and procedures, most banks follow very similar processes when making loans. Equity financing, particularly through sources other than venture capitalists (Chapter 12), has no real standard procedures or processes. Each deal and each equity investor can vary significantly. However, there are some common elements to equity financing negotiations, particularly regarding the key documents that are used by most potential equity investors. The specific requirements may vary, but most will require the following items.

Business Plan

The business plan can take many forms and use different formats depending on the audience and intended use of the document. Almost any business plan will include a discussion of the various component plans, including the marketing, financial, operating, and staffing plans. Equity investors expect four specific elements in addition to the traditional parts of the plan. First, a clear description of the company, including its history, developmental stage, and goals. The discussion should be an honest appraisal and not a sales pitch. For example, if there is only a limited probability that the goals will actually be met, that should be stated in this plan. Second, the product and market description should be factual and cautious. Overselling potential will only lead to problems with investors down the road. A thorough and factual description of competition also should be included. Third, there should be a realistic description of the management team, including any specific deals or commitments made to these individuals by the company, such as stock options or profit sharing. Finally, a clear and factual assessment of all risks should be fully disclosed. Experienced investors understand that any entrepreneurial venture has risk and uncertainty associated with it. The business plan should provide them with as full and complete description of the potential downside aspects of the venture as possible. Rather than scaring these investors away, the plan will show that the venture has been fully thought through and will provide them with vital information to assign the true risk of the deal in negotiating an ownership stake in the company. Although experienced investors realize that surprises will occur, they do not want any information withheld that is known by the current ownership, because once the investment is made, they are part of that very group.

Confidentiality Agreement

Before any detailed information is shared, a confidentiality agreement should be signed by the entrepreneur and the potential investor. More experienced investors will often have their own form of confidentiality agreement. Any confidentiality agreement should be reviewed or written by the entrepreneur's attorney. In fact, it is advisable that an attorney with expertise in mergers and acquisitions be used throughout negotiations for equity investments. Confidentiality agreements for equity investments typically bind both parties to limit the sharing and use of any information used in discussions and negotiations. The entrepreneur needs to protect proprietary competitive information and the investors will most often seek to keep their financial information secret. Most agreements will require that any written information that is shared be returned if the deal does not go through. Violation of the terms of a confidentiality agreement used in equity financing can have significant consequences. Agreements should therefore be entered into carefully and with complete understanding of the terms of the agreement.

Letter of Intent

If the investor is interested in pursuing ownership in the venture, and the basic terms of the investment are agreed upon, a letter of intent is usually issued by the investor and signed by the entrepreneur. This letter commits both parties to take the necessary steps to complete the deal, including full disclosure of required information. However, such negotiations often fail, and the letter allows for both parties to withdraw under reasonable circumstances. Such a letter usually restricts the entrepreneur from negotiating with other potential investors while current negotiations are under way. Although a letter of intent is a commitment to negotiate a deal *in good faith,* the majority of deals will fail before they reach a final agreement.

Modifications of Shareholder Agreements

If an agreement for a private investor to invest in a venture is reached, modification of existing shareholder or partnership agreements is usually required. For example, the investor may require participation as a member of the board of directors, there may be limitations on distribution of earnings until certain milestones are reached, or there may be a change in the decision-making responsibility of the chief executive officer, keeping more authority with the board for strategic decisions and for commitment to purchase significant new assets, such as a new factory building.

The level and means of communication with the new shareholders or partners should be agreed upon fully and clearly from the beginning. Investors have their own criteria to determine when they want to be notified outside of normal meetings and reports to shareholders. Some investors require regular updates and notification if any variations from the plan arise. Others only want to be notified if significant events occur, good or bad. The definition of *significant* should be clear to both parties. For example, one angel investor considered any event that could end up in the newspaper or in court as significant. For anything else he would wait until the normal monthly reports were given at the meeting of the board of directors. The most important thing to remember is that the investor is now in most cases a full partner in the business and should be treated with the honesty and integrity that a partner deserves. The investment is based in large part on trust, and that trust should be respected and valued by the entrepreneur.

DEVELOPING A FINANCING PLAN

The vast majority of entrepreneurs use some combination of the debt financing mechanisms discussed in Chapter 10 and the equity funding strategies discussed in this chapter. Although venture capitalists are often discussed in association with entrepreneurial ventures, the actual number of new businesses funded by venture capital amounts to only a fraction of a percent. Therefore, before moving into high-growth venture capital financing in Chapter 12, a model for developing a basic financing plan (using debt and equity) that applies to most entrepreneurial ventures will be discussed.

An effective financing plan first and foremost is derived from realistic and complete forecasts. Knowledge of all fixed assets needed by the business and the cash flow projections showing operating cash flow shortfalls during start-up are critical for the development of financing plans. The tools and techniques discussed in Chapters 4–6 should give a reasonable view of the financing that is required. The assumptions used in financial forecasts can be more important than the actual statements produced in the forecasting process, so these should be clearly outlined and then evaluated to assess their accuracy.

Entrepreneurs rarely raise all the funding they initially think they must have for their ventures, so a clear understanding of priorities for funding should be developed. What expenditures are critical, that is, those without which the business will never get started? This category could include key equipment or money to pay the salary of key staff. As discussed in Chapter 8, overhead expenses can be the undoing of many start-ups. Initial funding should be targeted for the operation of the business, and any nonessential expenses should be delayed, which may require operating out of a basement, bedroom, or garage. Effective bootstrapping can drastically reduce the actual need for financing and should be part of the financial planning process.

While the entrepreneur may initially assume that a single source will provide funding, the reality is that most ventures are funded by an array of sources. In their book *Guerrilla Financing,* Blechman and Levinson (1991) recommend that an entrepreneur first create a list of all assets that can directly or indirectly be funded through debt. The entrepreneur should then match those assets with the most appropriate source of funding, which may include either debt or equity investment.

For example, let us assume that Sally Warner, an entrepreneur, estimates that she will need about $500,000 to start her business. She derived this estimate from talking to other entrepreneurs with similar businesses. In developing her financing plan, Sally determines what assets her business will have to fund her venture. Table 11-1 displays the list of assets and the loans that they may help to support. These loans may

TABLE 11-1   Example of Assets and Potential Funding Generated

Asset	Estimated Value	Percentage Financed	Potential Funding Generated
Customer purchase orders	$ 50,000	70	$ 35,000
Accts. receivable (< 60 days)	80,000	70	56,000
Inventory	20,000	30	6,000
Leasehold improvements	10,000	50	5,000
Building	120,000	70	84,000
Undeveloped land	40,000	40	16,000
Equipment	15,000	80	12,000
Total of Business Funding Sources	**$335,000**		**$214,000**

come from a variety of sources. For example, the entrepreneur may be able to get a bank to issue a line of credit based on accounts receivable and customer purchase orders, a real estate lender to finance land and buildings, and a leasing company to fund equipment purchases. In this example, the entrepreneur is able to fund—through various sources of debt—as much as $214,000 from the $335,000 in assets that the business owns or will own once operational.

The forecasted financial statements developed for Sally's business show cash flow projections that include both operating cash flow needs and assets that will need to be purchased. She has carefully evaluated these projections and determined there is some room for bootstrapping the venture during start-up. The total financing required is thus estimated to be about $380,000, rather than the $500,000 initially estimated.

The entrepreneur's personal assets (such as bank accounts, retirement accounts, and publicly traded stocks) are worth $150,000 and another $120,000 can be borrowed by pledging these assets. Therefore, between debt financing of $214,000 using the various business assets and investing personal equity of $120,000 raised from personal assets, the entrepreneur will have $334,000 of the $380,000 to fund the venture, which leaves $46,000 in equity that needs to be raised to fund the assets of the business. She is reasonably confident that she can go to friends and family for this amount of funding. This example demonstrates the variety of funding sources that can go into the financing plan of a single deal.

SUMMARY

The typical sources of equity financing include friends and family, strategic partners, angel investors, private placements, and SBICs. Equity financing, although an effective means of raising funds for many entrepreneurial ventures, brings with it some potential disadvantages in the form of dilution, shark investors, and additional business partners. The process of working with equity investors varies significantly, but most deals share basic documentation, including the business plan, a confidentiality agreement, and a letter of intent. A financing plan should be developed that incorporates both debt and equity financing. The next chapter will examine a more specialized form of equity funding known as venture capital.

DISCUSSION QUESTIONS

1. Discuss the various types of equity financing. What are the best uses for each type? What should an entrepreneur do to generate each form of equity financing?
2. What are the key steps in the private placement process? Be sure to discuss any limitations or restrictions on this equity strategy.
3. What are the roles of the SBIC and the government in the SBIC program?
4. Discuss the advantages and disadvantages of equity financing for entrepreneurial ventures.
5. Discuss the relative advantages and disadvantages of debt and equity financing. What are the key differences between these strategies?

OPPORTUNITIES FOR APPLICATION

1. Choose one form of equity financing, and conduct two interviews, the first with a person who is a source of such financing and the second with an entrepreneur who used such financing. Describe the form of equity financing from both the source's and the entrepreneur's point of view.
2. Write a plan to build relationships with sources of equity financing for a new business venture you are developing.
3. Write an overall financing plan (including all sources of debt and equity financing) for a new business venture you are developing.

REFERENCES

Bagley, C., and Dauchy, C. (1998). *The Entrepreneur's Guide to Business Law*. New York: West.

Blechman, B., and Levinson, J. (1991). *Guerrilla Financing*. Boston: Houghton Mifflin.

Freer, J., Sohl, J., and Wetzel, W. (1996). Technology due diligence: What angels consider important. In P. D. Reynolds, et al. (eds.). *Frontiers of Entrepreneurship Research*. Babson Park, MA: Babson Center for Entrepreneurial Studies, pp. 359–360. http://www.sba.gov/financing

Kelly, P., and Hay, M. (1996). Serial investors: An exploratory study. In P. D. Reynolds, et al. (eds.). *Frontiers of Entrepreneurship Research*. Babson, MA: Babson Center for Entrepreneurial Studies, pp. 329–343.

CHAPTER
12

Financing the
High-Growth Business

Entrepreneurs with ventures that have the potential for high growth can face major challenges in financing the operating and capital needs that these businesses face throughout their development. Although high-growth ventures are relatively rare, their impact can be significant. Companies such as Dell, Intel, Microsoft, and Gateway have not only created wealth for their founders and investors but also created thousands of jobs that have transformed their home communities. Some have even created entire new industries. High-growth ventures most often require financing on the scale of millions of dollars, which is normally the domain of equity investors known as venture capitalists (see Box 12-1). Venture capitalists manage venture funds. A fund pools investments from a variety of large investors, such as pension funds, life insurance companies, and even some very wealthy individuals. The purpose of a fund is to invest in high-growth and high-potential companies. Because these investments carry significant risks, the investors' expectations of returns can exceed 70 percent capital appreciation.

INTEGRATING PROFITABILITY EXPECTATIONS IN THE BUSINESS PLAN

Raising money for a high-growth venture is one of the most difficult activities that an entrepreneur can undertake. When making a request, one should be aware that the potential investor's time is just as valuable as the money. Because venture capital firms have such high expectations of returns on their investments in growing companies, it is critical to integrate these expectations into the financial forecasts in the business plan. Therefore, before approaching a venture capitalist or any other financing source, it can be valuable to revisit the business plan applying a technique called the *reverse income statement,* which is based on the discovery-driven planning model first discussed in Chapter 1.

The concept of the reverse income statement is to start with the required level of profit and work backwards. The required level of profit is the minimum profit necessary to pay an adequate return to the investors.

BOX 12-1

In Their Own Words ... A Venture Capitalist

Venture capitalists are often closely linked to high-growth entrepreneurial ventures. Here is a description of what a venture capitalist looks for when working with entrepreneurs *in his own words:*

Venture capitalists look to invest in companies that are trying to make a major advance in their market by developing a product or service that is fundamentally better, faster, or cheaper than the alternatives. We typically invest in a company when they are still in the development stage and have yet to make a sale or validate their product. In exchange for taking the risk associated with investing at this early stage, investors in venture capital funds expect to generate compound annual returns well above what is offered in the broader public markets—typically targeting 20 percent or more across the portfolio of companies.

To find these returns, venture capitalists screen for several key attributes. First, we like to see a large and growing market opportunity, typically in excess of a billion dollars at maturity. Large markets are more likely to support new company formation and generate large returns. The rate of growth is also an important measure of the value creation potential that exists in the market—when a small company catches or creates a rapidly growing wave, great things can happen.

The second area of focus for venture capitalists is on the management team. We are looking for an entrepreneurial team with the skills, experience, passion, and "chemistry" necessary to build a great business. There is much more art than science involved in management assessment, but most venture capitalists would agree that the quality of the team is a critical factor in shaping their interest in an opportunity.

Finally, we are looking for companies that possess some form of enduring competitive advantage. In order to achieve market leadership, an emerging company must have something special that will allow them to prevail in the market. Their advantage could come in the form of differentiated technology, a unique team, or other relationships that contribute to a compelling offering. We spend a great deal of time during due diligence in testing and validating the degree to which this advantage exists.

Interview with Michael Gorman, St. Paul Venture Capital, St. Paul, Minnesota.

$$\text{Minimum Rate of Return} \times \text{Amount Invested} = \text{Required Level of Profit}$$

Once this required level of profit is approximated, the forecasting template that is included with this book can be used to determine the assumptions that will be necessary for the enterprise to generate that level of profit. This can be done by first inserting assumptions that the user believes are supportable and seeing if the spreadsheet model generates an income greater than the required level. If yes, this part of the exercise is finished. If no, then the entrepreneur must experiment by changing assumptions until the spreadsheet eventually records a projected profit that is greater or equal to the required level.

All the assumptions that have been made in order to achieve this calculated level of profit should be recorded and compared to experience or double-checked with other sources to see if they are reasonable. If they are not, the endeavor should not be pursued because the firm will not be able to earn an adequate return for the investors. If a reasonable and supportable set of assumptions generates the required level of profit, then the pursuit of funds can take place. Venture capitalists operate in an environment where investment proposals are based more on assumptions than historical facts because high-growth firms are not traditional, mature enterprises. Therefore, they will be especially interested in the underlying assumptions of the proposal. If unreasonable assumptions have to be created to make a proposal profitable, venture capitalists will probably not be willing to take the risk.

STAGES OF THE FIRM

Entrepreneurs, especially inexperienced ones, have some very serious problems when it comes to raising money. Without a track record of success in creating other companies, the job of convincing potential investors that this particular opportunity is an excellent use of funds becomes more difficult. Even if an entrepreneur does have a track record of success, the task still is not easy. Raising funds is a lot like being a salesperson. One should expect to be told "no" a number of times before getting a "yes." This, however, creates a risky situation for the entrepreneur for a number of reasons:

1. The economic window of opportunity may pass before the funds can be raised.
2. Key employees may not be willing to start work until funding is secured.
3. Sharing information with a potential investor may result in exposing the company's "trade secrets."

This last issue, protecting intellectual property associated with a new business venture, can be one of the most contentious. An entrepreneur is probably not going to have a successful high-growth venture if the plan is to start a firm in a preexisting industry and do what everyone else does. Typically, an opportunity exists because an entrepreneur believes that he or she has discovered a new market that few people know about or a new way to do business in an established market. In other words, a successful business must have some sort of competitive advantage. This advantage could be technological, strategic, or geographic; and it must be of a nature that is unique to this company. However, if that advantage is fully exposed to others, then the door is open for others to do the same thing, thus eliminating that advantage. In a perfect world, it would be optimal for an entrepreneur to share the secret only once and raise a sufficient amount of money at that time. However, it is more likely that several "sales pitches" will have to be made before successful fund-raising takes place, and each time a sales pitch is made, the circle of people who now know of the firm's competitive advantage gets wider and wider.

Typically, funds are raised in stages and not in one lump sum at the front end. Staging of financing allows investors to deal with the uncertainty of the validity of the idea and the untested nature of the management in the enterprise. Stages of funding are typically tied to the stages of business development, which generally progress as follows:

1. *Pre-start-up.* In the pre-start-up stage, the focus is on product research and development. The firm is not ready to invest in infrastructure or employees to actually produce or distribute the product. The firm generates no revenues and has negative net income and cash flow. Cash flow will continue to be negative as the firm invests in development equipment and pays development-type employees, such as engineers and designers.

2. *Start-up.* The start-up phase occurs when the company purchases equipment and hires the employees who will actually produce and distribute the product. Net income and cash flow are still negative as investments in manufacturing equipment and working capital are made. Working capital consists of the increases in inventory and prepaid expenses. This is in addition to the salaries, space rent, and utilities that must be paid during this phase.

3. *Early Growth.* During the early growth stage, cash flow and net income are again still negative. Revenue is now being generated, and potentially the rate of revenue growth could be quite high in percentage terms. However, the actual dollar amount of revenue is low relative to the expenses and investments in working capital, such as accounts receivable and inventory.

4. *Rapid Growth.* This stage is similar to early growth in the sense that cash flow is still negative. However, the negative cash flows will be much higher. A high sales growth rate in percentage terms calculated on a much larger starting base of sales in dollar terms would require very large financing amounts to be needed immediately. This is because of the immediate expenses and working capital that are required now to be able to satisfy the larger volume of sales anticipated to occur in each succeeding sales period.

5. *Mature Growth.* The mature growth phase is a point where the market has become saturated with the product so that the rate of growth, while still positive, is much lower. In this situation, the net income and operating cash flow are ideally positive. The revenues generated in a particular month should be sufficient to cover the investment in working capital necessary to get the firm through the next month and so forth. Some entrepreneurs choose not to operate their firms in this phase. They may hire professional managers to take over at this point, or instead, they may choose to jump to the next phase.

6. *Exit or Harvesting.* The exit or harvesting phase is a time where the purpose of the firm is to generate cash flows and returns for the investors. There are two ways to get cash flow to the investors. One method would be to sell all or part of the firm to other investors or to another company. Another strategy to generate cash flow for the investors would be to operate the firm in such a way as to maximize available cash and allow the investors to take this cash out of the firm through dividends and so on. With this kind of strategy, only the minimal necessary expenditures for working capital and investments in replacement equipment are made. Ironically, a firm can generate its maximum amount of cash during a period of declining sales. Generating cash flow by killing the firm with a slow death is unlikely to be popular with firms that used a number of outside stockholders in the earlier stages. This is because one cannot attract outside investors without a concrete, or at least reasonably thought-out, exit strategy spelled out for the investors at the time the pitch for funding is made.

STAGES OF BUSINESS FUNDING

Funding for high-growth ventures typically parallels the development of new ventures as they emerge and grow. There are four generally recognized stages of funding for such ventures:

1. *Initial-Stage Financing.* The first stage of the firm may have to be initially financed by the founder(s). Sometimes this stage is financed simply with sweat equity and a lot of creative bootstrapping. Angel investors often will play an important role in this stage of a high-potential business. In this "seed round," the firm is still a very early start-up. Initial funding is generally tied to the first one or two stages of business development. Beyond this very initial stage, a high-growth venture may require a much more formal request for funding from a venture capital fund.

2. *First-Round Financing.* For the first round, the company should have refined its business plan, have some of its management team in place, and should be willing to start to develop products and sales. The first round of financing could be large enough to cover the first two stages of business development—pre-start-up and early start-up.

3. *Second-Round Financing.* For this round of financing, the company should have made acceptable progress toward achieving the goals and benchmarks described in its business plan. For instance, at this point the company's sales should have started to increase and the business should be expanding. This round of financing should be of an amount that is consistent with the early and rapid growth phases of the business.

4. *Late-Round Financing.* At this point the company should have been successful in selling to the market and its product should be refined. The idea behind this round of financing is to prepare the firm for eventual exit through an initial public offering or some other major development.

As was stated earlier, in order to raise funds for a new venture, an entrepreneur does not have the same access to liquidity and past history that a publicly traded firm would. Therefore, benchmarks and milestones have to be used in place of statistically based risk and return measures to assess performance. If a firm can achieve the milestones that it set out for itself in the previous stage of financing, then it will have increased its odds of successfully convincing investors to supply funds for the next round of financing. These benchmarks can sometimes be quantitative goals, such as the volume of sales to be achieved by a particular date, or they can be specific accomplishments. The types of goals that are appropriate in a funding request depend upon the stage of development and the corresponding financing round. Some possible milestones include:

INITIAL-STAGE FUNDING

- File for incorporation
- Write business plan
- Find office and development space
- Complete initial design
- Hire key development personnel
- Complete prototype unit
- Complete prototype testing

FIRST-ROUND FINANCING

- Secure key vendors
- Hire key service or manufacturing personnel
- Rent or build manufacturing facility
- Purchase manufacturing equipment
- Market testing
- First sales contract
- Production of first manufactured unit
- First 100, 1,000, 10,000 units, etc.

SECOND-ROUND FINANCING

- Breakeven level of sales
- Development of next generation of product

LATE-ROUND FINANCING

- Initial public offering or sale of business

THE DARK SIDE OF VENTURE CAPITAL FINANCING

Venture capitalists are only really interested in projects that have an extremely large potential payoff. This is because they may take on several proposals and only a minority will succeed. Therefore, the returns of the one that does succeed must cover the costs of the ones that did not. The pressure to realize the returns expected by the fund investors can create significant conflict between the entrepreneur and the venture capitalist, which can have an impact on decisions about staffing, product design, marketing strategy, quality, and rate of growth.

To achieve the desired returns, venture capitalists may insist upon a very large percentage of ownership of the company, which may result in the founders having a minority stake. Venture capitalists want a large percentage of ownership for two reasons: (1) it means that if the company were to succeed the venture capitalist would get a large proportion of the return, and (2) it gives the venture capitalist the ability to take control to protect the investment if confidence is lost in the management team. And this is the rub. The entrepreneurs who founded the venture may soon find themselves on the outside of their own venture if the venture capitalists are not satisfied with their management of the business. Such was the case for the founder of Roller Blade. He found himself out of a job as later-stage financing resulted in ownership that was not pleased with his management of the company and its lack of financial performance in terms of their expectations.

However, there are also examples of businesses that fail because they are *not* willing to take the risk of working with venture capitalists. One of the authors once tried to help some research chemists who claimed to have developed an extremely cheap and extremely fast test for the existence of gram-negative bacteria such as *e. coli* and salmonella. The standard test requires an incubator, a laboratory, and 24 hours. Their test supposedly required a solution that could be squirted on a sample of food or water and a paper test strip that would change color if the bacteria were present. This test could be done in less than 10 minutes at a cost of pennies per trial. The failure to arrange financing that was acceptable to them arose from their unwillingness to accept less than 50 percent ownership under any situation. The funding sources rightly saw that these individuals did not have a history in entrepreneurship and neither did their board of directors. They also had no established system of distribution. In addition, the chemists refused to disclose the formula for their solution or release a sufficient quantity of the solution for outsiders to test because they feared reverse engineering. Hence, the unwillingness of either side to give up control caused this business to not move beyond the most preliminary stages.

INITIAL CONTACT WITH A VENTURE CAPITALIST

Venture capitalists find themselves bombarded with as many proposals from hopeful entrepreneurs as a Hollywood agent is bombarded with scripts from would-be screenwriters. Therefore, to avoid wasting their time, an entrepreneur should do some homework to see which type of venture capitalist is right for a particular proposal. For instance, venture capitalists tend to specialize in particular industries. As an example, if the intention were to start a manufacturing company, it would not do any good to approach a venture capitalist who concentrates exclusively on computer software. Likewise, if a firm is in need of late-stage financing, there is little value in approaching a venture capitalist who specializes in seed-round financing.

Once appropriate potential venture capital firms are identified, the following checklist of information should be created in anticipation of the venture capitalists' requests:

1. *Funding Amount.*   Be specific about the net amount of the loan or equity. Stipulate the actual net amount needed in your hands at draw-down. Be prepared to demonstrate milestones for when additional funds are to be injected.

2. *Duration.*   Although venture capital is an equity investment, the fund managers will want to understand the time frame of their commitment to the deal. A clear exit plan is critical. This will generally be tied to either an initial public offering or some type of sale. No venture capital firm is looking for long-term investments. Typically, three to seven years is the expected duration for most deals.

3. *Summary of the Project.*   Give a brief but factual, detailed summary of the project or transaction. This is most often the executive summary of a fully developed business plan.

4. *Use of Funding.*   Have a clear summary of how the funds will be used and over what period of time. Show milestones when funds are to be injected.

5. *Confirm How the Transaction Will Be Liquidated.*   One of the foremost thoughts in an investor's mind is "How am I going to get my money back?" Be able to show the investor that this has been worked out. The investor might be more inclined to invest if there was not only an exit strategy but also back-up strategies. It also might be helpful to include the following details for the first five years:

   a. Projected revenue stream
   b. Projected cost of goods sold
   c. Projected gross profit
   d. Projected overheads/expenses
   e. Projected net profit
   f. Net present value
   g. Sinking fund or reserve that will be available out of retained profits to repay principal, interest, and so on
   h. Exit strategies for equity investors (IPO, buy-back, merger, etc.)

6. *Investment in the Project.*   State how much money has already been invested in the project to date, and how the funding was used.

7. *Bankers, Lawyers, Accountants, and Consultants.*   Provide the names, addresses, telephone and fax numbers, and e-mail addresses of any person or persons dealing with the transaction.

8. *Unusual or Sensitive Information.*   Be aware that it will be necessary to provide any additional information in support of the application that may be relevant or unique. Disclose negative factors that could affect the project. If requests for funds have been made to other sources and were rejected, one should be prepared to answer why. Due diligence will probably reveal problems anyway.

Standard due diligence as performed by venture capitalists often includes a market review of the product, a background check on the principal agents of the company, a look at competing companies, interviews with potential customers, financial projections, and an analysis of the firm's management. In addition to standard due diligence, a formal legal due diligence will take place as well. A prospective entrepreneur should develop good filing and document-management skills so that when prospective funding sources request documents, the entrepreneur can have them ready. Among the documents to keep handy are sales contracts, lease contracts, employment agreements, confidentiality agreements, the corporate charter and bylaws, and any intellectual property documents such as patents and copyrights. In addition, the minutes and the consents of the board of directors should also be available. Last but not least, there should always be a copy of the company's business plan within easy reach.

Once a venture capitalist is satisfied with the information that the entrepreneur has provided, a term sheet may be issued. A term sheet is a list of proposed terms and provisions for investing. It is not a legally binding contract but it does show a rather serious level of interest on the part of the venture capitalist. Terms or conditions that could be on the term sheet are:

1. The amount of money that the venture capitalist wishes to invest.
2. What percentage of ownership, or at least the number of shares out of the total, that would belong to the venture capitalist.
3. The nature of the investment, such as loan, stock, warrants, and so on.
4. The rights of the venture capitalist vis-à-vis the board of directors.
5. The right of the venture capitalist to eventually register shares for a public offering.
6. Any remaining conditions that have to be met by the entrepreneur, such as periodic reports, financial statements, and so on.
7. An estimate of the valuation of the company.
8. Any specific requirements on what the money is to be used for or specific assets that must be purchased with the funds.

After both parties agree to the term sheet, the next step is the preparation of the stock purchase agreement. The venture capitalist's attorney typically prepares this document. Unlike the term sheet, the stock purchase agreement is official and legally binding. The stock purchase agreement will be more detailed and will outline who is required to pay or be reimbursed for various legal fees and costs.

INITIAL PUBLIC OFFERING (IPO)

Engaging in a public offering means that some of the company's stock is now sold to outside investors through the public stock markets. An IPO is a frequent goal of an entrepreneur, but it is not an absolute requirement. The decision to do an IPO or not do an IPO depends upon weighing the various pros and cons.

Advantages of an IPO

1. *Diversification and Liquidity.*   These are the main reasons that most entrepreneurs would like to bring their firms to an IPO. As an original founder of a company, an entrepreneur finds almost all of the wealth tied up in one enterprise. An IPO allows the original founder to diversify a portfolio and thus reduce investment risk by selling some stock to others, thereby reinvesting that cash into other investment vehicles. Selling stock directly to another investor is not as easy as selling stock directly into an actively traded market where the value of the company is determined by the market rather than individually negotiated.

2. *Ability to Raise New Cash for the Company.*   If new opportunities present themselves to a company that is still closely held, then the ability to raise money can be quite constrained by (a) the inability of the original owners to supply more of their own cash, (b) the regulatory restrictions placed on insiders to transact with others to raise cash, and (c) the general level of outsider skepticism to investing in a closely held company. If the firm transacts an IPO, then the increase in liquidity and reporting requirements of a public market can reassure investors and provide more opportunities in the future for cash to be raised.

3. *Valuation.*   Having an established market determine a valuation for a company can be useful for raising funds in the future, assessing the performance of the company, determining tax issues, and providing incentives to key employees through stock options.

4. *Future Business Deals.*   Being publicly traded can assist in finding potential business partners through stock swaps or even mergers that can be paid for with stock.

5. *Publicity.*   A publicly traded company gains visibility that not only can help its stock to be sold but can also translate into a larger awareness of the firm's product.

Disadvantages of an IPO

1. *Reporting Costs.*   This is the major downside of going public. Companies that go public must file quarterly and annual reports with the SEC and other agencies. In addition, each type of stock exchange can have different reporting requirements. To be listed with the smallest stock markets can add up to an extra $250,000 per year in accounting costs when compared to a privately held business. To be listed on a major

exchange like the NYSE, (New York Stock Exchange) the reporting and regulatory requirements can theoretically add an additional $10 million in annual costs compared to those of a privately held firm.

2. *Disclosure of Information.*   Closely held companies have a flexibility of operation that is sometimes not appreciated by entrepreneurs until after they have gone public. First, the formal disclosure of information to the stock market also means that the information is available to competitors. Second, internal transactions that are possible in a private company to minimize tax liability may no longer be an option. Another issue is that the rules of disclosure are theoretically for the purpose of releasing information to investors as simultaneously as possible. Therefore, the company's employees may have to undergo an extreme behavioral adjustment—such as forgoing the practice of "talking shop" with others—because it could result in an unintentional but illegal release of information. Another change in behavior may be required by maintaining investor relations. Top managers in the company frequently find their job descriptions changing dramatically. In addition to performing their regular duties, top executives will now have to budget substantial amounts of time to deal with major stockholders and influential stock analysts.

3. *Maintenance of Control.*   Just like the previous stages of financing, an IPO involves a further reduction in the voting rights of the original founders and all the issues that result.

THE PROCESS OF THE IPO

Step 1: Selecting an Investment Banking Firm

Once a company chooses to go public, it must select an investment banking firm. If a company has used venture capital funding at an earlier stage, it might be an extremely good idea to use the investment banker that is recommended by the venture capitalist. This would especially be true if the venture capitalist and the investment banker have substantial experience working together. Theoretically, it would be nice to have a purely competitive situation where all the investment bankers lay out proposals and fee schedules and the offering firm picks the most economical one. The only instance where a competitive bid process of side-by-side comparisons of investment banking fees and terms is possible is when the instruments being sold are extremely standardized (certain debt issues) and there is very little risk. The typical IPO does not fall into this situation. The actual process can take upwards of several months before an offering can be made, and full disclosure of information is not physically possible until the process is almost completed. Typically, this creates a case of having no choice but to make a commitment to "dance with the one who brought you." Switching relationships at midstream and constantly being on the hunt for the best deal is probably not a good option because of time constraints caused by either running out of cash or having the financial market conditions change before the offering can take place. In addition, such an action would be hard on the offering firm's reputation among investment bankers. Therefore, capitalizing on a preexisting relationship between the venture capital firm and the investment banker is typically the best and most seamless way to go.

In the absence of a venture capitalist/investment banker relationship, one must do some shopping. A beginner might be tempted to take the preliminary valuations from various investment bankers and choose the highest one. However, a preliminary valuation is just that, preliminary. Frequently, the final offering price is quite different from the preliminary valuation because of the information that is gleaned through the due diligence process combined with the changing conditions in the financial markets. As a result, one should select an investment banker on the basis of qualitative factors such as these:

1. Relationship with the venture capital firm that handled the company's earlier financing.
2. Experience with doing IPOs for companies in that same industry.
3. Reputation for "making things happen" and following through on offerings.
4. Reputation for being "aboveboard" in all its dealings (no SEC investigations etc.).
5. Respected research staff that has the ability to make clear presentations during the road show for firms that have unique proposals.
6. Ability to organize syndicates of the necessary size to match the needs of offerings.

The market-making capability of the investment bank is a key consideration. If the IPO is to be conducted on an exchange that is not as large and famous as the NYSE, then secondary market liquidity becomes even more crucial in attracting investors to the offering. An investment bank provides the following things in the IPO process:

POOL OF INVESTORS

The investment bank can provide a mechanism to sell stock because it has a large pool of existing customers. This pool may consist of certified investors, that is, investors who have a level of wealth and income to invest in above-average risk investments. Institutional investors such as mutual funds can also be part of this pool.

ANALYSTS

When an investment bank agrees to take on a firm as a client, it also agrees to supply an analyst so that its brokerage arm will have regularly distributed reports for investors. The involvement of a highly respected analyst can be helpful in promoting an active secondary market to provide liquidity, which in turn encourages investment.

CERTIFYING THE STOCK PRICE

By assessing a value for the IPO, the investment bank is attempting to convince its investors that the stock is not overpriced. Theoretically, what the investment bank is providing is an assurance that if investors buy this stock, they are likely to earn a good return. Note that the investment banker therefore has an incentive to at least slightly underprice the offering. This, of course, is not what is best for the firm pursuing the IPO.

Step 2: The Decision to Underwrite or Not Underwrite

For some people, underwriting means to make explicit and implicit representations to investors about the value of the shares; underwriting means more than this to others. It could mean that the investment banker directly purchases the shares and then resells them to the market. This is a very dramatic way to help an issuing firm deal with risk, and this is usually not done during IPOs. In IPOs, underwriting usually means that a syndicate has agreed to buy the entire security offering. This protects the firm pursuing the IPO by guaranteeing that the funds will be raised. An alternative approach is called "best efforts," in which there is no guarantee that the issue will be completely sold out. Everything else being equal, a company would obviously prefer underwriting, but things are not always equal and the cost as a percentage of cash raised will be quite a bit larger for an underwritten offering.

Step 3: Getting the Paperwork in Order and Certifying the Price of the Offering

The SEC has jurisdiction over all public stock offerings. Therefore, at least 20 days before a public offering, a registration statement called Form S-1 must be filed. The purpose of this document is to disclose legal and financial information to the SEC. Another document also needs to be prepared, called a prospectus, which is a summary of the S-1 and is meant for potential investors.

To properly fill out these documents, a substantial process of due diligence and price certification must take place in which an investment banker plays the role of intermediary between the issuing firm and the investing public. Generally, the price of securities rise after an IPO, thereby suggesting that offerings are typically undervalued. This comes from the asymmetry of information between the seller of shares and the buyers of shares. The seller naturally would like to raise funds with the least loss of company control. Buyers of shares know much less about the company than the issuer but are aware of this informational disadvantage. Therefore, they will have an incentive to demand a discount in purchase price. One can imagine this discount using a used car market analogy. Some used cars are mechanically sound and some are "lemons." If there is no way to fully inform the potential buyers of which are which, then a natural result will be a pricing discount on all used cars because every car purchased has a risk of being a "lemon." The better the information shared with the potential car buyers, the smaller the discount from fair value.

In the IPO market, this same situation takes place. When an investment banker with a good reputation conducts a thorough due diligence, the size of this pricing discount is reduced from what it theoretically could have been if the investment banker did not exist. Even with an investment banker, a small discount always exists on average because it is impossible to share all relevant information with all potential investors. This is especially true when intellectual property is the competitive advantage. Nevertheless, reducing the problems caused by information asymmetry is part of the intermediary role that an investment banker plays. Due diligence helps to ensure that the investment banker uncovers any information that would have a negative effect on the buyer, and hence the valuation. Frequently, the due diligence process is sufficient to scare off charlatans from issuing securities in much the same way that a certified mechanical inspection would keep a car seller from lying about whether or not a particular vehicle is a "lemon."

The majority of the work to certify the price is done in this third step of the process, but it also occurs in other steps in the IPO process as more feedback is gained. One can think of the pricing process as one that runs concurrently with the other steps of the IPO process:

1. Company and investment banker meet and explore whether there is a good fit between the two of them. If the answer is a potential "yes," then they continue.
2. Data is gathered by the investment banker.
   a. Finding valuations of comparable firms that are already publicly traded.
   b. Comparisons to similar IPOs that have recently been completed.
   c. Estimating future cash flow for the entity and performing several discounted cash flow valuations.
3. The information from (2) is used to create a preliminary estimate of value.
4. The offering company decides whether to formally commit to using the investment banker.
5. Due diligence commences and new information is gathered from the financial markets.
6. The investment banker issues a preliminary filing range (possible values) in a preliminary prospectus.
7. The road show takes place. This is done to market the offering and gauge demand for the shares. At the same time as the road show, the investment banker is also watching the financial markets for any possible changes.

The final issuing price and amount to be raised is reported in the final prospectus. The valuation and the amount of funds to be raised can be quite different from what was perceived in (3), depending upon changes in the financial markets in recent months, what was discovered during due diligence, and the perceptions of demand from the road show.

Step 4: The Road Show

At this point, the top management and lawyers of the company, along with the investment bankers, make a series of presentations to potential investors. Usually these investors are large clients of the investment bank. A crucial aspect of the road show is that the managers are not legally allowed to say anything that is not in the registration statement. This "quiet period" is mandated by the SEC and is required to last from the day the registration is effected to a period 25 days after the stock has begun trading. This does not stop the potential investors from asking many questions during the presentation, however. By many accounts, this is a physically and mentally exhausting experience, especially because the presentations may be given as frequently as once or twice a day in many different cities for up to two weeks.

Step 5: Determine the Size of the Book

The investment banker tabulates the information gathered up to this point. During the road show, information on the demand for the offering was gathered through nonbinding requests from possible investors. However, the price certification process must eventually come to an end and a formal offering price must be declared, given all the information gathered from the due diligence process, the nonbinding indications of interest from the road show, and any other information that comes to light. After the road show, the investment banker asks potential investing clients if they are interested in buying shares, a process called "book building." A positive situation would be for the offering to be oversubscribed, meaning that more shares are desired for purchase than are currently offered. The night before the offering, the investment banker should have the offering price officially set.

Step 6: The First Day of Trading

In a typical offering, there will be a significant price run-up during the first day of trading. This is because the market is aware of the incentive for the investment bank to at least slightly underestimate the initial offering price to help guarantee that the stock actually gets sold.

SUMMARY

As was stated at the start of this chapter, raising funds is one of the most difficult, if not the most difficult, activities that an entrepreneur must perform. The type of financing requested is dependent upon the stage of development that the firm is currently in, and as a result, the funding is typically provided in stages that have milestone goals that are used as the benchmarks of success or failure. Venture capitalists are active players in the financing of new firms, and like any potential investor, demand a substantial amount of information and control from the firm. The final end point of the investment for some of these investors is an IPO, which can be a very involved and expensive process but one that allows the initial founders to diversify their holdings.

DISCUSSION QUESTIONS

1. What is a reverse income statement and what is its relevance to raising funds?
2. Why do the financial markets traditionally raise funds in stages rather than supply the whole amount to an entrepreneur at the start?
3. In which funding stage is angel financing most likely to occur, and why?
4. Why are venture capitalists interested in owning a large percentage of a business?
5. What issues should a firm take into consideration when choosing a venture capitalist?
6. What is the relevance to entrepreneurial finance of having an exit or harvesting strategy?
7. What are the reasons that could make a firm desire to undergo an IPO?
8. Why is due diligence such a crucial activity?
9. When various investment bankers offer preliminary valuations for a company that wishes to do an IPO, why is it not necessarily the case that the investment banker with the highest valuation is the best?
10. What causes the disparity between the initial offering price and the trading price that exists afterwards?

OPPORTUNITIES FOR APPLICATION

1. Conduct two interviews, the first with a person who is a source of venture capital financing and the second with an entrepreneur who used such financing. Describe the venture capital financing from both the venture capitalist's and the entrepreneur's point of view.
2. Write a plan to build relationships with venture capitalists for a new business venture you are developing.

REFERENCES

Batterson, L. (1986). *Raising Venture Capital and the Entrepreneur.* Upper Saddle River, NJ: Prentice Hall.

Churchill, N., and Lewis, V. (1983, May–June). Five stages of small business growth. *Harvard Business Review,* 2–11.

Higashide, H., and Birley, S. (2002). The consequences of conflict between the venture capitalist and the entrepreneurial team in the United Kingdom from the perspective of the venture capitalist. *Journal of Business Venturing,* 17, 59–81.

McGrath, R., and MacMillan, I. (1995, July–August). Discovery-driven planning. *Harvard Business Review,* 4–12.

Smith, J., and Smith, R. (2000). *Entrepreneurial Finance.* New York: Wiley.

C H A P T E R

13

Business Valuation

Entrepreneurs do not have the time to read a thick, technically oriented book on business appraisal nor the excess cash to hire a professional appraiser on a whim. As a result, proposals for sale or investment are frequently rejected or accepted on the basis of some vague valuation ratio, or absent that, on the basis of emotions. The purpose of this chapter is to provide a brief synopsis of valuation so that an entrepreneur can economically and rapidly determine which offers are unreasonable and which are worthy of further consideration.

It must be stressed that an appraisal is an estimate or opinion. Business valuation is not an exact science. Instead, one might prefer to call it the "art" of business valuation because a certain amount of judgment must be used in conjunction with the mathematical principles. The techniques learned in this chapter should help the entrepreneur to utilize judgment to separate the relevant information from the irrelevant.

GENERAL CONCEPTS THAT GUIDE
THE DETERMINATION OF VALUE

There are seven general principles that should govern any valuation. This section will examine each of these principles in detail. The seven valuation principles are:

1. Fair market value
2. Going-concern value
3. Highest and best use
4. Future benefits
5. Substitutes and alternatives
6. Discounted cash flow analysis
7. Objectivity

Fair Market Value

Having a clear definition of value is important during negotiations because the other side may try to justify its proposed price by referring to comparable firms that have been recently sold. However, just because someone else sold a company does not mean that the price received is directly related or relevant to another business.

The definition of fair market value as used in this chapter comes from the Institute of Business Appraisers. This definition also seems to be consistent with general legal precedents and IRS rulings. Fair market value means the price, in cash or equivalent, that a buyer could reasonably be expected to pay and a seller could reasonably be expected to accept, as long as the property were exposed for sale on the open market for a reasonable period of time and both buyer and seller are in possession of the pertinent facts, with neither being under compulsion to act.

Therefore, a price is *not* fair market value if:

1. ***The payment was not made in cash on or near the date of the deal.*** If payment were to be deferred, for instance, then the amount received was probably adjusted to allow for the time value of money. In other words, if the buyer is going to give the seller a note that promises to make payment at some future date, then the total amount that the entrepreneur should receive should be greater than the fair market value to allow for the interest that could have been earned. This does not rule out seller-financed arrangements; it simply means that the parties should use the cash equivalent price as the starting point for negotiation.

2. ***It was a less than arm's-length transaction.*** For example, a transaction between two family members cannot be used as the basis for a market comparison. Such situations are not open markets.

3. ***The offering period was excessively short.*** Suppose someone offers a firm for sale for such a brief period of time that only a person with beforehand knowledge could have submitted a bid. This roughly would be the equivalent of insider trading—not a fair open market.

4. ***Information was withheld or not pursued by one or both parties.*** This situation does not necessarily nullify the agreement to buy or sell at the specified price (unless criminal intent was involved). All it means is that the acquisition might not be taking place at a price that fully reflects fair market value in the conceptual sense.

5. ***One of the parties was operating under duress or is legally required to consummate the agreement regardless of the terms.*** A price cannot be deemed a fair market value unless the parties have the right to reject an offer or bid. For instance, some partnerships have a legal agreement that forbids selling a share of the business to anyone other than a partner. In this case, the buyout price should probably not be used as a market comparison. Another example would be a seller who is forced into a quick sale rather than face a probable bankruptcy. However, it should be noted that dire financial distress, by itself, does not automatically mean the same as "under compunction to act" and that the price is not fair market value. It could be that *all* sellers in that industry are desperate, so reasonable buyers and sellers would expect a low price.

Going-Concern Value

Going-concern value is the value of a business as an operating concern rather than the sum value of all the individual assets that are owned by the firm. Another way to explain going-concern value is to view buying a business as if it were a traditional investment that will be paying income. Most businesses are purchased based on the anticipated cash flows expected from these businesses in the future. Therefore, the purchase price would be based on the value of the income to be generated by the business rather than the resale value of the inventory, office furniture, and so on that make up the firm.

The approach of valuing the real assets of a business sometimes is referred to as *liquidation value*. This implies that the equipment and property of the firm are sold individually. For the sake of brevity, we offer no advice on how to estimate liquidation value. Volumes could be written on this topic alone because the individual markets for real estate and used equipment would have to be studied to arrive at this value.

As a side note, if a business is being sold, it is important to be aware that potential buyers sometimes try to use liquidation value as a rationale for suggesting that the price should be lower. In most cases where the firm is a going concern, liquidation-value estimation is merely a "red herring."

Highest and Best Use

The concept of highest and best use means that the price that one pays for a business should be based on the activity or use of the company's assets that generates the highest economic value. For example, suppose the business in question is an eight-track cassette repair shop (an obsolete activity) in downtown Manhattan. In this particular case, it would be safe to assume that the going-concern value would probably be much less than the value of the real estate upon which the shop sits (liquidation value). Therefore, the highest and best use would be to sell the real estate of the business rather than to value the business on the basis of its income.

Future Benefits

While historical information is very useful for valuing a traditional business, it may be a luxury not available to an entrepreneur. In addition, even if a firm does have a track record, one should always remember that it is irrational for someone to pay extra for *past* good performance if the economic conditions have changed. For instance, one's business may have had a long string of successes because there was no other competition in town. If new competitors have now moved in, one should not expect those large cash flows to continue and neither should a potential buyer. The technique of discounted cash flow is consistent with the concept of future benefits because it attempts to value the firm on the basis of future prospective cash flows. Valuation techniques that involve multiplying historical profits or revenues by valuation multiples should be viewed as "reality checks" rather than definitive valuation techniques. This is a "quick-and-dirty" method of valuation that should be used only for a rough estimation of the potential value of a business. Again, it is the *future* potential benefits that should really determine the value of a business, not its past benefits.

Substitutes and Alternatives

This principle means that the value of a business is related to the value of alternative investments. The process of selling a home offers a good example of this principle. Home appraisals are conducted on the basis of how much similar homes sell for in the same neighborhood. As applied to business, there are many techniques that borrow valuation ratios (such as price to earnings ratios from companies in that same industry) to assist in valuing a particular company. While substitute or alternative investment is the basis for these techniques, we will see later in this chapter that it is extremely difficult to apply these so-called market comparison techniques without ironically violating this principle. At the very least, the buyer should keep in mind that buying that *one* particular business is *not* the only alternative. The buyer will always have the option of taking that same money and investing it in something else with a comparable or even lower level of risk. For instance, if higher returns were available from risk-free U.S. government securities than from owning a risky business, why would someone buy it under this principle?

Discounted Cash Flow Analysis

Discounted cash flow analysis is a technique that intrinsically incorporates all of the previously mentioned principles. It builds upon the capital budgeting techniques that one would find in a traditional corporate finance textbook. This process uses the current income of a business as a starting point. Income is almost always measured using earnings before interest, taxes, depreciation, and amortization (EBITDA). EBITDA creates a consistent measure of profits that removes the specific income tax situation and financing strategy from valuation, as these will vary widely from firm to firm and do not really reflect the true performance of a business entity. EBITDA also removes the noncash items of depreciation and amortization from net income, as investors are interested in assessing the future *cash flow* that a business can generate. Therefore, it is important for entrepreneurs to keep track of the EBITDA measure of profits in their businesses.

Using EBITDA as the starting point, one then estimates as objectively as possible what the cash flows should be over the next five years. A key element to discounted cash flow analysis is choosing accurate assumptions. For instance, one may make assumptions such as a sales growth rate of 5 percent, salaries increasing or decreasing based on hiring plans, and the planned replacement of a machine during a specific year.

At the end of the five-year forecast, a terminal value of the firm is estimated that represents the approximate value of all the cash flows expected to be generated beyond year five. The five years of forecasted cash flows and the terminal value are then adjusted through the discounting process to determine what those

---

BOX 13-1

Valuation: The Buyer's Perspective

From the buyer's perspective I know all too well how difficult it can be to pass over a "dream." I had the opportunity to conduct a leveraged buyout (LBO) of a firm that was located in the town where I grew up. Moving back and taking over the company would have offered an exceptional quality of life in addition to the "psychological benefits" of serving my home community. Most exciting of all, my partner could have raised the necessary financing for us without putting a large sum of my personal funds at risk. Despite all of this, I had to honestly admit to myself and to my partner that the firm would not be able to repay the debt holders and other investors who would be part of this transaction. In addition, there were 40 other offers to buy this firm, so there was a strong likelihood of the "winner's curse" taking place. In other words, the entity that purchased this firm by beating out all other offers probably would be paying too much and would have an even harder time paying off all of the creditors. As a result, I had to pass on this deal because the objective facts required me to.

David Vang, professor of finance and consultant.

---

future cash flows are worth as of today's date. The value of those cash flows as of today's date is called *net present value*. The process of calculating net present value requires the use of a rate of return that would represent appropriate compensation for the business's risk.

The end result of this process is a value calculated in today's dollars that would be a fair price in exchange for all the estimated cash flows that this particular business is expected to generate in the future. Therefore, the technique should represent the concepts of fair market price, going-concern value, future benefits, and substitutes and alternatives. The issues of whether going concern is the highest and best use and whether the cash flows have been estimated objectively will have to be determined by the entrepreneur. A full discussion of the method for computing discounted cash flow, including examples, will be presented later in this chapter.

Objectivity

To perform a valuation it is absolutely essential to be objective. As a businessperson, one must confront the reality of the situation. A buyer must never allow the "dream" of business ownership to cloud sound judgment. A seller must accept the fact that the buyer will be interested only in the economic value of the business. The entrepreneur may have worked very hard to build the business and may have taken great risks along the way, but all of that will be irrelevant to a potential buyer. Only supportable data should be used to ensure a consistent and objective analysis of business valuation. Box 13-1 and Box 13-2 offer examples of this principle in action.

BOX 13-2

Valuation: The Seller's Perspective

Another experience, this one from my consulting practice, highlights the importance of objectivity from the seller's perspective. I was hired as a valuation consultant to a corporation that was contemplating the acquisition of a family-owned business. During this assignment, the patriarch and other members of the family consistently demanded a price that was 50 percent over the maximum possible value that our analysis could determine. Since it appeared that no deal would take place anyway, I suggested that the corporation disclose to the family all of its information and its process for valuation to show that the difference between our bid and their offer was not due to any sort of negotiating strategy. Even with all of this information supplied to them, this family still could not calculate a value on their own that was anywhere near ours. I discovered at a much later date that members of the family had serious health issues that would not allow them to run the business in the future. Nevertheless, they turned down what was a more than fair offer (which I can attest to) with no guarantee that a similar offer would ever be extended again. While it is perfectly okay to turn down a fair offer for whatever personal reasons one may have, in this particular case, the other party's emotions did not allow them to even recognize that the offer was fair. This was borne out one year later. During this time period the family had invested a tremendous amount of energy and money to make their business 30 percent larger. Due to the above-mentioned health issues, they wound up recontacting my client and selling their much larger business for roughly the same price that was offered before. It took the passage of time before they could emotionally "let go" of the firm, and the result was that they gave away 30 percent of their business for free.

David Vang, professor of finance and consultant.

BASIC INFORMATION REQUIRED FOR A VALUATION

The following is a checklist of the basic requirements for performing an effective valuation of a business venture:

1. *Income Statements and/or Tax Returns.*   A general rule of thumb in business valuation is to ask for copies of the most recent five years of financial statements, including statements of cash flow if possible (or for every year of its existence if the firm is less than five years old). If the firm is a sole proprietorship, it may not have official income statements. In this case, tax returns combined with other information may have to be used to estimate the firm's actual cash flow so that the discounted cash flow technique can be used.

2. *Balance Sheets and/or List of Assets and Liabilities.*   The request for five years of financial statements should include both income statements and balance sheets. If the firm can legally operate without a balance sheet, then one may have to be constructed from a compiled list of the assets owned by the firm and the liabilities that the firm owes.

3. ***Rates of Return That Are Consistent with the Risk Level.*** This is the kind of information that will be needed so that the valuation analysis is consistent with the principle of substitutes and alternatives. In other words, this information will help determine whether the potential business owner will get a return that will be commensurate with the amount of risk undertaken. The process of estimating a firm's specific required rate of return will be discussed later in this chapter.

4. ***Interviews with Current Owners and Staff.*** For privately owned companies, access to the owners and staff will be essential to gain information that does not show up on financial statements. Table 13-1 displays a checklist of the type of information that is often required during interviews with staff. Some business owners filter expenses through their company that are not 100 percent essential for the business in order to reduce taxes. Providing information on items such as (1) and (2) would generally be in the seller's interest because removing such expenses from the estimate of cash flows would increase the assessed value of the firm. For example, it is unreasonable to expect the new owner to continue to employ Uncle Bill as the receptionist at three times the going wage or to continue paying the previous owner's life insurance. For items (3) through (11), however, the seller may not have an incentive to be quite as open with the buyer. In this case, the buyer may have to get outside confirmation from someone familiar with the industry, a professional appraiser, or an experienced acquisition attorney.

5. ***An Assessment of the Future Business Environment for This Firm.*** Such an assessment should begin with a thorough analysis of competitors and

TABLE 13-1 Information Checklist for Management Interviews

1. A list of employees and salaries.
2. A list of all personal expenses that the owner(s) may have loaded into the company.
3. A summary of any equipment that may need to be fixed or replaced in the near future.
4. A discussion of which key employees will stay with the company and how the firm usually recruits new staff.
5. A list of all judgments or potential judgments against the firm. For example, does the firm have possible problems with OSHA, the IRS, the EEOC, or potential lawsuits?
6. A list of receivables that are unlikely to be collected.
7. A list of payables that are past due.
8. The owners' opinion on why customers choose their product or service and what expectations must be met to keep their customers satisfied.
9. What are the most common problems that the owners must deal with?
10. Do they have cost accounting capabilities to estimate cost per unit?
11. What is the outlook for the industry?

potential competitors. Is the industry shrinking or growing? Is the number of competitors increasing? Where does this particular firm fit in the industry? Picking up the lunch tab for other people in the industry is a small price to pay for such insight. If the business is local in nature, then the local chamber of commerce or the city development office might have information on the economic outlook for that community. For broader-based information, possible contacts are the Chamber of Commerce of the United States, the National Association of Manufacturers, the National Federation of Independent Business, the Small Business Administration, or industry trade associations.

DISCOUNTED CASH FLOW

With an income-oriented approach to valuation, a company can be viewed as an income-generating machine. Given this, what one is willing to pay for this machine is dependent upon how much income it can produce. Discounted cash flow analysis estimates the value of the income a business can produce. As mentioned earlier, EBITDA (earnings before interest, taxes, depreciation, and amortization) in most cases is a closer representation of the actual cash flow of the firm than the "taxable income."

For example, suppose that a firm has a constant EBITDA every year. The value of the firm could be found by dividing the EBITDA of the firm by a rate of return that represents a fair compensation rate for the risk of the firm.

$$\text{Value of Firm or Investment} = \frac{\text{EBITDA}}{\text{Rate of Return}}$$

If the firm is capable of generating $26,600 per year in income as measured by EBITDA and if a 27 percent rate of return is required to compensate for the level of risk of this investment, then

$$\text{Value of Firm} = \frac{\$26,600}{.27} = \$98,519$$

The most that one should be willing to pay for the firm is $98,519 because $98,519 placed in an investment of equal risk that earns 27 percent would generate just as much income per year.

There are two component parts to this valuation—the numerator (EBITDA) and the denominator (the rate of return). The annual income measured with EBITDA should reflect the expected future annual income rather than past income. A more accurate measure for estimating future EBITDA would be to add back all of the nonbusiness expenses that the previous owner has loaded into the firm. This would give the "true" level of income that the owner actually received.

At this point, a judgment also must be made as to whether this level of income is sustainable in the future.

The other component for estimating value is determining the appropriate rate of return with which to capitalize the firm's future sustainable income. The rate of return required on the buyer's equity is not something that can be looked up in some official publication, but it can be inferred from the rate that could be earned on other opportunities. At a minimum, it should be several percentage points above the calculated, long-term rate of return on a common stock mutual fund that is devoted to small company stocks. A rate of such magnitude, given the principle of substitutes and alternatives, should be relevant because of the following issues. First, equity ownership is more volatile in terms of rate of return than government securities, hence the use of a small company mutual fund as a starting benchmark rather than a treasury rate. On top of this, the diversification effect of a mutual fund invested in many different companies would cause it to have a much lower overall risk than the "all-your-eggs-in-one-basket" position the buyer would have with direct investment in just one company. In addition, a mutual fund is a liquid investment that can be easily sold on the investor's whim. Direct ownership in a company, on the other hand, may take months or more to liquidate. Because of these last two items, an owner should demand a rate of return that exceeds the return on the previously mentioned mutual fund.

Long-term returns on stock indexes such as the Standard and Poor's 500 or the New York Stock Exchange are occasionally published in periodicals such as *Barrons* and *The Wall Street Journal*. However, these indexes represent only large companies. For small company stock returns an excellent source that can be found at most libraries is *Stocks, Bond, Bills and Inflation* by R. G. Ibbotson and R. A. Sinquefield. This source has calculated stock returns measured over periods of 60 years or more. Typically, when measured over long periods of time, small company tradable stocks have an average return between 12 and 18 percent. This return should be adjusted to deal with the observation that investment values are frequently reduced by between 10 and 50 percent in the absence of a liquid market in which to sell them. Furthermore, the value of an investment can fall even more if it is not of a diversified nature. Table 13-2 displays general guidelines for expected returns from different types of investments.

Suppose an appraiser consulted *Stocks, Bonds, Bills and Inflation* and found out that small company stocks had an average return of approximately 18 percent over the past 10 to 20 years. The appraiser then believed that this rate should be increased by about 50 percent (30 percent to reflect a lack of liquidity premium and another 20 percent to reflect that this will not be a diversified investment like the mutual fund). So, the required return on equity in our example should be

$$18\% \times (1.50) = 27\%$$

The reader should be aware that this is a crude approach to approximating the required return on equity. It is a tremendous simplification of the process that

TABLE 13-2 Perceived Expected Long-Run Annualized Returns	
Publicly traded companies	12–18%
Privately held companies (with substantial history)	20–35%
Angel investors	20–50%
Venture capitalists	35–80%

a professional appraiser would and should perform. Many volumes of research have been written on this topic, and part of the reason that one hires an appraiser is because professionals are familiar with the most recent findings. However, under the assumption that the buyer has chosen to not hire a professional, the practice of adding a premium that doubles or more than doubles the stock fund rate would not be unreasonable. For instance, if an investment has a value 50 percent less than a similar but liquid investment, its ratio of profit to price will result in a rate of return that is double the liquid investment.

The moral to entrepreneurs is that a direct purchaser of their business will not be shy about demanding a rate of return in the range of 20 to 70 percent (about two to three times the rate on the stock market) on the equity that has been invested. On the other hand, if the purchaser is a large corporation with publicly traded stock or if stock is sold directly into a well-established market (i.e., IPO), then investors might not demand such a high liquidity or risk premium, which would result in a higher value for the business. For instance, if investors demanded only a 20 percent rate of return, then the firm in our example would be worth

$$\$26,600/.20 = \$133,000$$

Notice the inverse relationship between required rates of return and value. When investors demanded a lower rate of return, the value increased by almost $35,000 (from $98,519 to $133,000).

This simple example demonstrates the forward-looking aspect of valuation. However, the use of a single number to represent average future income may be too simplistic to accurately capture the specific circumstances of the firm. We can now add more sophistication.

Instead of using a single number to represent future earnings, it might be better to estimate the annual cash flow for a number of years (usually five or more) into the future. These estimated cash flows are then discounted at the appropriate rate to determine their present value (today's cash equivalent). In addition, a *terminal or ending value* of the investment is estimated at the end of this forecasted time period. This terminal value is also discounted back to today's cash equivalent, just like all of the other cash flows. The terminal value represents the value of all cash flows expected to continue beyond the end of the analysis. The sum of these discounted cash flows represents the cash value of the investment as of today. Financial calculators, spreadsheets, or regular calculators can rapidly perform such calculations. The following example will demonstrate how.

Suppose a more thorough valuation of the firm is desired. Closer examination may reveal that while $26,600 was the EBITDA according to the official financial statements, the actual cash flow or *adjusted* EBITDA that was generated this year was $27,000 due to a combination of factors. It was also discovered that 5 percent growth in sales per year is a reasonable expectation, but the future beyond five years is totally indeterminate. In addition, this company has a machine that will wear out in two years and will cost $20,500 to replace. Given these assumptions, one can estimate the next five years' worth of cash flows as follows:

Today + 1 yr	$27,000 × (1.05)	= $28,350 CF_1
Today + 2 yrs	$28,350 × (1.05) – $20,500	= $9,268 CF_2
Today + 3 yrs	$29,768 × (1.05)	= $31,256 CF_3
Today + 4 yrs	$31,256 × (1.05)	= $32,819 CF_4
Today + 5 yrs	$32,819 × (1.05)	= $34,460 CF_5

In other words, each year's cash flow is 5 percent larger than the previous year's, except for the second year, when $20,500 was subtracted out to represent the cost of replacing the machine at that time. Cash flows in year 6, 7, and so on are assumed to be the same as in year 5, based on the belief that growth beyond year 5 is indeterminate. The valuation technique discussed previously can be used plus the assumed rate of return of 27 percent to estimate what the firm theoretically could be sold for five years from now (i.e., its terminal value):

$$\frac{\text{Cash Flow Yr 6}}{\text{Rate of Return}} = \frac{\$34,460}{.27} = \$127,630 = \text{Terminal Value}$$

The next step is to discount all of these cash flows back to a cash equivalent in today's dollars using the 27 percent rate of return. If a regular calculator is used, the math would be as follows:

Year 1	$28,350/(1.27)	= $ 22,323
Year 2	$9,268/(1.27)^2$	= 5,746
Year 3	$31,256/(1.27)^3$	= 15,259
Year 4	$32,819/(1.27)^4$	= 12,616
Year 5	$34,460/(1.27)^5$	= 10,430
Terminal	$127,630/(1.27)^5$	= $ 38,631
Total equivalent cash value		$105,005

If a financial calculator were used, the typical keystrokes would be

0	CF_0	
28350	CF_i	
9268	CF_i	
31256	CF_i	
32819	CF_i	
162090	CF_i	(Please note that 162,090 is equal to 34,460, the year 5 cash flow, plus the ending value of 127,630 added together.)
27	I	
NPV		>>>Answer would be displayed as 105,005*

*If the answer is not reasonably close to this, double-check to see that (1) the calculator is set on END mode, (2) the display is set to four or more decimal places, and (3) the calculator is set for annual, not monthly compounding.

Thus, the estimated value of this firm is $105,005, compared to the crude estimation of approximately $100,000. The difference of $5,000 was the result of the discounted cash flow approach's ability to incorporate the additional information learned about this company. The output of this analysis is only as precise as the assumptions that went into its calculation, of course, but the advantage of discounted cash flow analysis is the ability to reestimate values by varying the assumptions. For instance, one might want to repeat the analysis using a range of growth rates from 3 to 10 percent. The actual price to be offered within this range would depend upon the perceived likelihood of sales growth being above or below 5 percent. As was mentioned earlier in this chapter, business valuation is an art, not an exact science.

ESTIMATING A FIRM'S CASH FLOW AND DETERMINING ITS VALUE

The basic view that someone *should* have when buying a small business is "How much should I be willing to pay to get a decent salary (if I were to run the business myself) *and* a reasonable return on my investment?" Of all of the techniques for valuation, the discounted cash flow approach is the best at answering this question. The only way to make a fully informed decision is to formally calculate the level of cash flow of the firm to see if it currently is providing an appropriate salary and return on investment. The market comparison approach of multiplying a ratio by one piece of business information would not automatically provide such insight.

Performing a discounted cash flow analysis is a worthwhile activity for both the buyer and the seller. The buyer should know whether the firm will provide sufficient personal income, and the seller should know whether or not he is being too generous to the buyer. It also provides a nice direct decision rule for the buyer. If the net present value of the estimated cash flows is greater than the offering price, buy the company. If the net present value is less than the offering price, do not buy.

DEFINITION OF CASH FLOW

Cash flow, sometimes referred to as "free" cash flow, represents the cash that is left over *after* covering operating costs, debt repayment, capital expenditures such as asset replacement, *and* paying the owner/manager an economically reasonable wage.

This definition fits in nicely with the principle of substitutes and alternatives and the concept of future benefits because one alternative to buying a business is to get a job working for an established company. The supposed economic benefit of owning a business, however, is that the buyer should get an income in excess of what one would get working for someone else. Sometimes people refer to buying a business as "buying yourself a job." In principle, it does not make sense to pay a huge sum of money just to "buy yourself a job." But it does make economic sense to pay money (i.e., make an investment) to have incremental income above and beyond the market value that the buyer can earn in the open job market. Therefore, cash flow must be carefully estimated so that the buyer is not paying for:

1. Cash flow that could have been gotten without the risk of business ownership (the income from working for a company).
2. Cash flow that has to go for future asset replacements that will be the responsibility of the new owner. These are payments to the bank, lender, or equipment dealer, so the new owner cannot use them.
3. Cash flow that must be used to pay the normal expenses that allow the business to run on a day-to-day basis, such as salaries to employees, production costs, the light bill, and so forth.

In other words, a firm could be generating large annual revenues, but the amount that the owner can consider discretionary income might only be a very small percentage of that revenue. It is very likely that this amount is very different from the reported "EBITDA." For instance, it could even be the case that a firm may officially be making a profit but have a negative cash flow. This situation frequently occurs in years when the company has to make major asset purchases.

ESTIMATING THE CASH FLOW FOR A PARTICULAR YEAR

To determine what the "free" cash flow for a business is in any particular year, start with the official operating profit or EBIT (earnings before interest and taxes) of the business and make the following six adjustments:

1. Add back the owner's salary and benefits.
2. Subtract out a more reasonable compensation for the work performed by the owner.
3. Add back any of the owner's personal expenses that have been filtered through the company.
4. Add back any depreciation and amortization expenses that were claimed this year. Remember, these are noncash expenses. They are not actual

payments made to someone, but merely a number from a table or formula that the IRS allows the owner to subtract out before the calculation of the firm's taxable income.

5. If a major piece of equipment or asset is to be purchased in this particular year, then subtract this amount.

6. Subtract the amount of money it would take to bring the inventory of the company up to a reasonable level. For instance, sometimes when a business owner knows that the company will be sold, the owner may "sell out of inventory" rather than reorder new inventory. Therefore, by the time the new owner takes possession there may be nothing on the shelves to sell. As a result, the new owner may need to invest in inventory or other types of "working capital" *before* the business is able to operate and generate income. An analogy might be the way that people sell their cars. One typically does not buy new tires, a brake job, a battery, a tune-up, and fill the gas tank the day before a car is sold.

AN EXAMPLE OF ESTIMATING CASH FLOW OVER A SIX-YEAR PERIOD

Let us suppose the following situation:

1. A corporation is interested in purchasing a company from an entrepreneur whose financial statements report that this year's EBIT was $200,000.

2. Other information gathered revealed that the owner paid himself salary and benefits of $100,000 when a more reasonable compensation given the local job market was $50,000.

3. There was $20,000 in depreciation expense this year.

4. The owner had $10,000 in personal-type expenses such as lease payments on a Lexus as a "company" car.

5. In addition, the firm will need a net investment of $200,000 next year to replace worn-out equipment. Buying this new equipment will cause depreciation expense to increase by $50,000 each year for four years.

6. It is believed that sales will increase by 7 percent per year for the next five years given the productive capacity of the firm and the nature of the product market. Beyond five years, a reasonable estimate of growth is neither possible nor relevant because the buyer should not have to pay for growth that would come from one's own efforts and future investment.

7. The firm has an outstanding loan of $500,000.

8. The "cost basis" of the firm is $100,000. In other words, the original investor has $100,000 of his money invested in the company. If the firm were to sell for more than $100,000, then the difference between the sale price of the firm and the $100,000 invested would be considered capital gains income to the seller. Further suppose that the original investor would fall in a combined state and federal tax bracket of 40 percent.

9. One last point, the firm has a history of maintaining an average inventory balance of $80,000. Since the firm first appeared on the market the owner has not purchased any new inventory and has allowed the level to drop to $65,000, thus suggesting that the buyer will probably need to invest $15,000 in inventory just to bring the firm's inventory back up to a safe level.

Given all of the above information, Tables 13-3 through 13-9 demonstrate how to construct a forecast of cash flows for the next six years. Please note that Table 13-3 determines the cash flow for year zero as a baseline starting point. This would be the cash flow for the firm *this year*. The first cash flow to be received by the new owner will be cash flow for year 1.

So, if this firm were purchased, it could theoretically have the following cash flows:

First year	+79,000
Second year	+308,980
Third year	+321,509
Fourth year	+334,915
Fifth year	+349,259

and an approximate amount per year thereafter of +$349,259.

Notice that EBIT was *never* equal to the actual cash flow. Also note that even though revenues were growing at 7 percent per year, cash flow did not steadily increase at that same rate. In fact, cash flow actually dropped significantly in the first year from what it was originally.

TABLE 13-3

Year 0		
Official EBIT	$200,000	
Add back owner salary	+ 100,000	
Subtract out more reasonable salary	– 50,000	
Add back depreciation for this year	+ 20,000	
Add back "personal" expenses	+ 10,000	
Estimated EBITDA		$280,000
Subtract new equipment purchased	0	
Subtract inventory investment	0	
"Free Cash Flow"		= +$280,000
vs.		
Accounting EBIT $200,000		

TABLE 13-4

	Year 1	
Official EBIT	$214,000*	
Add back owner salary	+ 100,000	
Subtract out more reasonable salary	– 50,000	
Add back depreciation for this year	+ 20,000	
Add back "personal" expenses	+ 10,000	
Estimated EBITDA		$294,000
Subtract new equipment purchased	– 200,000**	
Subtract inventory investment	– 15,000	
"Free Cash Flow"		= $ 79,000
vs.		
Accounting EBIT $214,000		

*This number is last year's official EBIT times 1.07 to represent a 7 percent growth [200,000 × 1.07].
**This represents the purchase of the new equipment needed this year.

TABLE 13-5

	Year 2	
Official EBIT	$178,980*	
Add back owner salary	+ 100,000	
Subtract out more reasonable salary	– 50,000	
Add back depreciation for this year	+ 70,000**	
Add back "personal" expenses	+ 10,000	
Estimated EBITDA		$308,980
Subtract new equipment purchased	0	
Subtract inventory investment	0	
"Free Cash Flow"		= + $308,980
vs.		
Accounting EBIT $178,980		

*This number is last year's value of $214,000 times 1.07 to represent 7 percent growth, and then subtracting out the extra $50,000 in depreciation.
**This is last year's depreciation plus $50,000 from the newly purchased equipment.

TABLE 13-6

	Year 3	
Official EBIT	$191,509*	
Add back owner salary	+ 100,000	
Subtract out more reasonable salary	− 50,000	
Add back depreciation for this year	+ 70,000	
Add back "personal" expenses	+ 10,000	
Estimated EBITDA		$321,509
Subtract new equipment purchased	0	
Subtract inventory investment	0	
"Free Cash Flow"		= + **$321,509**
vs.		
Accounting EBIT $191,509		

*This is the previous year multiplied by 1.07 [178,980 × 1.07].

TABLE 13-7

	Year 4	
Official EBIT	$204,915*	
Add back owner salary	+ 100,000	
Subtract out more reasonable salary	− 50,000	
Add back depreciation for this year	+ 70,000	
Add back "personal" expenses	+ 10,000	
Estimated EBITDA		$334,915
Subtract new equipment purchased	0	
Subtract inventory investment	0	
"Free Cash Flow"		= **$334,915**
vs.		
Accounting EBIT $204,915		

* This is the previous year multiplied by 1.07 [191,509 × 1.07].

It is from these cash flows that the new owner will have to recover the purchase price of the firm. If these cash flows have a discounted present value that is less than the seller's proposed purchase price, one should *not* buy this firm. Such a situation means that the cash flows are not sufficient to do all of the following at the same time:

1. Pay back the debt part of the financing that would be used to purchase the firm
2. Earn an acceptable return on the personal equity investment that would be used to purchase this firm
3. Pay the buyer a reasonable compensation for his or her own labor

TABLE 13-8

	Year 5	
Official EBIT	$219,259*	
Add back owner salary	+ 100,000	
Subtract out more reasonable salary	− 50,000	
Add back depreciation for this year	+ 70,000	
Add back "personal" expenses	+ 10,000	
Estimated EBITDA		$349,259
Subtract new equipment purchased	0	
Subtract inventory investment	0	
"Free Cash Flow"		= **$349,259**
vs.		
Accounting EBIT $219,259		

* This is the previous year multiplied by 1.07 [204,915 × 1.07].

TABLE 13-9

	Year 6	
Official EBIT	$269,259*	
Add back owner salary	+ 100,000	
Subtract out more reasonable salary	− 50,000	
Add back depreciation for this year	+ 20,000**	
Add back "personal" expenses	+ 10,000	
Estimated EBITDA		$349,259
Subtract new equipment purchased	0	
Subtract inventory investment	0	
"Free Cash Flow"		= **$349,259**
vs.		
Accounting EBIT $269,259		

* This is the same official EBIT as year 5 (zero growth) because it is difficult to reasonably predict what will happen in the marketplace after five years. To this amount, however, we added $50,000 to represent that the equipment we purchased in year 1 that will now be fully depreciated [219,259 + 50,000] in accounting terms, but operationally still useful.
**A reduction of $50,000 to reflect equipment that is now fully depreciated.

Suppose that the required rate of return is still 27 percent. If the preceding information is accurate and reasonable, then the potential value of the expected, future cash flows of this firm can now be calculated.

First, find the year 5 terminal value by using the investment value approach:

$$\frac{\text{Terminal Value}}{\text{at Year 5}} = \frac{\text{Cash Flow Year 6}}{\text{Cost of Financing}} = \frac{\$349,259}{.27} = \$1,293,552$$

The next step is to discount all of the cash flows back to a cash equivalent in today's dollars using the 27 percent rate of return:

Year 1	$ 79,000 / (1.27) =	$ 62,205
Year 2	$ 308,980 / (1.27)^2 =	191,568
Year 3	$ 321,509 / (1.27)^3 =	156,957
Year 4	$ 334,915 / (1.27)^4 =	128,742
Year 5	$ 349,259 / (1.27)^5 =	105,713
Ending	$1,293,552 / (1.27)^5 =	$391,530
Total cash equivalent value as of today:		$1,036,715

Using a financial calculator, the typical keystrokes would be

0	CF$_0$		
79000	CF$_i$		
308980	CF$_i$		
321509	CF$_i$		
334915	CF$_i$		
1642811	CF$_i$	< < < < < < < <	1,642,811 is equal to 349,259 + 1,293,552, which is the year 5 value cash flow plus the terminal value.
27	I		
NPV		> > >	Answer would be displayed as 1,036,715, allowing for rounding differences.

By using different sales growth assumptions that can be considered reasonable, the value of this firm, if purchased today, is in a range with a reasonable middle value of $1,036,715. If the seller is absolutely adamant about a price that is significantly greater than $1,036,715, then the potential buyer should probably refuse. The cash flows that have been estimated perfectly correspond to a 27 percent rate of return if the company is purchased for $1,036,715. If the company is purchased for more than $1,036,715, the buyer will be earning less than 27 percent. In other words, if more than $1,036,715 is paid, the buyer will not be able to pay the principle and interest on the money borrowed, get a reasonable rate of return on the equity investment, and receive the reasonable salary of $50,000 all at the same time. Something has to give and mostly likely it will not be the banker—it will be the buyer. Likewise, the lower the price, the easier it will be to accomplish all of these things.

TABLE 13-10

Price > Net present value	Buyer earns less than the required rate of return.
Price < Net present value	Buyer earns more than the required rate of return.
Price = Net present value	Buyer earns exactly the required rate of return.

Now let us look at the seller's perspective. An amount of $1,036,715 has been received from the sale of the business. From this the original owner can now pay off the outstanding $500,000 loan (see assumption number 8). However, also remember that the original investor had a cost basis of $100,000 and sold the business for $1,036,715. In the eyes of the IRS, the person just made income of $936,715. Given a tax rate of 40 percent, the seller now owes $385,486 in taxes. Altogether,

Proceeds from sale	$1,036,715
Minus debt to be paid	– 500,000
Minus capital gains tax	– 386,486
= Net proceeds	$ 150,229

At this point, the potential seller of this business should go back to Chapter 2 of this book and see if achieving wealth of only $150,229 is sufficient to achieve personal goals.

SUMMARY OF THE DISCOUNTED CASH FLOW APPROACH

The basic view that someone *should* have when valuing a business is "How much should I be willing to pay to get a decent salary and a reasonable return on my investment?" The only way to make a truly informed decision is to formally calculate the level of cash flow of the firm to see if it can provide for repayment of debt, an appropriate salary, and an appropriate return on investment. If the calculated net present value of the cash flows is less than the offering price, the answer is no, it cannot. If the net present value is more than the offering price, the answer is yes, this firm can provide these things. From the seller's perspective, the effect of debt repayment and income taxes should be taken into account to determine if the size of the wealth accumulation from the sale of the business is significant enough for the entrepreneur to achieve his or her personal goals.

MARKET COMPARISON TECHNIQUES AND THEIR DRAWBACKS

There are a number of different techniques for valuing companies, but when it comes to determining going-concern value these techniques fall into two broad areas—those that use some sort of market comparison and those that discount future earnings or cash flow. Although the latter approach is advocated in this chapter, information on market comparison techniques is included because of their widespread use. Ideally, this section will give businesspeople the necessary "ammunition" to distinguish the reasonable from the unreasonable when approached with market comparison ratios.

The market comparison approach goes by many different names in the literature of business valuation, such as market multiples, market data, market comparables, sales comparison, and so on. Regardless of the terminology, the general process is to identify recent company sales or use publicly traded prices of companies that are comparable to the specific company to be valued. If the companies used for comparison are not 100 percent comparable to the firm of interest, then those prices must be adjusted. The adjusted selling prices of the comparable firms are now used as the basis for estimating the value of the company in question. Usually, this is done through some sort of ratio formula. Table 13-11 displays a list of possible variables and corresponding ratios that may be used in conjunction with company acquisitions or stock prices to estimate values with the market data approach.

Not all of these variables are used in every valuation. Which ones are used would depend upon the kind of sales data collected and industry convention. For instance, if data are available for actual purchases of companies in the industry, take the selling price and divide by the respective net income for each company. The result is a series of total price to total net income ratios that can be multiplied by the net income of a particular firm to estimate its possible value.

The underlying principle of the market comparison approach is the concept of substitution and alternatives. The idea of using market comparisons as "sanity checks" or a "quick-and-dirty" way to assess offers comes from the idea that if one uses firms from the same industry, then the risk should be approximately equal to the firm to be valued. Therefore, one is valuing a company by using the values of

TABLE 13-11   Possible Ratio Formulas for Market Data Approach

Variable	*Ratio*
1. Net income	1. Price\Earnings
2. Earnings per share	2. Price\Earnings
3. Pretax earnings	3. Price\Pretax earnings per share
4. Cash flow	4. Price\Cash flow
5. EBITDA	5. Price\EBITDA
6. Dividends	6. Price\Dividends
7. Gross revenue	7. Price\Sales
8. Total assets	8. Price\Assets
9. Book value per share	9. Price\Book value per share
10. Number of total customers	10. Price\Customer
11. Industry specific measurements	11. Price\Unit

what should be equally desirable substitutes. The commonsense appeal of this general approach has caused it to be frequently used by valuation experts and courts of law. The actual application of the market comparison approach, however, is fraught with difficulties. For instance, its successful use depends on having access to information on several different company acquisitions. Furthermore, its validity is dependent upon these sales being sufficiently comparable to a given situation.

The first difficulty with market comparisons is access to information. There are data files of recent sales of companies, but access is usually reserved for professional appraisers who pay fees for memberships in organizations such as the Institute of Business Appraisers. Another source might be industry trade journals, but again there is usually an annual fee for a subscription. For laypeople, access to such information can be very difficult, and even professional appraisers may have trouble. One reason is that data are more frequently collected on only very large company transactions. Also, most data are recorded in summary fashion rather than being fully detailed.

The market comparison approach has a second potential difficulty: the occasional need to adjust for comparability even when one has access to information. This is an area where concept six, objectivity, is sometimes tainted. In a previous section, an experience was mentioned where a family refused a more than fair offer because they were unable to recognize it as such. One of the reasons was their insistence on using the price to earnings ratio of the purchasing company to value their firm without allowing for any differences. A single division of the purchasing company was over 30 times larger than their firm, and the parent company had three different divisions. In addition, the parent company's stock was traded on a major stock exchange. In other words, the family ignored three issues of comparability. First, they were comparing themselves to a firm that was approximately 100 times larger. Second, they ignored the difference in risk between the diversified parent company and their single-product firm. Last, they ignored the difference in liquidity between a publicly traded stock on a major exchange and ownership in a family business. In other words, they probably should have adjusted the price to earnings ratio downward three times before they applied it to their company.

Using a market comparison approach is not as simple as it first seems because of the potential need for value adjustment. There are many possible issues that can interfere with finding a set of truly comparable company sales. Truly comparable company sales would involve firms that have these same basic characteristics:

1. *Line of Business.* This item may be extremely obvious, but it may be difficult to achieve because many small businesses operate in niche markets for which there is no direct comparison.
2. *Geographic Area.* As an example, a gas station that operates in a large metro area by any measure would probably sell for more than a similar firm in a rural area because of the difference in the number of potential customers. In other cases, the value may be different because of geographic differences in the cost of financing or the cost of living.

3. ***Production Process and Age of Assets.*** If a firm operates with an outdated technology, it should not be expected to have a price similar to a firm that has recently modernized. If the firm needs new equipment in the near future, this will reduce the future cash flows of the enterprise.

4. ***Listing Status or Form of Ownership.*** Firms whose stock is traded on a major stock exchange are highly liquid. That is, investors can change their minds on a day-to-day basis on whether to own the stock or not. As a result, investors are willing to pay extra for ownership in this form as compared to the illiquid investment in a company that is not listed. There can even be differences in liquidity between different stock exchanges.

5. ***Costs of Inputs or Other Competitive Advantages That Affect the Level of Profitability.*** Because of the principle of future benefits, valuation ratios that do not directly relate value to cash flow or profits should probably be viewed with skepticism. It may seem like common sense to say that when the cost of servicing the customer exceeds the revenue collected, there is no value. Despite this simple logic, false industry conventions sometimes arise, such as valuing firms as a multiple of total revenue, total assets, or some other basis that does not allow any difference in profitability.

6. ***Level of Establishment, Name, Trademark, or Industry Position.*** Direct comparisons between a firm that has a 1 percent market share and another that has a 75 percent market share would probably not be appropriate because the latter has the economic power to influence product price and industry behavior while the former would not. Likewise, a firm with a widely recognized trademark or a historically recognized location has an advantage over a recently started company. For instance, one client used to experience a slight increase in sales *when a competitor* ran TV ads because of the location, name recognition, and the fact that it was listed first in the Yellow Pages under that product heading. Obviously, an upstart company should not be given a comparable value in this market.

7. ***Sale Terms.*** Buying or selling a business is more confusing than buying a car or a house. Theoretically, the basic starting point of negotiation should be the cash price, with further negotiations dealing with the terms of the sale. In reality, terms may be so important that the cash equivalent price need only be an approximation rather than a precisely determined number. Sale terms may include issues such as the timing of payments, who absorbs the financing fees, whether it is an asset purchase or an equity purchase, and so on. Many times there are advantages, just like in real estate, to roll some of these issues into the purchase price rather than deal with them separately. As a result, the official "price" that may get quoted may not be very close to a true cash price equivalent.

8. ***Standing of Ownership.*** This issue deals with whether a purchase is of all or most of the company (majority ownership) or a minor holding in the company (minority interest). A direct value comparison should not

be made between an acquisition of a minority interest—say, 5 percent—and the total acquisition of a company because a majority owner would have control over how the firm operates, whereas a minority owner generally does not. For example, if the interest is 5 percent of the company, one does not calculate the total value of the firm and pay 5 percent of that amount. Instead, one should pay less than that amount because the future benefit of that 5 percent ownership stake is dependent upon the continuing wisdom, fairness, and general good management of the controlling majority owner.

9. ***Size of the Business.***   Depending upon the valuation measure, small companies usually sell for a discount compared to large companies due to many of the previously mentioned issues such as differences in risk, profitability, industry standing, and economies of scale.

10. ***Financing.***   Buying a business can be similar to buying a house in that when interest rates go down, one can afford to spend more. As a result, firms that have been purchased with low-cost financing may have a higher price than similar companies for which the buyers could not access cheap financing.

11. ***Time Period.***   Economic conditions can change substantially over time. Therefore, a company purchase that was recorded more than a year or two ago probably would not be a good comparison because the conditions for economic growth and the level of interest rates could be very different than today's.

12. ***Similar Buyer.***   The value of a particular business can be different for different types of buyers. To illustrate, if the only buyers are individuals who need to retain all of the company's staff in order to run the business, then the fair market price probably would be less than in another time or place where the buyers are all large corporations who have the luxury of laying off redundant personnel. An organization that already owns one or more businesses in the industry may assess a value that is more than the fair stand-alone value for a company because of potential synergies and/or economies of scale.

Summary of the Market Comparison Approach

To summarize this discussion of the market comparison approach, it should be said that valuation techniques that use price-to-earnings ratios or other market comparison measures are susceptible to large errors unless the companies used for comparison are very similar to the company of interest. If the companies are not almost identical, then subjective judgment must be inserted into the process to adjust the values. At this point, the objectivity of the valuation becomes highly suspect. On the plus side, such techniques have two advantages. First, they are mathematically simple. Second, they have a wide range of acceptance by the general, but not necessarily informed, public.

DISCUSSION QUESTIONS

1. How does the discounted cash flow approach incorporate many of the other principles of valuation?
2. Market comparables are theoretically based on the principle of substitutes and alternatives. What are some of the ways that market comparables actually contradict this principle?
3. Explain why liquidation value is typically not the method that should be used for evaluating the harvesting strategy for a company.
4. Under what conditions would the concept of highest and best use be in conflict with the concept of discounted cash flow?
5. What would be the effect on valuation if the discount rate was too high? What if it is too low?
6. Give some examples of how income in accounting terms can be different from cash flow.
7. What are some of the reasons that the return on U.S. Treasury Bills should not be used as the discount rate in the valuation of a business?
8. Why would two businesses that are identical except for the fact that one is publicly traded and one is privately owned have two different values?
9. If a transaction took place a couple of years ago, why would it not necessarily be applicable to a business sale that is taking place today?
10. Is it possible for an entrepreneur to experience a reduction in wealth when a business is sold even though the value of the business is much greater than the amount invested? Under what conditions would this take place?

OPPORTUNITIES FOR APPLICATION

1. Suppose a firm generates an annual cash flow of $100,000, has zero growth, and has a required rate of return of 15 percent. If the offering price is $50,000, should you buy it?
2. You believe you need a 50 percent return on equity to compensate you for risk. How would this affect the value of the firm in problem 1?
3. Your firm had an EBIT of $105,000 last year, and you expect it to be the same this year. You have $15,000 in personal expenses annually paid by the company. Depreciation expense was $2,000, and you will purchase new office equipment at a cost of $5,000. You paid yourself a salary of $200,000, but you know you could hire someone else to be a manager for $75,000. What was your EBITDA and free cash flow this year?
4. Free cash flow: Year 1, $100,000; Year 2, $90,000; Year 3, $110,000; Year 4, $120,000; Year 5, $125,000; Year 6 and beyond, $125,000. The required rate of return on equity is 30 percent. What is the most one should pay for this firm?
5. Redo problem 4 under the assumption that the firm has $65,000 in debt that must be paid off. What will be the proceeds from the sale of the business to the seller after paying off the debt, but before paying capital gains tax?
6. Redo problem 5 under the assumption that the tax rate is 40 percent, and the cost basis of the business was only $10,000. What will be the net proceeds after the payment of the debt and the taxes?

7. Your firm's free cash flow per year is as follows:
   Year 1 = $120,000
   Year 2 = $140,000
   Year 3 = $150,000
   Year 4 = $160,000
   Year 5 = $170,000
   The cost of capital is 20 percent.
   a. What would be the terminal value at year 5 if there is no growth expected beyond the fifth year?
   b. What is the present value of the free cash flow for the first five years?
   c. What is the value of the firm today?
8. A business has an EBITDA of $220,000. If a comparable firm recently sold at a price to EBITDA ratio of 2:1, then what would be the theoretical value of this business using the market comparables approach?
9. A privately held business has the same EBITDA as a publicly traded one. It is assumed that the liquidity discount is 25 percent. What theoretically should be the value of the privately held business if the publicly traded one is worth $1,500,000?
10. A firm's discounted cash flow value is $1,600.000. Its market comparables value is $1,550,000 and its liquidation value is $100,000. Using only an average of techniques based on the principle of highest and best use, what should a valuation report claim as this firm's value?

REFERENCES

Bowers, A. Business valuation explained. www.office.com

Damodaran, A. (2002). *Investment Valuation*, 2nd ed. New York: Wiley.

Mills, R. C. (1984). *Basic Business Appraisal.* New York: Wiley.

Pratt, S. (1998). *Valuing a Small Business and Professional Practice.* 3rd ed. New York: McGraw-Hill.

Sherman, A. J. (2001). Methods of company valuation. www.entreworld.com, accessed August 2001.

CHAPTER

Exit Planning

At some point, the founding entrepreneur will leave the venture. This can happen in a variety of ways, including selling the business, transitioning to the next generation in a family business, bankruptcy, or even through the death of the entrepreneur. The process of preparing for the transition of both the entrepreneur and the business is called *exit planning*. This chapter presents a model of exit planning that is tied to the self-assessment first presented in Chapter 2. Many experts believe that exit planning should begin at the very inception of the business; that is, a person should plan for the end of the business from the very beginning. Taking this approach, the exit planning process integrates the personal aspirations of the entrepreneur with the starting point of the exit planning process. This chapter will examine the various options for the actual exit process.

SELF-ASSESSMENT REVISITED

The first major component of an exit plan is an assessment of the wealth the entrepreneur aspires to realize from the sale of the business. As stated throughout this book, the entrepreneur is best served by integrating wealth and income goals into the planning process. Wealth in a business is created by excess cash flows that potential buyers believe will continue into the future and that can provide an adequate return on their investment. This requires a history of positive cash flow, an industry that holds the promise for continued growth or stability, and, most often, a business that can continue after the entrepreneur exits the firm. This last item is why many small service businesses have very little value in a sale. Because the owner is the main source of revenue, that revenue is dependent on the reputation and relationships of the entrepreneur. The promise for continued cash flow is not there. Therefore, the entrepreneur should make sure that aspirations match reality and that there are not unrealistic expectations for wealth from the exit from the business. An understanding of valuation, as presented in the previous chapter, is beneficial to creating realistic wealth objectives.

For example, a husband and wife team ran a successful commercial landscaping company for over two decades. Although during the peak season they employed dozens of seasonal workers, there were only four full-time, year-round employees, including the two of them. The business had several hundred thousand dollars of profit every year. They started the process of selling their business, thinking they could sell it for several times their annual profit. However, when potential buyers looked at the business, they consistently shied away from serious negotiations. All saw something that the owners failed to recognize: All of the contracts the business had were based on long-term personal relationships the couple had with a few customers. None of the potential buyers believed that these customers would stay on once the company was sold. This is an example of a service business that is too dependent on the entrepreneur to have much value once the owners exit the business.

Another key part of exit planning involves the issue of timing. One part of timing considers the personal preferences of the entrepreneur, where life and career planning come into play. When does the entrepreneur want to retire? Does the entrepreneur want to participate in more start-ups? Would the entrepreneur enjoy a change in career after leaving the venture, such as consulting, teaching, or working with other entrepreneurs on their ventures? The other component of timing to consider is the market opportunity for a sale. In some industries, the sale of a business is a fairly rational and consistent process over time. In other industries, periods of consolidation may be episodic, requiring quick decisions about selling because the next opportunity for the desired price may be far in the future, if it occurs at all. This has been the case in many emerging industries, such as personal computers in the 1980s, managed health care in the early 1990s, and Internet companies in the late 1990s. Many entrepreneurs in these industries failed to understand that the sustainability of these industries, or at least the sustainability of their growth, would not last indefinitely. Many held on to ownership of their businesses well beyond their real peak in value, hoping that the value would continue to go up. When high-growth industries reach their peak, the drop in value after that peak can be so rapid that many entrepreneurs fail to implement an exit strategy in time to get any real value out of their ventures. Knowing when to exit, therefore, requires attention to both personal and market factors, and these two factors do not always intersect. Ignoring either one can result in exiting too early or too late.

As discussed in Chapter 2, the process of self-assessment plays an important role throughout the life of an entrepreneurial venture. Aspirations for income and wealth can change over time due to factors such as a change in the entrepreneur's family situation, situations where ventures either exceed or fall well short of initial expectations, or dramatic changes in market conditions. Such changes will have an impact on the expectations these entrepreneurs have when exiting their businesses. The exit process, if well executed, relies on careful and thoughtful self-assessment throughout the growth and development of a business venture. Exit planning should be an ongoing process because most business exits do not happen as the entrepreneur originally intended.

For example, market fluctuations dramatically changed the exit plans of a group of entrepreneurs in the health care industry. During start-up, their plan envisioned building a modest business that would generate strong cash flow for about 15 to 20 years until the time came for the partners to retire. However, their concept caught fire in the marketplace and the business appeared to have potential well beyond even their most optimistic start-up assumptions. Realizing that their initial exit plan failed to focus accurately on the wealth generated by the value of their growing venture, the entrepreneurs changed their plans and their expectations. Their time frame for exit decreased to roughly 7 to 10 years due to the newfound potential of their business. Then a major change developed in the health care industry. Large sums of money flowing in from public offerings persuaded these companies to go on an acquisition binge. The entrepreneurs realized that their window for exit had just shortened to about 2 to 3 years, and they began to prepare their business for sale. They no longer believed the company could grow as large as they once thought, but they could realize a good return from a sale. Again, they had to adjust their expectations to be consistent with the new reality.

Not all changes in exit plans are financial in nature. For example, a highly successful retail coffee store chain was sold because the owner's wife became seriously ill. The entrepreneur wanted to help care for her and wanted to be more available to parent their teenaged child. Up until his wife's illness, the entrepreneur had no intention of selling his business.

When a business has more than one owner, the challenge becomes one of giving adequate consideration to the potentially differing aspirations of the various partners. The self-assessment process becomes not just an individual activity but also one that all of the partners should share openly with each other. An example of the challenges this can create can be seen in an engineering firm in which the three partners had quite different aspirations and expectations. One was interested in building a large, possibly national company. The second wanted to create a sustainable business and possibly move into other ventures. The third hoped simply to harvest as much wealth as possible, as quickly as possible. The partners did not openly discuss these differences during the start-up phase. A consolidation period began in their industry, and an opportunity arose to sell the business for an excellent return. This caused the partners to squabble, however, because one was anxious to sell, one was not at all ready to exit, and one was uncertain and hesitant. The buyers were concerned with the dissent among the owners and eventually walked away from the deal. The partner who wanted a quick exit grew bitter over the failed sale, and the three never fully regained the trust they had in each other. Clearly, a full and frank discussion of aspirations before they started and throughout their growth could have prevented this type of situation.

THE ETHICAL SIDE OF THE ENTREPRENEUR'S TRANSITION

Much of the focus on exit up to this point has been on financial matters. After all, the basic purpose of the exit is to execute a transition in the ownership of the business. However, the entrepreneur still retains the opportunity to fulfill the original vision during this final transition. That is, the culture and the values the entrepreneur brought to the business can be factored into the exit process. Who is chosen to be the next owner and how the transaction is structured can be deliberate decisions made in a way that is consistent with the entrepreneur's values. For example, some entrepreneurs take great care to find buyers for their businesses who espouse cultures consistent with their own. Their intent is to ensure that employees, customers, and other stakeholders will continue to be treated as they have been under the original ownership. These entrepreneurs believe in a commitment to these stakeholders even as they leave the business. Factoring in these types of considerations can limit the number of potential buyers, however, and the law of supply and demand suggests that such an exit strategy can reduce the ultimate sale price.

A decision not to take the venture public can result in even more money being left on the table in an exit. While public offerings can create tremendous wealth, they often create a fundamental shift in the business to a more financially based culture due to the pressures for financial returns in the public equity market. For example, when Dale Merrick, Bob Wahlstedt, and Lee Johnson started Reell Precision Manufacturing (RPM), a small midwestern company, they envisioned a very specific culture they wanted to foster in their business. When they decided to exit the firm they founded, they could have easily taken their business public or sold it to a public firm, but they wanted to make sure that the unique culture they had created in their business would continue for the benefit of the employees and their customers. With that in mind, they opted to pursue an employee stock ownership plan (ESOP) that resulted in the founders realizing only a fraction of the value they could have received with other exit strategies. Their feeling of obligation toward those who helped them build their company was more important than the money they earned from the sale. The exit process can require courageous acts if the entrepreneur intends to focus on more than just the financial considerations of the exit transaction.

A MODEL OF EXIT PLANNING

Several additional steps are involved in an exit plan beyond the setting of goals and time frames through the self-assessment process as discussed thus far in this chapter. Figure 14-1 displays a model of exit planning.

Manage Financial Statements

Analysis of the balance sheet may reveal several items that can impact the exit process. If possible, reducing outstanding loans is advantageous. In most business sales, the seller uses the proceeds to pay off any outstanding loans. Even if the buyer does agree to assume the liabilities, bankers can be hesitant to move loans to a new entity with which they have no history. To illustrate this point, assume that

Self-assessment: goals related to financial, professional, family, etc.

Establish exit time frame

Manage financial statements

Conduct external audit

Develop business plan for sale of business

FIGURE 14-1

three different businesses each have a sale price of $1 million. All three are S-corporations and none have significant assets that could be subject to the capital gains rate of tax. That is, assume that the proceeds of the sale will pass through to the owner as regular income (not an unusual situation for a service-related business). Two have used bank debt to fund their business and still have balances on their loans. Company A's sale is a distress sale, and it still owes the bank $750,000. Company B owes $250,000. Both companies borrowed working capital using accounts receivable.

	Company A	Company B	Company C
Sale Price	$1,000,000	$1,000,000	$1,000,000
Loans due	750,000	250,000	-0-
Gross proceeds	$ 250,000	$ 750,000	$1,000,000
Personal tax (assume 40% rate)	400,000	400,000	400,000
Net proceeds	$ (150,000)	$ 350,000	$ 600,000

Taxes on all three sales are based on the proceeds of the sale and do not take into account any liabilities that are outstanding. Company B's owner will receive only 35 percent of the sale price; Company C's owner will receive 60 percent. Company A is a distress sale and its owner will owe more tax on the sale than received after paying off the loans!

Certain assets can actually be a detriment to a sale. Any nonproductive assets—buildings, vehicles, or equipment not in use—should be sold off prior to entering into the sale process. Nonproductive assets lower the buyer's perception of the potential return on investment. Moving property and buildings into a separate entity may also be beneficial, because many buyers do not want to own real estate. The entrepreneur can then either keep the property and buildings and receive rental income or sell the property to someone who specializes in owning commercial real estate. If the buyer wants the property, the seller can sell both the operating and the property businesses in the same transaction.

Any property leases should be kept short term toward the time of a sale. Such leases are considered liabilities that must be "assumed" and can actually reduce the cash flow value to the buyer. The buyer may already have space in which to consolidate operations or may have other, cheaper space in mind.

The income statement and statement of cash flows should be monitored to ensure progress is being made toward the desired level of profitability. Remember that the key objective is to maximize cash flow, because EBITDA is the main component of valuation. Minimizing nonproductive overhead also can be a significant benefit, for example, keeping administrative staff as small as possible and not over-spending on space for administrative offices. Furthermore, unless it is essential to the operations or perceived quality of the business, expensive office space should be avoided so that the maximum amount of cash flows to the bottom line.

Conduct an External Audit

Most buyers will request three years of financial statements audited by an outside public accounting firm. A review of the financial statements is cheaper and usually adequate for bankers, but most buyers will want an audit. However, this is generally not the case for smaller businesses, especially those with sales under $500,000. Audits cost about $10,000 to $25,000 for businesses under $10 million in sales if they are performed each year. A retroactive audit for three years (one going back in time at the time of sale) is much more expensive. If the business has significant inventory, it will need a supervised inventory count for at least a few years even if a retroactive audit is completed. It is a good idea to begin the audit process if a sale is expected to occur in the next few years.

Chapter 7 contained suggestions for hiring and managing outside accountants. The same suggestions apply when hiring and managing an auditing firm. It is wise to get bids from two or three auditors, as their fees and procedures can vary significantly. Price is not the only factor to consider; a good personality match with the business and its team is also important. The auditors' understanding of the industry can also have a major impact on the quality and cost of the audit. During negotiations, billing procedures should be discussed up front and any concerns over charges should be raised openly and honestly. To use resources efficiently, the business's own staff should handle the most routine tasks rather than incur unnecessary auditing expense.

Develop a Business Plan for the Sale of the Business

A well-developed business plan can assist the process of selling the venture. What is being purchased, in effect, is the potential of the firm. If that potential can be supported and substantiated by a business plan, the buyer may be willing to pay more for the business. The plan should be comprehensive, including a thorough industry analysis, marketing plan, financial plan, and operating plan for at least three to five years in the future. Of particular interest to the potential buyers is the marketing plan and its link to future revenue forecasts, as discussed in Chapter 4. If the plan strongly supports future growth, the seller may be able to negotiate for a higher multiple. In addition to most-likely-case forecasts, the plan should include a best-case scenario to show the upside potential of the venture and all assumptions tied to this scenario.

EXIT OPTIONS

An entrepreneur may consider a number of different exit options before choosing one. Often, several of these options may present themselves simultaneously. The notion of transfer of ownership most likely emerges when an entrepreneur thinks about an exit strategy. However, some options may not represent such a clean transition, and a few involve the business simply ceasing operations entirely. A variety of factors should be considered when evaluating each alternative exit strategy. Which gives the best financial return? Which generates the most cash to the entrepreneur? How do the various options fit with the nonfinancial aspects of the entrepreneur's aspirations? Are there overriding tax implications that come into play? How can the entrepreneur ensure that the vision, culture, and values nurtured in the business continue beyond the present ownership and control? Figure 14-2 summarizes the options discussed in this section.

Ownership Transfer

The most common form of ownership sale is an *asset sale*. In an asset sale, the buyer purchases all of the assets tied to the operations of the business, usually excluding cash and accounts receivable. The liabilities remain the responsibility of the seller. Buyers usually prefer an asset sale because they can depreciate many of the assets they purchase, thus reducing future taxes. Buyers also desire to avoid any unknown liabilities, including such items as unforeseen tax assessments or lawsuits that may be filed postclosing. There are some disadvantages to the seller in an asset sale. First, any taxes owed by the seller that arise from the sale of the business accrue at the time of the sale in their entirety. In some types of transactions, some of the tax liability can be deferred. Also, the price in an asset purchase is usually less at face value than with other kinds of transactions. The advantages to the seller are that the purchase is with cash and that the sale allows the entrepreneur to make a clean break from the business if both sides agree.

In some asset sales, the buyer and seller cannot agree on a price, but both sides are eager to move ahead with the transaction. In such cases, the deal can be structured with an earn-out option. With an earn-out, a base price is mutually determined. Then, if the business realizes the growth that the seller predicted, the buyer pays an agreed-upon premium or bonus. However, if the business fails to

FIGURE 14-2   Summary of Exit Options

Type of Exit	Advantages to the Seller	Disadvantages to the Seller
Ownership Transfer		
Asset sale	Cash sale	Immediate tax on full sale
	Clean break for entrepreneur possible	Lower face-value sale price
	Earn-out possible if price disagreement cannot be resolved	
Stock sale*	Higher face value of sale price	Potential volatility of stock received from sale
	Tax deferment of sale price	Restrictions on sale of stock received from sale
Partial or Limited Transfer		
Merger	Potential synergies of companies brought together	Cultures may clash
	Tax deferment of sale price	Limited opportunities to receive immediate cash
IPO	Taking some cash out of business possible	Limits on sale of stock
	Can use funds to bring in professional management	
Strategic alliance	Reduces risk to existing value of business	May take a long time, if at all, to actually exit
ESOP	Can maintain culture of business	May take a long time, if at all, to actually exit
Family business transfer	Can maintain culture of business	Challenges of generational succession
Bankruptcy as Exit	Orderly end to business	Ethical challenges
		Results in no realization of wealth from business
		Can hurt entrepreneur's ability to fund future deals
Liquidation	May result in more value, especially for service business	No value for going concern
		Can be viewed as "failure"

*For this discussion it is assumed that a stock sale is for stock in the acquiring company rather than cash.

meet expectations, the price that was paid probably reflects a fair price. Both sides can thus benefit from an earn-out.

Another form of ownership transfer is a *stock sale*. In most stock sales, buyers exchange stock in their companies for all of the stock in the selling company. The advantage to buyers is that they pay for the company with stock, so cash is not required for the transaction. The advantage to sellers is that they will typically get a much higher valuation than they would with an asset sale using cash. There also is the opportunity to realize even more proceeds from the transaction if the buyer is a publicly traded company with an appreciating stock price. On the other hand, a significant disadvantage to the seller involves potential volatility in the buyers' stock. Once held by the seller, there are usually restrictions on the sale of the stock in the buyer's company, such as how many shares can be sold at a time and when they can be sold. Thus, stock sales can hold considerable risk for the seller.

For example, a publicly traded company called Coastal Health Care used its company stock in the late 1980s and early 1990s to purchase physician practices. The stock showed many months of consistently increasing prices, which was very attractive to physicians wishing to realize an even greater return for the sale of their practice. Some saw the value of the stock they now owned in Coastal double in value in only a few months after they closed their sale to Coastal. However, the Coastal stock began to fall into disfavor and experienced a sudden and dramatic fall in market price. Many sellers were unable to sell their Coastal stock before it had lost most of its market value. Consequently, the high prices they thought they had received for the sale of their businesses vanished.

This is not a unique story. A major bust occurred in the speculative health care stock market during the early 1990s, and an even bigger bust emerged in the speculative bubble of dot-com stocks in the late 1990s. Many sellers in this industry never truly realized the gains they thought they had received on the sale of their businesses due to the crash in the dot-com equity market.

Partial or Transitional Transfer

Several exit strategies do not involve a complete or at least an immediate transfer of ownership. These strategies are varied in their structure and intended outcomes, yet all of them typically include an ongoing ownership and often a management role for the entrepreneur.

In some instances, two or more businesses are brought together to form an entirely new entity, a transaction called a *merger*. A merger may be preferred if both entities are approximately the same size and the desire is to demonstrate that neither side is taking over the other's business. The shareholders of both entities would trade their stock for stock in a new company at a predetermined ratio based on the relative value of each company. For example, assume that Company A is valued at $4 million and Company B at $5 million and that both have the same number of shares outstanding. They may agree in this case that Company A shareholders will receive four shares in New Company for each share they currently own and Company B shareholders get five shares in New Company for each of their Company B shares.

One major challenge in the merger of two companies is blending two distinct cultures that may be very different. This has certainly been the experience in the merger of large corporations. The merger of Chrysler and Daimler-Benz resulted in many clashes between two entrenched and proud corporate cultures. Even in smaller companies mergers can be traumatic. Cultural fit should be examined during negotiations and due diligence for any potential merger. In fact, both parties should recognize cultural fit as a deciding factor in whether or not to proceed with the merger. Failing the recognition of the importance of this factor, mergers can go terribly awry. For example, two service companies were considering a merger. One had a strong market position in two states, and the other in three neighboring states. One was known for its marketing strengths, and the other for its operating efficiencies. The lead entrepreneurs of both companies believed the complementary nature of the fit between the two companies was compelling. Because they were of comparable size, both having revenues between $10 and $20 million, a merger was considered to be the best form of integrating the two companies. Additionally, because one of the entrepreneurs was interested in phasing out his day-to-day operation of the company, management control was not a contentious issue. However, as the negotiations began to move to detailed discussions and disclosures, it became clear that the businesses had fundamental cultural differences. In one of the businesses, the financial function was viewed as a supporting system aiding managers to make quality decisions, whereas in the other it was a watchdog that constantly challenged even the smallest expenditures and used the budget to keep operating units under its control. One of the companies sought out new opportunities, but only after detailed planning and evaluation. The other company preferred taking risks and was consequently willing to start new ventures with little or no formal planning. One of the companies had a decentralized structure; the other had a highly centralized and formalized structure. Even the boards of directors, which would be merged in the new company, operated differently. In the end, the companies realized that trying to blend two somewhat opposite cultures would create overwhelming obstacles to a successful merger, and the negotiations were terminated.

Another strategy for ownership transfer is an initial public offering (IPO), discussed in Chapter 12. With an IPO the founding entrepreneurs may have the opportunity to move out of day-to-day management if they so choose or if it is in the best interests of the shareholders. An IPO also can provide the founding entrepreneurs with the chance to take some money out of their business. Entrepreneurs will normally be limited to how much and how often they can sell stock, however, and the market will likely look negatively or suspiciously on those who sell too many shares. But, an IPO can often mark the beginning of a transitional time for many entrepreneurs.

Some entrepreneurs find a *strategic alliance* to be a useful transitional strategy. A typical strategic alliance is a long-term fixed contract between two companies to engage in a defined business relationship. An entrepreneur may make a strategic alliance with a much larger firm that could result in a sale of the entrepreneur's business to that company at some point. Sometimes a strategic alliance may involve some equity investment in the entrepreneurial venture by the larger firm. Larger companies use the strategic alliance to help in new product or market development. For example, Vical is a company located in San Diego, California that is currently developing new DNA-based pharmaceuticals. Large drug manufacturing companies like Merck were among the early investors in Vical. A strategic alliance like the one between Vical and Merck can provide an entrepreneurial venture access to capital and expertise from the larger company. No matter what the structure of the strategic alliance initially, the larger company often decides to purchase the entrepreneurial venture outright should its product become marketable or show signs of rapid growth.

An Employee Stock Ownership Plan (ESOP) is a tax-advantaged mechanism whereby employees become investors in the company. Employees can use the company's pretax dollars to fund the plan or to support an ESOP loan. The Internal Revenue Service and the Department of Labor tightly regulate ESOPs, so care must be taken to properly structure and administer the program. There are reasons beyond the financial advantages for using an ESOP as an exit strategy. For example, Reell Precision Manufacturing established an ESOP to ensure the continuation of the culture and values that the founding partners had established for the business. Many of the employees had come to work for Reell because of its appealing culture, and the founders wanted to create an exit strategy for themselves that would allow these employees to carry this culture well into the future. After several years, the ESOP still does not have total ownership but shares it with the founders and their families. An ESOP is not a strategy that leads to a quick and clean exit for the entrepreneur, but it does create a mechanism to begin to liquidate the founders' ownership in the firm.

Family businesses are those that desire to pass on ownership and control of a venture over multiple generations. By definition, family businesses face transitions as they pass from generation to generation. In some family businesses, the transition involves a buyout and transfer of control from one generation to the next. In others, the process is more gradual and integrates estate planning in the transition of ownership. No matter what the planned transition strategy, a succession plan is essential, as it not only designates who will succeed the current generation's management but how those successors will become prepared to fill the leadership role. This often includes a policy requiring family members to work outside the family business for a number of years.

Bankruptcy and Termination of Operations

Some entrepreneurs do not have the opportunity to take an exit strategy that provides for the realization of wealth from their businesses. Due to a variety of causes that are not always within the control of the entrepreneur, the business no longer has the viability to continue into the future. Typically, the business faces *insolvency* when its ability to meet future liabilities is in doubt. Some businesses find that the process of bankruptcy is the best method for facing this problem. A business bankruptcy can take two basic forms. The first, Chapter 11, allows a business to reorganize. The terms of its debts are changed, and a plan is submitted to a bankruptcy court that will allow the business to again become a going concern. Management keeps control of the assets necessary to ensure the operation of the business. The court protects the company from any actions by its creditors to attempt to collect debts outside of the plan. Under a Chapter 7 bankruptcy, the court appoints a trustee to oversee the liquidation of the assets of the business, the proceeds of which are used to pay the business's creditors. Under a Chapter 7 bankruptcy, the business ceases operations. Ethical issues come into play with a bankruptcy, and the entrepreneur should not use bankruptcy as a convenient way to reduce debt obligations. Many of the creditors involved in a bankruptcy are likely to be entrepreneurs and small business owners themselves; they can be adversely affected by a nonpayment of money owed to them. One entrepreneur noted in a speech to a class of young entrepreneurs that he was now a millionaire but it took him three bankruptcies to get rich. What he did not acknowledge is the damage he caused to others on his path to financial success.

Some entrepreneurs exit their businesses through a planned liquidation without the need of bankruptcy protection. This strategy is most effective if the parts of the business—that is, its assets—are worth more than selling the company as a going concern. The entrepreneur sells off the assets, pays off any outstanding debts, and then keeps any residual proceeds as the wealth taken out of the venture. Many service businesses find that their ventures have very little value as a going concern. The owner of a successful landscaping company, for example, with over $2 million dollars in revenues found that the value of his business as a going concern was less than he was able to get by selling off his equipment and buildings separately.

Figure 14-3 displays a checklist that summarizes the exit planning process. The next section will discuss the specific process of selling a business, should that become the exit option of choice for an entrepreneur.

THE PROCESS OF SELLING A BUSINESS

When contemplating the sale of a business as a going concern, some entrepreneurs mistakenly look to their book value or retained earnings to assess value. However, as discussed in Chapter 13, valuation is based on the buyer's expectations of future cash flows. Even historic cash flow matters only to the degree that it predicts future cash flow. For example, a corrugated box manufacturer decided to sell his business after learning that a large national company was going to build a plant in his geographic market. Although historically quite profitable, the national competitor would likely have a devastating impact on his sales, because he would be unable to compete on price. When he decided to sell his company, he tried to value the business based on a steady record of historically positive cash flow. As soon as

1. Reexamine all shareholders' goals and aspirations from the business.
2. Determine the estimated time of the exit, considering both shareholder preferences and market forces that may effect valuation.
3. Use stakeholder analysis to list all ethical concerns related to the exit process.
4. Set specific financial goals and the time frame to achieve these goals, based on owners' aspirations related to wealth.
5. Establish a specific plan to meet financial goals, including
   - Selling all nonproductive assets
   - Keeping all leases short term
   - Developing financial reports that focus on net cash flow (EBITDA) from the business
6. Begin external audits at least three years before the planned sale.
7. Evaluate advantages and disadvantages of all possible exit options as they specifically relate to the goals, aspirations, industry trends, tax issues, and ethical considerations of the business.

FIGURE 14-3 Checklist for Exit Planning

potential buyers learned of the new competition in his market, any interest immediately vanished. A purchase is based on future cash flow, and this business's future was clearly in jeopardy. A realistic estimation of value should be the starting point for any attempt to sell a business. Figure 14-4 illustrates the sale process.

The sale process normally begins with an initial inquiry by a prospective buyer. The entrepreneur's potential interest in selling is determined, and some

FIGURE 14-4 Sale Process of a Business

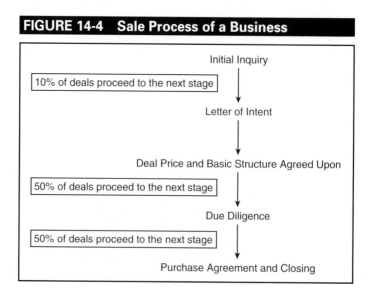

basic information is exchanged. Until a confidentiality agreement is signed, only general, nonfinancial information should be shared. Only about one in ten inquiries typically go to the next stage, the letter of intent. This stage generally begins with both sides entering into a confidentiality agreement. The letter of intent includes a proposed initial price and will require exclusive negotiations in return for the costs the potential buyer will incur going forward. The sale of a business most likely will be characterized by tough negotiations. Initial offers are not always close to true value. Once a price and basic deal structure are agreed upon, the deal moves into a more complex stage. However, about half of the deals will never get beyond the letter of intent.

In the next stage, the parties enter into due diligence. At this point, it is no longer possible to keep the sale secret from employees because of the process itself. In due diligence, all details of the company are disclosed, including an analysis of accounts, inventory, contracts, employee records, and so forth. The seller needs to honestly disclose everything, even possibly embarrassing details, as surprises that are discovered without being disclosed up front can adversely affect the sale price or even derail the deal. The price can change significantly during due diligence based on the information that is disclosed. The seller also should use this time to learn about the buyer by contacting other companies purchased by the buyer and gathering data to help assess the culture of the buyer. Again, about half of the deals do not proceed past the due diligence stage of negotiation.

In the final stage, attorneys will develop the purchase agreement and prepare for closing. Even at this late stage about half of the remaining deals will end before the final closing due to disagreements over document language and specific terms of the purchase agreement, which means that less than 1 percent of inquiries ultimately result in a closed deal. Therefore, it is important to continue to run the business wholeheartedly, because the entrepreneur will own it up until closing, which may not even happen.

Transaction costs to sell a business are high. Most experienced entrepreneurs and experts will recommend that only an attorney with expertise in mergers and acquisitions should handle the sale. However, they also will recommend that the entrepreneur make sure to stay in control of the process.

POST EXIT ISSUES

Obviously, life does not end for the entrepreneur after exiting the business. Many entrepreneurs experience what is known as *seller's remorse*. That is, the entrepreneur may have second thoughts about the wisdom of selling the business, the specific terms of the deal, or how the new owners are running the venture. One entrepreneur reported feeling quite depressed upon the realization that she would never be able to just walk into her business at any time she felt like it—because it was no longer hers! Experts in mergers and acquisitions find that seller's remorse is actually quite a common feeling and will often warn their clients that they will likely experience some degree of remorse when they sell their businesses.

These same experts also caution their clients to take time before starting new endeavors. Just like a jilted lover, entrepreneurs can make impulsive decisions "on the rebound" from selling their business. By taking the time to do periodic self-assessments and by remembering their personal aspirations, entrepreneurs will be more likely to make wise and reasoned choices about their "next steps." Making sure that one's career choices are a part of a broader life plan can help keep such decisions in perspective.

SUMMARY

This chapter presented a model for exit planning. By preparing well in advance of the actual sale of the venture, the entrepreneur has a better chance of meeting the objectives for the business. The process of exit planning includes doing ongoing self-assessment, determining the desired time frame of the exit, managing the financial statements, hiring an external auditor, and developing a business plan for the sale. A variety of exit options are available for the entrepreneur to pursue based on the situation and the entrepreneur's personal and professional goals. These options include a complete or partial transfer of ownership or the possibility of simply ceasing operations. Whichever option is finally chosen, it is important to use personal aspirations as a guide to this critical process.

DISCUSSION QUESTIONS

1. Why is timing such an important issue in planning to exit a business?
2. Discuss factors that should be considered by entrepreneurs when planning their exit strategies.
3. Discuss the advantages and disadvantages of the various exit options. Give specific examples of each.
4. Examine the ethical issues related to the exit options discussed in this chapter.

OPPORTUNITIES FOR APPLICATION

1. Interview an entrepreneur to determine what exit planning he or she has done for the business. Evaluate any gaps that exist in the exit plan and how those gaps may be remedied.
2. Write an exit plan for a new business venture you are developing. Reflect on the self-assessment you completed in Chapter 2 to understand specific goals and aspirations that shape your plan. Make sure to examine any post exit plans that you can or should make at this time. Remember, it is never too early to begin exit planning, even during the start-up process!

REFERENCES

Bagley, C., and Dauchy, C. (1998). *The Entrepreneur's Guide to Business Law*. New York: West.

Fenn, D. Family-business planning. www.inc.com, accessed July 1, 1998.

Fraser, J. What do buyers really want? www.inc.com, accessed July 1, 1999.

Gabriel, C. Selling your business. www.inc.com, accessed November 1, 1998. www.fed.org, accessed November 1, 1998.

Bankruptcy basics. www.findlaw.com, accessed October 24, 1999. www.vical.com, accessed February 1, 1991.

Payne, W. (2002). Choosing your exit strategy. www.entreworld.org/Content/EntreByline.cfm?ColumnID=16

Rosen, C. Employee ownership: The basics. www.inc.com, accessed September 1, 1998.

Savage, D. (2000). *Cases on Reell Precision Manufacturing*. Unpublished.

Index